THE TELLING LINE

CHARLES KEEPING

FAITH JAQUES

VICTOR AMBRUS

NIGEL LAMBOURNE

BRIAN WILDSMITH

SHIRLEY HUGHES

JOHN LAWRENCE

JAN PIEŃKOWSKI

HELEN OXENBURY

JOHN BURNINGHAM

RAYMOND BRIGGS

QUENTIN BLAKE

JANET & ALLAN AHLBERG

ANTHONY BROWNE

MICHAEL FOREMAN

THE TELLING LINE

ESSAYS ON FIFTEEN
CONTEMPORARY BOOK ILLUSTRATORS

DOUGLAS MARTIN

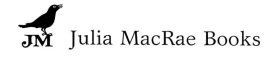 Julia MacRae Books

A DIVISION OF WALKER BOOKS

First published in 1989 by Julia MacRae Books,
a division of Walker Books, 87 Vauxhall Walk,
London SE11 5HJ

Text © 1989 Douglas Martin

The matter on p.6 constitutes an extension to this
copyright in respect of the illustrators whose
work is included

British Library Cataloguing in Publication Data

Martin, Douglas
 The telling line: essays on 15
 contemporary book illustrators
 1. British Illustrators: Illustrations for books,
 1900−1980−Biographies
 1. Title
 741.64'092'2

ISBN 0−86203−333−0

Designed by Douglas Martin
Phototypeset in Compugraphic Garth Graphic
by Armitage Typo/Graphics Ltd, Huddersfield
Printed and bound in Italy
by L.E.G.O., Vicenza

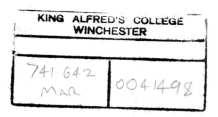

CONTENTS

ACKNOWLEDGEMENTS

All photography from original drawings and printed books by Ian Wood Photography, Oadby, and K & S Commercial Photography, Leicester, except for plate 78 supplied by Robin Johnson, London, and plates 127–140 by Zul Mukhida, Hove. Line copies by Grant Studio, Leicester. Oxford University Press generously made available duplicate film of certain subjects by Victor Ambrus, Charles Keeping and Brian Wildsmith, for which the original drawings were inaccessible. Similarly, Heidelberger Druckmaschinen AG kindly supplied film for plates 171, 175 and 178; Victor Gollancz Ltd for plate 81, William Heinemann Ltd for plate 157, and Penguin Books Ltd for plate 124.

COPYRIGHT PERMISSIONS

Every effort has been made to trace the copyright holders for the illustrations which appear in this book. The author and publisher express their thanks to the individual artists and to the following for kind permission to reproduce material for which they hold the copyright. [Numbers refer to the plates.]

Abelard-Schuman Ltd 142; Addison-Wesley 40, 42, 77; Janet Ahlberg 156, 161; Victor Ambrus 44; Estate of Edward Ardizzone 7; Atheneum Publishers 24, 153; Edward Bawden 2; A. & C. Black (Publishers) Ltd 42, 158; Blackie & Son Ltd 143; The Bodley Head Ltd 79, 80; Raymond Briggs 138, 140; Anthony Browne 168; Jonathan Cape Ltd 31, 96, 97, 98, 107, 119, 120, 121, 122, 123, 124, 144, 147, 149, 150, 151, 154; Century Hutchinson Ltd 174; William Collins, Sons & Co Ltd 28, 176, 177; Coward McCann 128, 129, 130, 135; Thomas Y. Crowell 45, 88, 106, 123; Crown Publishers, Inc 125; Delacorte Press 180; J. M. Dent & Sons Ltd 146; Andre Deutsch Ltd 148, 155; Dial Books for Young Readers 115, 116; Doubleday & Co, Inc 178; Faber & Faber Ltd 29, 75, 76, 141; Farrar, Straus & Giroux Inc 151; The Folio Society 11, 20, 49, 50, 51, 52, 85, 87; Michael Foreman 173, 179; Victor Gollancz Ltd 23, 81, 83, 178, 180, 181, 182; Rigby Graham 9; Greenwillow Books 157; Hamish Hamilton Ltd 35, 88, 127, 128, 129, 130, 131, 132, 133, 134, 135, 136, 137, 139, 167; Harper & Row, Publishers, Inc 149; Harrap 183; William Heinemann Ltd 3, 24, 33, 38, 99, 100, 101, 103, 104, 105, 106, 111, 112, 113, 114, 157, 160, 163; Hodder & Stoughton Ltd 13, 14, 32, 82; Holt, Rinehart 28, 122; Shirley Hughes 78; Internationale Jugendbibliothek, Munich 47; Faith Jaques 26, 27, 34, 36; Alfred A. Knopf, Inc 104, 105, 147, 154, 164, 165, 166, 169, 170; John Lawrence 84; The late John Lehmann 4; Lion & Unicorn Press 145; Little, Brown & Co 134, 163; Longman Group Ltd 17; Lutterworth Press 93; Margaret K. McElderry Books 118; Macmillan Publishing Co 46; Julia MacRae Books 91, 94, 95, 164, 165, 166, 169, 170; Henry Moore Foundation 8; William Morrow & Co, Inc 113, 114; Orchard Books, London and New York 25, 37; Helen Oxenbury 117; Oxford University Press 6, 12, 15, 18, 22, 39, 40, 43, 45, 46, 48, 60, 61, 62, 63, 64, 65, 67, 68, 70, 71, 72, 73; Oxford University Press, New York 15, 22; Pavilion Books Ltd 175; *Pegasus Magazine* 171; Penguin Books Ltd 21, 79, 89, 90, 102, 125, 126, 152, 159, 162; Jan Pieńkowski 108; John Piper 5; Private Collections 1, 3, 19, 21, 26, 53, 54, 55, 56, 57, 58, 59, 69; Hugh Tempest Radford 92; *Radio Times* 10; Random House 119, 120, 121, 127, 136; Routledge 172; Schocken Books, Inc 133, 138, 139, 175, 181, 182; Simon & Schuster 110; Unwin Hyman Ltd 30; Viking Penguin, Inc 89, 124, 126, 167, 174; Walker Books Ltd 74, 109, 110, 115, 116, 118, 153; Franklin Watts, Inc 61, 62, 63, 75, 111, 112; Brian Wildsmith 66.

LIST OF ILLUSTRATIONS

'Every picture tells a story' –
if it don't – it ain't.

Walter Richard Sickert (1860–1942)
as recalled by Nigel Lambourne, who studied under Sickert;
a gloss on a famous slogan of the day
advertising backache pills

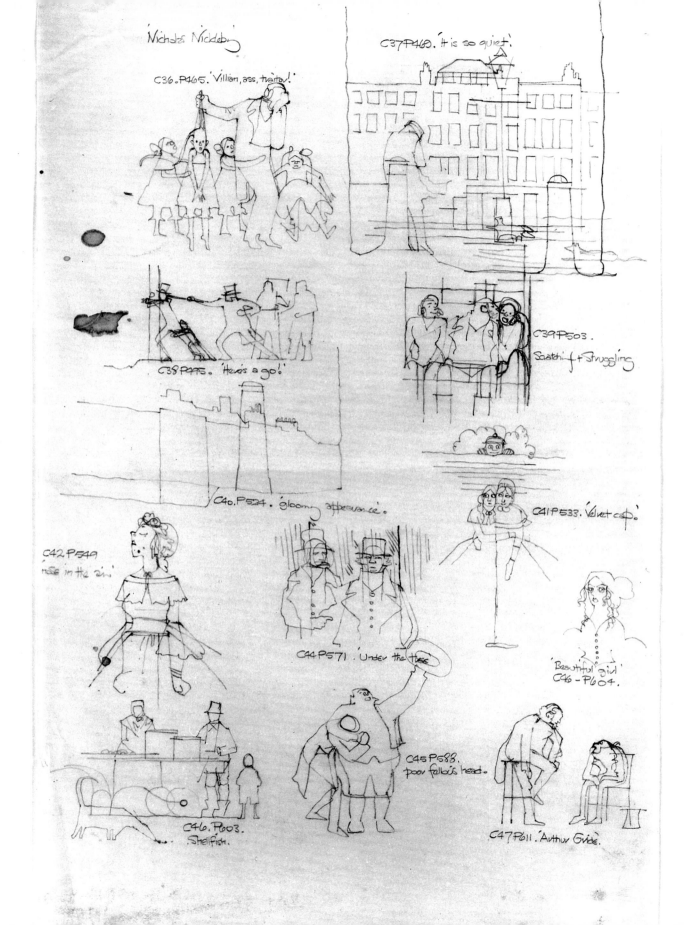

'Nicholas Nickleby'

C36.P465. 'Villian, ass, traitor!'

C37P468. 'It is so quiet.'

C38 P475. 'Here's a go!'

C39 P503. Snatching + Struggling

C40.P524. 'gloomy appearance.'

C41 P533. 'Velvet cap.'

C42 P549 'rose in the air'

C44 P571. 'Under the tree'

'Beautiful girl' C46 - P604.

C46. P603. Shellfish.

C45 P583. 'Poor fellow's head.'

C47 P611. 'Arthur Gride.'

PREFACE

ILLUSTRATORS and their work have always been very much part of the fabric of my career as a (non-illustrating) book designer. They are a most intriguing group of individualists and yet very little has been written about their professional lives, save for the occasional newspaper interview, or monographs of the type reserved for the most illustrious of an earlier generation such as Ardizzone or Bawden – though there have recently been signs that this situation is changing. My aim in this book has been to record the approach, views and achievements of a small number of distinguished artists through conversations and correspondence, in the hope that the resultant essays might also bring out those contrasts and contradictions in theory and practice which make the world of illustration so diverse and exciting.

To acknowledge the inevitable restrictions of such an approach – at first to ten, then to twelve, and in the event to fifteen artists – has been extraordinarily difficult; and it must be emphasised that no sort of list or ranking is in any way implied: another selector would find no difficulty in fielding a strong alternative team of fifteen, and it is a testament to the fecundity of the scene that this should be so. On the other hand, one restriction which did not seem either practical or desirable was to confine the study purely within the area of children's book illustration, since comparatively few artists allow themselves to be exclusively restricted to that major field of practice in any case, and since often it is what they do in the rest of their time – whether for other categories of book (especially in the imaginative illustration of adult literature whenever the rare opportunity presents itself), or in the form of independent painting, drawing or printmaking – that makes possible the interpretation of the overall picture.

Illustrators are generally preoccupied with the project that is on the drawing board at the moment, and their evaluation of their own early work may well range from relative indifference to an active desire for its suppression – perhaps an understandable consequence of having to accept whatever commissions are available in the initial struggle for recognition, as well as of possessing a self-critical and unforgiving eye for shortcomings. In many cases, illustrators have little recall of early

1 Charles Keeping's initial notes made on reading *Nicholas Nickleby*

books. It is also noteworthy that few have more than a small portion of their published repertoire in print or available from lending library stock at a given time, and this adds impetus to the hunt through catalogues and bibliographies, rummage sales and publishers' files for the submerged part of the iceberg. Much is difficult to trace, some virtually impossible even at this short remove of time; but little is devoid of interest. It is against this background that the lists of selected titles illustrated by each artist should be seen; they record the pattern of titles published year by year, but jacket commissions and occasional drawings have generally been omitted, and in one or two cases it is possible that a significant out-of-print volume may yet come to light.

In a very few instances, where the original drawings could not be found, but where their intrinsic importance was clear, it seemed best to include them here despite having to reproduce from printed copies.

In a book of this nature, it goes without saying that I am deeply grateful for the kindness and cooperation extended to me by the participating artists. What I could not have foreseen, though, was the extreme patience and generosity with which they have responded throughout, and their contribution to the overall shape and direction of the volume. As they know, my thanks go to them all.

I am much indebted to Anthea Bell, David Chambers, Mabel George MBE, Rigby Graham, Dr Hans A. Halbey, Ron Heapy, Keith Hogg, Antony Kamm, Gisèle Kearley, Barbara Lambourne and Geraldine Waddington for their kind and ready help over the years and with specific queries; and to the staffs of Book Trust, the British Library, Leicestershire Libraries (Humanities Reference Collection), Leicester University Library, New Zealand Department of Education (School Publications Branch), and the St Bride Printing Library for invaluable advice, information or research facilities. Finally a special word of thanks to my publisher, Julia MacRae, for her unconditional confidence and support from the initial idea onwards; to my wife, Sue, for her creative and constructive role in this book as well as for coping at the same time with the stresses it generated; and to Riley (1971–1988), studio cat *extraordinaire*.

D. M.

Oadby, November 1988

1 · INTRODUCTION

The post-war climate for book illustration

During the course of the Second World War, all forms of activity in the arts were closely monitored and many came to a virtual standstill. In contrast to the conditions imposed under the Third Reich which had hounded Germany into cultural suicide long before the war, the main consequence of the conflict in England was that in a sense each of the arts was held in the caretakership of a very few and much cultural life was mothballed. Reading and talking about the arts over this prolonged period of stasis and deprivation created a knowledgeable public eager for direct experience through the other senses as soon as the return to relative normality could take place. First viewings of Henry Moore's drawings of Underground shelter scenes, Ronald Searle's of Japanese PoW camps in Siam and Malaya, or John Piper's of Windsor Castle and Coventry, will remain quite as vivid in many people's minds as anything seen subsequently. And for the child growing up in wartime the inter-war years seemed no distance away, because most available books, whether fictional or informational, dated from that time or earlier.

In another sense the clock had been stopped for the duration of the war, and those who returned were deemed in theory free to resume their civilian activity from the point at which they had left off. The artistic losses were not to be compared to those of the Great War, but those lost to book illustration include Eric Ravilious and Rex Whistler. Artists of fame or promise, including those such as Edward Ardizzone, Edward Bawden, Barnett Freedman, Anthony Gross, Paul Nash (d.1946) and John Nash who had served as official war artists, came back to private practice and to teaching. Many of their first pupils had similarly been involved in active service or in the war effort and this meant that their average age, experience of life and critical perception at the point of commencing or resuming art studies was higher than any intake before or since; and this in turn was to have a positive effect in those areas, of which illustration is one, where art and design have to come into contact with professionalism and the real world.

The academic tradition in drawing, all-prevailing at the beginning of the period and still alive and well in a small cluster of institutions, will be approvingly cited by one illustrator after another as the strongest formal grounding in their craft. The influence of the Arts & Crafts Movement still held sway in the immediate post-war era in applied courses within schools of art before it was largely supplanted, until fairly recently, by neo-Bauhaus theory. Although the Arts & Crafts ethos is once again side-tracking designers for industry into irrelevant handicrafts, perhaps its most permanent achievement in disciplines contingent to illustration has been to set and maintain a climate in which distinguished British schools of wood engraving and of calligraphy have flourished from the early years of the century to the present.

A tradition of decorative graphic design and illustration had also evolved through various stages of sophistication since the early 1920s, culminating in the work of artists such as Ravilious and Bawden amongst others who had established themselves before the war; this was to stimulate many book illustrators to develop and discover outlets for a decorative style as an adjunct to a narrative one. Together with a grasp of the ornamental formulae of the baroque and rococo, this was to prove invaluable to artists such as Faith Jaques and Val Biro early in their respective careers, and there are signs from the colleges and in recently published work that the pioneers of this decorative style are coming back into fashion.

British painters enjoyed an unaccustomed vogue at the time, their work being popularized through enterprising Arts Council touring exhibitions and that attractive and influential series, Penguin Modern Painters, the first seventeen titles of which appeared between 1944 and 1950. With a few obvious exceptions, there is a predominant leanness about the work of these painters, in which the visible bones of draughtsmanship rather than virtuoso handling of pigment make the telling effect. This linear quality made it possible for several to function successfully as painter/illustrators – a conjunction normal in France but rare in England – in a way that was no longer to be viable for British artists not already active prior to about 1950 as a consequence of the waning of neo-romanticism and the drift towards more highly chromatic or non-figurative trends in painting.

Penguin Books, and John Lehmann's Penguin New Writing in particular,[1] provided one of the few channels through which the public was able to keep in touch with current developments in the arts as a whole in wartime and after, and here regular glimpses could be had of current work by Sutherland, Ayrton, Craxton, Rosoman, Minton and Vaughan amongst others including John Piper, whose *British Romantic Artists* had appeared in 1942. From these and other sources it was possible to see a bridge linking this contemporary group to the line-and-wash of the great eighteenth-century topographers and caricaturists, to the watercolour tradition exemplified by the still under-regarded Norwich School, and above all to the romantic visionaries: Blake, Palmer and Calvert.

This takes us to the heart of the English vernacular – just as Britten's music

2 Edward Bawden, *Gulliver's Travels*, 1965

resonates in closer affinity to that of Purcell, his seventeenth-century ancestor, than to that of any of his European contemporaries. In the evolution of major compositional forms in either music or art the emphasis frequently shifts from a national to an international scale of values, often within the work of the same composer or in response to the historical destinies of the state; but one of the constantly delightful things about book illustration is that it never has to strive for such effects, since for much of the time it is content to mirror the literature and character of a place.

That is not to say that illustrators do not possess the greatest curiosity about excellent draughtsmanship, regardless of when or where it was produced. There is an easy flow of international information, and normal relations were quickly resumed with Paris and New York, but Germany and Central Europe after the war presented quite a different problem. This was a matter of interest to a handful of illustrators at the time and so merits attention now, although most shared in the deep-rooted national disregard for these territories for which in 1945 there was no artistic present, no recent past to catch up on, no opportunity to visit and no-one with whom to communicate; there had only been a past of which very little was known or remembered, and there might be a future. But when a symphony by the almost unknown Mahler was heard in London (c.1954), the Berliner Ensemble visited (1956), and Kokoschka was shown at the Tate (1962); these events from what felt like another planet fired the public imagination and the rest, as it is said, is history.

But it would be a mistake to date awareness of a host of major artists purely from their first popular English monographs and London showings, since at any time during or just after the war, the work of draughtsmen of the calibre of Beckmann, Fronius, George Grosz, Hegenbarth, Kokoschka, Kollwitz, Kubin, Liebermann, Schiele and others could have been introduced to those who were sufficiently interested through the collections and contacts of Jewish intellectuals, who were glad to open windows onto the wider artistic developments that have taken place on the Continent in our time. Attention has only recently been devoted to the full extent of the role of the Jewish immigration in combating insularity, not only – in the present context – through individual creative work, teaching and art-historical studies, but also in promoting innovative thinking and a more receptive climate for new talent from inside the structures of publishing and the other media.

Another background feature of the period that should not be left out of account is the use to which some of the finest design intellects had been put as part of the war effort. Disciplined research and analytical thought were applied to propaganda ends – to ways of solving problems of visual and verbal communication to maximum popular effect – but by means of skills which no contemporary art school could have taught. There is need for research which would trace the origins[2] and explore the subsequent civilian use of these techniques in poster, packaging and advertising design, education and journalism.

3 Anthony Gross, *The Forsyte Saga,* 1950

4 John Minton, *Time was Away: A Notebook in Corsica,* 1948

It is necessary now to take a brief glance at the state of publishing and print, and at how immediate public needs and future possibilities were gauged at the time. This ground has been covered from different aspects elsewhere, but has to be mentioned here for its general effect on the working environment for book illustrators and designers.

Paper rationing is a constant complaint in publishing memoirs of the period, since stocks depleted by bombing could not easily be replaced and the related wartime economy standards were not lifted until some time afterwards, and thus it became increasingly reasonable for publishers to predict that these years of famine for themselves and their readers would be succeeded by years of plenty. The problem, on realising that the conditions for a book boom were gathering on the horizon, consisted in anticipating the directions and proportions it might assume. For many trade publishers a return to the pre-war *status quo* was all they asked, but there was also a hectic idealism and vision generated in many quarters in response to this unprecedented situation. In the summer of 1945 Allen Lane travelled to Basel in the company of Oliver Simon of the Curwen Press with the object of recruiting Jan

Tschichold to take charge of design for Penguin Books.[3] This was to prove momentous and decisive, not simply for Penguin but in setting the highest standards that mass production could be required to maintain.

Another aspect of this concern, traditional in German-speaking countries, that the book designer should have the final word in specifying materials and processes, was represented in Britain by the distinguished book designer Berthold Wolpe who was with Faber & Faber from 1939 until his retirement in 1975.[4] His was a complementary influence to Tschichold's in benefiting the trade at large; Wolpe's care in the selection of paper and bookcloth and his love of enterprising calligraphy for jacket and binding-case design were an inspiration to other designers in combating false economies and routine thinking.

Any designer or illustrator needs to have unswerving faith that a latent public responsiveness to positive design and craftsmanship exists, and that enterprising presentation can play a vital role in sales. This thinking produced many attractive and still collected little series of which the best known are Britain in Pictures[5] and King

5 John Piper, *English, Scottish and Welsh Landscape*, 1944

Penguins,[6] Miniature Books published by Rodale Press, and the post-war series of Ariel Poems from Faber, as well as leading to the launch in 1947 of the Folio Society. The idea that a popular book club could succeed in finding an audience for books on the basis of how they looked, and that the best in illustration, typography, printing and binding would actually spearhead the sales of a soundly selected but essentially conservative list, was both elementary and audacious.

Of course there were failures as well, where some of the smaller independent houses made courageous but uncompromising efforts to promote the contemporary arts including illustration, and the idealism which proved their undoing when the anticipated readership failed to materialise make their books a pleasure to seek out today. Contact Books, Paul Elek, Falcon Press, Grey Walls Press, John Lehmann, Max Parrish and John Westhouse are just some of the imprints which vanished in their original form or altogether. (Much could be said about the particular aims and personality of each publisher who ever commissioned an illustrator, since human qualities invariably influence the outcome in this situation, but these issues form part of general publishing history and are well covered in the memoirs and company histories which continue to appear.[7])

The endeavours of the quality printing houses (notably W. S. Cowell, Curwen Press, Jarrold's, Lund Humphries and Shenval Press) were of almost comparable importance, not only in the pursuit of technical excellence and innovation, but in their recognition that illustration and design had a vital role to play for the future. Whilst it remained unclear how responsibility for design and production initiative was to be divided between printer and publisher in the new dispensation, printers made strenuous and enlightened efforts to broaden the scope of their services, thus sharing a figurative umbrella with designers and illustrators. This situation resolved itself as it became apparent that printers were not well placed to respond to the individual demands of each and every book, whereupon designers and technical experts began to gravitate from the printing industry into publishers' production departments.

As observers and recorders of these developments, future generations will be indebted to the writings of Kenneth Day, John Dreyfus, John Lewis, Ruari McLean, John Ryder and Hans Schmoller, all practising designers as well as historians, who kept open the debate on illustration, design and production at an articulate level.

Any attempt at subjective recall of the immediate post-war era is now for me intrinsically linked with those fragments which that foremost of German artists in British exile, Kurt Schwitters, had shored against his ruins.[8] The way in which we as children had hoarded bus tickets, postage stamps, early cigarette cards and packs rescued from the gutter, comic papers (of which the first rare ones from America became the gold standard of playground barter), official ration coupons to be exchanged for goods sold loose in sugar paper: all this found its profoundly sad yet life-enhancing mirror image in his collages.

Similarly, for illustrators then setting out on their professional training or practice, it was apparent that things could only get better, if gradually, and that the day would come for media and industries long deemed non-essential to revive their fortunes. Then art workers would be needed at all levels: in print workshops and commercial art studios; as packaging designers, poster artists or strip cartoonists; specialists in technical drawing for the industrial press or in fashion and scraperboard for new magazines and catalogues; and not least for the long-awaited initiative in textbook, children's and general book publishing. The snag was that no-one at the time could say in precisely what order these opportunities would come about, and so it was sensible for artists to train as all-rounders and be prepared to bide their time until they could break into their chosen specialisation.

The children's book revival

The children's book area was eventually to prove the dominant market for creative illustrators by a margin that could not have been predicted, and it is tempting to try to recapture some of the excitement of this development from personal experience. I first came into contact with children's publishing as a book typographer in the late 1950s, and soon became fascinated by the art of illustration. It may have helped to have had no personal talents or ambitions in that field when it came to involvement with illustrators as an art editor,[9] but above all this was an ideal time and vantage point from which to observe a major shift in the pattern of publishing, for the chief process in use since printing had been invented – letterpress printing from movable metal type – was already on the way out. No cause and effect link with the parallel decline of black and white narrative book illustration can be established, although the availability of cheaper colour printing from the rival and ascendant process, offset lithography, was to determine the future course of events; and this was to entail a dramatic change in status for illustrators. The lists of titles appended to each essay will show that to illustrate a book each month was by no means a Stakhanovite achievement in the black and white days: it was simply a matter of economic necessity to take on as much as possible alongside part-time teaching. Nowadays for a well-known illustrator to produce more than one or two picture books a year is to tempt fate, and perhaps that shows how far this *métier* has travelled along the road from relative obscurity to stardom.

If, as the crudest of generalisations, the post-war period falls into two parts with a considerable overlap and for which the year c.1962 may be taken as the crossover point separating the black and white era from the full-colour one which succeeded but did not entirely supplant it, then there are two strata of out-of-print material to consider: the earlier, predominantly black and white, deposit being overlaid by more recent colour activity.

For long it was axiomatic that each and every children's book called for some form of illustration, and this extended to the large category of novels for the upper reading ages (a challenging market-place for line illustration), which was to suffer progressive attrition as print runs shortened. The level of activity in all areas of children's publishing remained considerable,[10] but it was run predominantly as a low-budget operation for most of the period and as such encouraged a fair amount of routine and mediocre work, although the finest artists seldom submitted less than their professional best. Therefore the black and white archive is part junk-shop, part treasure house; a wonderful place for research or for browsing, and one in which to make immediate finds or to begin to re-evaluate a fertile artistic phase. The real treasures are bound to return to public display, whether enduringly – through reissues of individual titles and new publications about the artists who illustrated them – or from time to time in the form of exhibitions of original books and drawings. There are signs that, after a period of neglect, this is starting to happen and the familiar processes of stylistic rehabilitation can be seen to be at work. In due course an enterprising publisher will see the potential for a series of classics of children's book illustration from this period either in facsimile reprint, or in freshly designed editions using the original artwork where it survives.[11]

As the new paths opened by full-colour offset printing became evident to publishers of children's books, the focus shifted towards the youngest age-groups and in favour of those illustrative styles most likely to have universal and lasting appeal, so that high production costs could be shared between as many subscribers to individual language editions as possible. At this revolutionary moment in its development, the picture book called for new artists and a wholly fresh approach to illustration.[12] Several countries produced an exciting crop of illustrators in response to this challenge, and, in close alliance with leading colour printers, publishers set out to interest the rest of the world in colourful and innovatory types of picture-story book. And it is interesting to note that although fashions are quickly adapted from country to country, it is national or even regional thinking that usually makes for an authentic contribution on the international scale; products become ersatz when designed in terms of the suppression of local characteristics and colours in pursuit of bland acceptability.

Britain was in the forefront of this initiative, its publishers ready to invest in the development of original talent as well as to encourage their established artists to make full use of the new resources. Of the new discoveries, Brian Wildsmith is now acknowledged as the true innovator of the 'painterly' picture book.[13] He adopted the time-honoured procedure of using the world of animals through which to address or appeal to children, and this convention, which affords incidental release from the constraints of modern dress as it affects place and time, contributes further to the likelihood that many of his books will continue to be passed down through the generations.[14]

Numerous other artists of distinction also originated picture books from a variety of standpoints and there is now a call, after more than a quarter century of intensive

6 Brian Wildsmith, *Tales from the Arabian Nights*, 1961

productivity, for some form of international stocktaking. Over such a time-scale many classics or near classics are inevitably dropped from the repertoire, at least temporarily, but the bank of full-colour material viewed as a whole has excellent survival prospects since so much intelligence and careful investment went into its creation in the first place.

There is also a correlative sense in which life may have become progressively more difficult for the younger artist as the potential scope for innovation in a well-tilled field has diminished, but recent achievement has been impressive none-the-less. There is a temptation to list names in the ascendant as well as those of artists in unmerited eclipse, but this situation is in constant flux and the contingent risks of omission too grave.

7   Edward Ardizzone, self-portrait, late 1960s

The imaginative illustration of adult literature

Unquestionably the illustration of books for children plays a vital functional and stimulatory role up to a certain age; in almost every country of the world today it is regarded as a prime adjunct in the ascent to literacy and learning. But this has not always been so, and, prior to the *Orbis Pictus* of the great Czech educator Comenius (c.1653),[15] the visual element in education must have been drawn largely from nature, folk-art or the resources of the individual teacher, since the published record is sparse and rudimentary in the extreme. In this sense children's books represent only a minor and recent episode in the total history of book illustration.

Does it follow from this that the wealth of decorative and imaginative illustration – implicit in the earliest artifacts of most cultures and abundant from the manuscript tradition onwards – should be regarded as material mainly introduced for the benefit of an illiterate and unsophisticated adult populace? Much scholarly interpretation tacitly subscribes to this view, or to the equally puritanical thesis that the march of literacy should be accompanied by the progressive elimination of any form of decoration or illustration that might stand in the way of the text.[16]

Perhaps there have always been public misgivings as to whether the illustration of creative literature should be attempted at all – just as there will always be those who incline to Dr Johnson's definition of opera as 'an exotic and irrational entertainment' rather than to the Wagnerian 'collective work of art' (*Gesamtkunstwerk*). The phenomenon of the dialogue between words and pictures is quite as fascinating as that between words and music; when it is successful the product is more than the sum of the parts. There is the further curious parallel that contemporaries of comparable stature in their respective fields often find it difficult to work together, and that a certain imbalance in the relationship can lead to interesting consequences.[17] For this among other reasons it has become highly unusual for a major imaginative work to be first issued in an illustrated edition, although it is unlikely that the view held by many artists that most modern fiction is unillustratable will prevail in the longer term.[18] A shift in time or geography is often all that is required to bring about a successful confrontation between great writer and committed illustrator, as where Delacroix illustrates *Faust* (1828), Barnett Freedman *War and Peace* (1938), or Werner Klemke *The Canterbury Tales* (1963).

A measure of agreement will be found to exist between artists and readers alike that certain writers are so self-sufficient that any form of illustration would be an intrusion, but this too can sometimes be disproved by events – Jane Austen is frequently cited in this context, and yet who would wish to be without Joan Hassall's wood-engravings (1957–63) for the Folio edition? Many of the artists featured in these pages touch on what for them are the boundaries of the possible in illustration, and, despite the contrasts and contradictions which ensue, remarkably little is in fact excluded. All but one or two have already made a significant contribution in some form to the illustration of adult literature, and most would like to be asked to do more.

The *livre d'artiste* and private press book categories can only receive isolated mention here; the former has never taken root in these islands, and the latter only merits consideration for those qualities of literary insight and purposeful execution brought to it by the rare artist for whom it serves as an authentic channel of communication.

Prometheus hurls defiance at the Gods in Goethe's dramatic fragment, nobly translated by André Gide, with colour lithographs by Henry Moore and typography by Henri Jonquières: *Prométhée* (Paris, Nicaise, 1951) is an undisputed monument of twentieth-century book illustration and production, in which the elemental theme and Moore's scale of thought humanise the traditional overblown page size. The same would naturally be true for works of the stature of Clavé's *Gargantua* (1955) or Chagall's *Bible* (1956), but it is difficult to think of comparable achievements by other British artists.

The neo-Romanticism which John Piper himself went a long way towards defining[19] has been kept alive by him, not through limited editions as might perhaps have been expected, but for the most part as a result of his involvement in carefully designed trade editions. Among a number of publishing involvements he found time for a long-term commitment to the Shell Guides as topographical illustrator[20] and photographer, and eventually as general editor, without in any way compromising his own vision. This association was begun at a time when illustrators with interests related to the countryside – ranging from local and architectural history to natural history – could still express their own enthusiasm in an unforced style before being rendered obsolescent as new academic disciplines and prescribed standards of colour photography took hold. For the best of these artists landscape had led directly into literature, and in Piper's case there can have been little conscious distance to travel from the Shell Guides to his own *Romney Marsh* (1950) and thence to *The Natural History of Selborne* (1962).

For younger artists, who shared a common outlook with Piper and Minton, it was soon to be too late to interest publishers in what had come to be regarded as a trend in retreat from commercial ends. Rigby Graham's work merits attention in this connection; for over thirty years now he has chosen to work prolifically for a variety of shoe-string printers rather than change his ground for the sake of achieving orthodox publication. In the course of his career he has produced some magnificently illustrated books which justify his concept of the scope of the private press, since they could have seen the light of day in no other way.

In contrast, the illustrative performance record of the established private presses has been dismal. The Ark, Rampant Lions and Lion & Unicorn Presses, and others of more recent vintage, have all produced distinguished work where professional illustrators have made guest appearances; but as a forcing-ground for talent – and of course this is not a role that has to be thrust upon them or that they need accept – at best they have failed to generate much more than quietly competent wood engraving. If the Folio Society did not exist then it would be necessary to invent it, if only to ensure that enterprising commissions to illustrate the classics, whether major or obscure, did not dry up totally. Folio Society, and the Limited Editions Club of New York, have consistently defended the middle ground between the apathy of the purveyors of standard texts and the elitism of the private presses and bibliophile societies.

8 Henry Moore, *Prométhée*, 1951

The critical interpretation of book illustration

Critical approaches to illustration via (a) the text, and (b) the supposed cognitive requirements of the reader at given stages in development may be perfectly valid but tell only part of the story, since these can never be more than adjuncts to the consideration of illustration as drawing. Studies in children's literature have in the main taken the above-mentioned paths, one consequence of which has been to reinforce the view that assigns to illustration a secondary, supportive or definable role *vis-à-vis* writer and audience, and another that those at the educational workface may be misled through the over-simplification of current orthodoxies.

Some children's book reviewers generally respond to illustration with sensitivity and common sense, but sadly it does throw others into considerable confusion. Misunderstandings can and do arise between an illustrator's intention and a literary critic's perception, in areas not reasonably to be taken as liable to deflect or dismay the child, and this helps no-one, yet unfortunately there is no context in sight for the evaluation of research into illustration and the establishment of a sounder critical basis.[21] This is not to be dismissive of a considerable volume of scholarly research,[22] merely to observe that much of it stands at several academic removes from the issues of everyday practice and response. Certain aspects of illustration have been studied and analysed under such headings as educational theory or the psychology of visual perception, although the findings usually relate to typologies of illustration rather than to the style of the individual illustrator. In other words illustration, currently studied as a science, may benefit from more rigorous consideration as an art, and it may be useful to look at one or two ways in which this could be brought about.

The prospect that illustrated children's books might receive more attention from art critics as opposed to literary critics is an intriguing one (if impractical on a day-to-day reviewing basis), and there is certainly room for more books of the quality of William Feaver's concise survey,[23] as well as for more expertise in the compilation of the monographs and exhibition catalogues which will be needed as the work of an increasing number of illustrators calls for retrospective evaluation.[24] A further approach for the art historian may prove to be the contemporary study of individual artists and their work, so that the documentation of sufficient and diverse cases begins to map out and define the outlines of this fascinating area of practice. This has developed as a particularly lively discipline in West Germany and Austria,[25] where it is seen as a mixture of detective work, biographical empathy, critical detachment and archival scrupulousness.

The bibliography of book illustrators is not extensive, but interesting beginnings for the period were made in the 1950s, mostly by practising illustrators and book designers,[26] and in recent years there has been a spate of useful publications on individual artists. Although few may choose to write autobiographically, there is quite a lot of potential here at present which is unlikely to go unnoticed by publishers; in the case of some satirical, journalistic and topographical artists – Steve Bell, Gentleman, Glashan, Hogarth, Scarfe, Searle, Steadman, Topolski, to name just a handful – their books and features form in effect an autobiographical work record in instalments. If the literature on illustrators is deficient it is surely in the area of collective studies of groups of artists, which is a pity since this method usually works well whenever it is essayed: Paul Hogarth's *The Artist as Reporter* and David Driver's *The Art of Radio Times* are two particularly successful examples.

For this volume, it seemed apposite to explore the critical reception of their work with illustrators themselves, and to solicit their views on the growing literature which is being generated as a commentary to their professional activity. The feedback received was complex, fascinating, and fell into no common pattern beyond some fundamental generalisations. Illustrators as a group appear to be as uncertain of their status as they were in the Victorian age, and this parallel is interesting because the risk of the professional indignity of the illustrator being told how to do the job, by anyone along the gamut from author to reader, can have changed as little as the human resources available for asserting autonomy and defending privacy.[27] Those interviewed for this book were all highly experienced practitioners, aware of how they had come to terms personally in this situation and learned for the most part to discount ill-informed criticism. There was almost full accord that – where the primary language is a visual rather than a verbal one – all statements have to be self-sufficient, and consequently there is little point in defending the communicative intent of drawings in print. Several artists expressed relative indifference towards any kind of personal publicity save that elicited by their work, but most shared a concern that the aims of the wider community of illustrators should be better understood by publishers, art students, and all those with a responsibility for introducing books to a wider public.[28]

Artists who may have spent a large part of their working life in a particular field – say black and white narrative illustration – may be entitled to consider, as some do, that the best days for that genre are past and that there will be little future demand; but my own impression after looking at thousands of illustrated books ranging in date over the past five decades was entirely to the contrary, and I emerged brimful of optimism for the future of book illustration. It does seem that excellence in draughtsmanship hardly ever remains outdated for long; fashions may look incongruous or even risible for a few years after banishment, but that is only part of the conditional basis for their future charm. Similarly, after years of publishing neglect, many idioms and illustrative resources only await the right creative talent in order to be reactivated to telling effect, not in the sense of that fraudulent work which borrows the clothing of a past master, but through an intellectual grasp of the expressive possibilities latent in valid technical procedures that have been temporarily abandoned.

9 Rigby Graham, *Leicestershire,* 1980

NOTES

1. *New Writing* (Penguin, 40 issues, November 1940 – September 1950). The firm's complete catalogue with dates of publication which appears in *The Penguin Story: 1935-1956* (Penguin, 1956), 63–124, is valuable for the picture it gives of the list at this culturally significant point in its post-war development.

2. The roots are to be found in the forms of expression that international social modernism found in England in the 1920s and 1930s through the planning of new towns and the London Underground, through Mass-Observation and the evolution of a rhetoric of cinema and graphics that would serve the nascent Welfare State. The Civil Service continued to operate a massive system of patronage under successive post-war administrations from ministries and marketing boards, the COI and other agencies, which linked into the same network of advertising agencies and printing houses used by such giant corporations as ICI, Shell (cf. *'That's Shell — that is!': An Exhibition of Shell Advertising Art,* Barbican Art Gallery and Shell UK, 1983) and

Unilever; what now seems remarkable is the parallelism between state and industry in their deployment of designers. It is fascinating that both should see value in commissioning the *signed* work of individual poster artists, illustrators and cartoonists, a practice based on a valid theory of mass communication which has only been eclipsed as part of a fashion cycle, and may well shortly come full circle to be in demand again.

3. cf. Ruari McLean, *Jan Tschichold: Typographer* (Lund Humphries, 1975).

4. cf. *Berthold Wolpe: A Retrospective Survey* (Victoria & Albert Museum and Faber, 1980).

5. Peter Eads, 'Britain in Pictures', *The Private Library,* 3rd series, 9/3 (Autumn 1986), 119–31; D. E. Wickham, 'A further look at Britain in Pictures', 10/3 (Autumn 1987), 118–24.

6. David J. Hall, 'The King Penguin Series', *The Private Library,* 2nd series, 10/4 (Winter 1977), 143–71.

7. The published material is extensive, but for the flavour of the period see the second and third volumes of John Lehmann's autobiography: *I Am My Brother* (Longman, 1960); *The Ample Proposition* (Eyre & Spottiswoode, 1966); also J. Maclaren-Ross, *Memoirs of the Forties* (Alan Ross, 1965).

8. cf. Stefan Themerson, *Kurt Schwitters in England* (Gaberbocchus Press, 1958).

9. At that time, this involved supplying the artist with a manuscript and a technical briefing together with typographical specimen pages printed on the correct paper and a guide to jacket dimensions. The artist was then left to get on with the job, able to discuss problems arising but protected from the extremes of third party caution. It was the art editor's job to ensure that the illustrator complied with any just criticisms or objections raised by author or publisher, whilst representing the interests of his freelances in house and affording openings to new talent.

10. Annual totals of children's books published or reissued in the UK have been averaged for each five-year period, with the percentage accounted for by reprints or new editions shown in brackets: 1940–44, 709 (19.9%); 1945–49, 1,206 (19.6%); 1950–54, 1,579 (27.5%); 1955–59, 1,941 (18.2%); 1960–64, 2,395 (11.7%); 1965–69, 2,348 (17.7%); 1970–74, 2,383 (23.4%); 1975–79, 2,858 (19.8%); 1980-84, 3,443 (19.0%); 1985, 4,410 (17.7%); 1986, 4,642 (20.7%). Source: *Whitaker's Cumulative Book List.*

11. The present whereabouts of original drawings is a fascinating study in itself. Until artists and agents began to insist upon its return, printers and publishers often took a philistine view of artwork – that once it had been transferred to metal or film it had served its purpose. Whereas it is clear that printers either returned material to publishers at the time or destroyed it shortly afterwards as instructed, some of the latter certainly have extensive holdings, normally of the full artwork for a particular title where this has survived. When drawings were dutifully returned it was not unusual in earlier days for artist or agent to break-up the set and send sample drawings to other publishers as mailing shots, but many artists are known to have conserved the significant bulk of their creation whilst sanctioning the gift or sale of individual drawings. Mel Calman opened 'The Workshop' in 1970, soon to be followed by other galleries offering interesting works on paper by cartoonists and illustrators, and the idea of these as 'collectables' has gradually taken firm root.

12. cf. Bettina Hürlimann, *Picture-Book World* (OUP, 1968), and also the children's book issues of the Swiss graphic design periodical, Graphis, for the years in question.

13. 'Brian Wildsmith's earliest picture books startled the children's book world with their textured pictures bleeding off the page in whirling, vivid colours. So began a vogue for similarly exotic work which led to the current domination of colour over line and painter over illustrator.' Joyce Irene Whalley and Tessa Rose Chester, *A History of Children's Book Illustration* (John Murray with Victoria & Albert Museum, 1988), 225.

14. When evaluating half a dozen animal stories (including Wildsmith's *ABC* and *The Lion and the Rat,* and Burningham's *Borka*) at the time, Margery Fisher wrote: 'Looking at books like these, I seem to be back thirty years, to the time when the work of Ardizzone and Lewitt-Him startled picture-books into new life.' *Intent upon Reading: A Critical Appraisal of Modern Fiction for Children* (2nd edn, Brockhampton, 1964), 360.

15. cf. John Amos Comenius, *Orbis Pictus*, a facsimile of the first English edition of 1659 introduced by John E. Sadler (OUP, 1968); also Bettina Hürlimann: *Three Centuries of Children's Books in Europe* (OUP, 1967), 127–43.

16. To paraphrase Adolf Loos: 'evolution der kultur ist gleichbedeutend mit dem entfernen des ornamentes aus dem gebrauchsgegenstande' [The evolution of culture goes hand in hand with the elimination of ornament from everyday objects], 'Ornament und Verbrechen', 1908; in Loos, *Sämtliche Schriften* (Vienna: Herold, 1962), I, 277.

17. Two celebrated musical instances: Beethoven sent his settings to Goethe, who barely acknowledged them because he preferred those of Zelter; Schubert immortalised the relatively minor poet Wilhelm Müller in his two greatest song-cycles.

18. The collaboration between Ted Hughes and Leonard Baskin forms a notable exception; it was also rather surprising that an illustrated edition of Richard Adams's *Watership Down* (by John Lawrence) should have appeared so soon after its first publication. These remarks do not apply in the particular world of children's books, where artistic dialogue between equals occurs freely and sometimes on a level as inviting to adults as to children, as in the books produced by Leon Garfield and Charles Keeping.

19. cf. Piper's introduction to his *British Romantic Artists* (Collins, 1942).

20. Topographical illustration lies so close to the heart of the English literary and artistic experience that it is surprising that no study has yet appeared bringing the story far enough forward to consider the work of Boswell, Casson, Foreman, Gentleman, Graham, Hogarth, Barbara Jones, Linda Kitson, Piper, Searle, Sorrell, Steadman *inter alios.*

21. At one time many book artists and typographers kept an open mind in the hope that the findings of experimental psychology, if never able to provide a lead, might at least confirm some of their own basic working observations. Practising typographers will be aware of two extremely damaging cases where they found themselves dismayed to be at complete odds with theories that had found uncritical lay acceptance: first, Sir Cyril Burt's correlation of age-groups with optimum size of type, etc. – in *A Psychological Study of Typography* (CUP, 1959) – which was subsequently shown to have been based on non-existent research; and second, the campaign to advocate the adoption of the initial teaching alphabet (ita) in the schools in the 1950s. If such things can happen in a field that looks deceptively amenable to psychometry, then illustrators as individualists are potentially at even greater hazard from such prescriptive theories. Perhaps if the working experience of book illustrators and designers could be solicited and collated in some way then a very different pattern of concern would register, and it might not be necessary to debate the 'controversiality' of a Maurice Sendak or a Charles Keeping at all.

22. An excellent bibliography of visual perception (basically typographical, but also germane to semiotic, diagrammatic and illustrative imagery) appears in Herbert Spencer, *The Visible Word: Problems of Legibility* (2nd edn, Lund Humphries, 1969), 85–107. The topic was pursued at the 1981 Brighton Conference: *Research in Illustration* (conference proceedings parts I & II, Brighton Polytechnic, 1982). A subsequent conference specialised in children's responses to illustration; the organiser, Dr Evelyn Goldsmith, has published *Research into Illustration: an Approach and a Review* (CUP, 1984).

23. William Feaver, *When We Were Young: Two Centuries of Children's Book Illustration* (Thames & Hudson, 1977).

24. This assumption is based on the vast growth over the past decade of exhibitions and publications (*see* General Bibliography), devoted to selected artists mostly of a senior generation, and bearing in mind how much of the work of their contemporaries and of that of successive waves of younger illustrators remains unexplored.

25. I remain indebted to Dr Hans M. Wingler for once convincing me of the urgency of all work of this kind; his books [in the English editions: *Oskar Kokoschka: The Work of the Painter* (Faber, 1958) and *Bauhaus 1919–1933* (2nd edn, Cambridge, Mass: MIT Press,

1968)] remain models of this approach.

26. A still useful series of little monographs, English Masters of Black-and-White, covers work to date by Bawden, Freedman, Fraser and Gross (Art & Technics, 1948–49); see articles in *Alphabet & Image, Image, Motif, Penrose Annual, Signature, Typographica;* see also Robin Jacques, *Illustrators at Work* (Studio Books, 1963).

27. For the great Victorian spats between authors and their illustrators see the nineteenth-century catalogue and bibliography pages in Edward Hodnett, *Five Centuries of English Book Illustration* (Scolar Press, 1988), 324–42, 358–9.

28. Some take the opportunity to talk about their work at book trade and educational gatherings, or to draw for children, and are natural performers able to communicate their individual stance compellingly.

10 Eric Fraser, *In Camera,* 1963

2 · CHARLES KEEPING

22 SEPTEMBER 1924 – 16 MAY 1988*

CHARLES KEEPING was born in Vauxhall Walk, close to the old Lambeth Walk Market. A London childhood has recurrently provided subject matter for his picture books and it pervades his graphic vision, this life-long love of the metropolis found its most recent expression in his illustrations for the full works of Charles Dickens. London itself is perhaps one of the best guides we have in studying continuity and development in the first three decades of the work of this rich and complex artistic personality – not simply the nineteenth-century London of Dickens and Mayhew, Turner and Doré, of working horses and dockland pubs, of fogs and vast brick walls; but the wastelands caused by the Blitz and later by crass development, and the bright lights of Carnaby Street which so quickly gave way to a bleaker outlook. In books such as *Railway Passage* and *Adam and Paradise Island* the point is made that this social dimension of cities, the options confronting young and old alike, can and should be presented to children without moral preconceptions.

For as long as he can remember, Charles Keeping has been an illustrator. When he was only five or six years old he used to make drawings with his sister for the stories she wrote. His grandfather had been to sea on windjammers in a long career as a merchant seaman, and both grandparents were great storytellers. His father worked for the *Star* newspaper and brought home lots of newsprint and placard paper to draw on. So storytelling and drawing were actively encouraged in a household which he was later to describe as 'comfortable working class'.

He drew what was about him in what was then a very lively community: the street market with its stalls and coster-mongers, the local people, many of whom lived in small Georgian or Victorian houses with even smaller gardens, the walks of ancient whitewashed cottages running down to the river, but above all the horses stabled there in proximity to the docks:

---

*This essay had been written and discussed with Charles Keeping prior to his death, and it is printed in unchanged form.

. . . and when it comes to my own actual work later in life, I tend to keep
within what I could see as a child. That was mainly a small garden, a fence,
and a large blank wall. Against that blank wall many things took place. It was
a yard which had cart horses, and I could see these vast shapes of horses
moving across this wall. These very simple images attracted me . . . I also
enjoyed being taken into that yard next door and sat on the backs of cart
horses. This was a very, very exciting thing for a child. It had an element of
fear, because the animals were so large, and it had a feeling of almost sensuous
comfort because the horses were furry and warm. When I got back home, I
used to draw those horses and what I had seen in that stable. [1]

Drawing became a way of life, to the point that he no more thought of not drawing
for a day than of not having something to eat. This pattern was shaken for the first and
probably the only time when, after his father's death, he had to make a career decision.
Having an elder sister still at school, it seemed advisable to seek out an apprenticeship,
and the printing industry was a natural choice since it was known that it afforded a
useful route into art school for the exceptionally talented. Of this time, whilst he was
briefly indentured to William Clowes & Sons Ltd (then in Blackfriars), he recalls the
typical early days of any apprenticeship. On being sent 'running-out' as an office-boy to
collect drawings from an artist and deliver them to the blockmaker, he re-affirmed his
resolve to be in the artist's position one day, and that never could he belong in the craft
world of the machine-minder, bookbinder, or whatever.

War broke out, but he continued to draw almost every day even during the Blitz –
and Kennington where the family had moved to was a heavily-bombed area. He joined
the Royal Navy in 1942 at the age of 18 and served for four years as a ship's wireless
operator. Working demands and crowded conditions on small ships meant that he
hardly drew at all during these years, but as soon as he came out of the Navy he started
to draw again. Immediately he entered art school. At first no grant was forthcoming so
he took a job as a gas meter man, work which he could get through in his own time in
order to get to art school as soon as he had finished. He puts this down to experience:

I was on really tough districts like Paddington and North Kensington; those
really rough, poor, slum areas, and I think it was a great help to me in
illustration. It gave me a great understanding of how people lived. I think the
recent whole series of Dickens I did for Folio Society – a lot there came from
my knowledge of those days – it wasn't exactly Dickensian, but some of the
conditions were almost Dickensian. I've been in houses where there's no
banisters, they've been chopped down for firewood. Where chickens roamed
around in the kitchen, and people used to sleep all night with their clothes on.
They were very poor indeed and living in dreadful conditions, and to get the
chance to go into those houses was a great experience and help to an illustrator. [2]

Keeping entered the Regent Street Polytechnic School of Art in 1946, but had to wait until 1949 for a grant to enable full-time studies, which lasted until 1952. He has said that the two greatest facilities an art school can afford an illustrator are 'free access to printmaking presses, and life models standing there every day waiting to be drawn'. Although no-one can teach someone else how to illustrate, or help channel natural responses to literature into appropriate and personal visual expression; there were three teachers in particular who recognised his exceptional talent and to whom he responded: Stuart Tresilian, Nigel Lambourne and Henry Trivick.

Nigel Lambourne recollects:

> The school was fine-art biased, and I don't remember anyone with the exception of Charles Keeping who emerged and succeeded in illustration. He is, and was then, one of the few *great* illustrators we've got. A superb draughtsman, and he had – for all his marvellously brash, outgoing manner – the ability to tear up purposively anything that didn't work. I don't recall anyone who could draw looking all around him, but then when you looked back at the sheet it was all there. In life classes he'd start from the model and chat and he would dash something off, but the result was anything but superficial. He was the most natural draughtsman I ever saw or worked with. [3]

After completing his studies in 1952, the year of his marriage to the painter Renate Meyer, he was allowed continuing use of the lithographic presses, and in 1956 was invited by Henry Trivick to join the staff of that department. He was visiting lecturer there until 1963, and at Croydon College of Art and Design from 1962 to 1978; since 1979 he has taught lithography for one day a week at Camberwell School of Art and Crafts.

For nearly four years in the early 1950s he produced the strip cartoon for the *Daily Herald,* a stint which ended in acrimony and to which he looks back with little affection. A chance introduction to the artist's agent, B. L. Kearley, produced a little commission within a couple of days, rapidly followed by an appointment with the *doyenne* of children's book editors, Mabel George. This meeting in 1956 established the happiest of relationships, which still continues, with Oxford University Press, for whom he has illustrated more books than for any other publisher.

The drawings for Rosemary Sutcliff's *The Silver Branch,* the first book to result from this collaboration, immediately established Keeping as a new and masterly presence on the scene. Almost as immediately the law that 'nothing is resisted with more savagery than a new form in art' [4] began to operate, and for much of his career Keeping has been regarded by some as a controversial illustrator. This strong critical undercurrent needs to be taken into account in respect of each successive group of books, or phase in his artistic development.

Most children's novels before the 1970s were printed by letterpress and the quality of paper and print effectively eliminated continuous tone, confining the artist to the mechanically-etched line block, or 'zinco'. This was a notoriously difficult medium to

11 *Bleak House,* frontispiece, 1985

work for, and, although a range of fascinating results had been striven for by British romantic artists of the post-war period, with few exceptions reticence, decorum and outmoded conventions prevailed in the field of children's books at the time. To the novels of Rosemary Sutcliff and Henry Treece, Keeping brought vigorous and exuberant handling. Of *The Silver Branch* he says:

> I tried to treat it a bit differently and I did margin drawings – up to that time people had done all these full page drawings and chapter head decorations and tailpieces and I didn't go in for all that – I did double-page spreads and fighting across pages and God knows what else. Anyway Mabel seemed to like it a lot and she commissioned me very quickly to do the next one of Rosemary's. . .

A new idiom was emerging for the illustration of historical fiction, in which, in their very different ways and followed by a host of imitators, the chief protagonists were Charles Keeping and Victor Ambrus. Keeping's views on the appropriate garb for Romans, Saxons and Vikings were typically forthright:

> I went to look up what Romans wore, and promptly forgot it. The same with Treece – nobody knows what Vikings dressed like – it's absolute nonsense. You can make up anything, because the probability is that most people were just covered in any old skins and rags they tied round their bodies to keep

12 *The Silver Branch,* 1957

13 *Horned Helmet*, 1963

warm, and that's how I drew them. (But someone said to me one day, 'You're quite an expert on the Vikings, and do you know all of our children at school draw the Vikings and they take it from you because you must know what they were like?'; I said, 'Me? I wasn't around, I made it all up.') And I do, because I believe you have a liberty to do that . . .

In sharp contrast to the restrictions of the letterpress printing process, lithography was being developed into a sophisticated medium for the illustrator by such leading printing houses as Curwen Press, Jarrolds and W. S. Cowell. This led on to the full-colour picture book explosion of the 1960s which swept Keeping and a number of his contemporaries into international prominence.

Cowells of Ipswich developed a material called 'Plastocowell' which was to prove historically significant for the development of illustration in this country, for it restored and even augmented the range of effects obtainable from working direct on stone, and no photographic screen was needed to transpose the artist's autographic colour separations to the conventional offset press, although how this was done was a closely-guarded secret at the time. The company issued liberal supplies of sheets of this grained plastic to art schools so that students as well as skilled lithographers could experiment, and Keeping became an early enthusiast. His own two picture books for Brockhampton Press, and several titles for the Folio Society, were done in this way and printed by Cowells. For Brockhampton he also produced superlative illustrations to a collection of tales and legends, *Knights, Beasts and Wonders*, which afford the opportunity for a fascinating comparison between his two approaches to black and white illustration at the time: on the one hand he was working within a linear

14 *Knights, Beasts and Wonders*, 1969

discipline which had not expanded technically since the incunabula period, and on the other in a new area where, in Geoffrey Glaister's words, 'the possibilities are limited only by the artist's skill and understanding of the medium'.[5]

In common with many other illustrators, Keeping at first felt that he had come into illustrating children's books largely as a result of the accidental existence of a market. He couldn't have foreseen how committed or distinguished his overall contribution to that field would become, but equally he was aware of a potential for illustrating adult literature that remained unexploited and neglected. He maintains that there are few books, good or bad, that may not have an extra dimension conferred through appropriate illustration, and one of his very few grounds for not entertaining any commission would be that it contained some propaganda element with which he refused to be associated.

One classic to come his way early was *Wuthering Heights,* his first book for the Folio Society. The story behind this is best told from his own conversational account, since it shows how an antipathy that some will find inexplicable was resolved through sheer professionalism:

> It so happened that I must have been one of the few, rare people who had heard of the book but didn't really know it at all. I read it, and I didn't particularly like it, and I'll tell you why. It struck me as the totally romantic conception of a woman who obviously had hardly ever known a man personally, let alone had had an affair with a man. There were these totally unreal people, like none that had ever lived or could have existed; they were just a wild figment of this sad woman's imagination. Therefore they had no faces to me, and no character or reality. Accordingly I drew them without faces and with no particular costumes of any sort. I knew they wore biggish dresses, and I left it at that.

Here's candour and integrity; the illustrator discards all that means little or nothing to him, not in order to shock or scandalise the reader but to distil the atmospheric and histrionic residue. How unorthodox Keeping is found to be in this and in certain other extreme cases will depend on how the role of illustration is to be defined. I certainly think that more than any other artist in this century he has expanded that role, and has attracted criticism for doing so from those unprepared for innovation.

It is often implied that illustration should be subservient to the text, but who is to say so? The relationship between drawings and words, has evolved – as that between words and music – through many stages of formal complexity and at diverse levels of artistic endeavour. In a discussion in 1970, Keeping said:

> Many people believe that an illustration should illustrate the story. This is something I don't really believe. I'm sick to death of the illustration that just shows an incident. It bores one doing it. I would much sooner make a drawing that has an evocative mood . . . It's like two jazz musicians playing together –

one plays piano, the other alto-sax, or one drums and another trumpet. You play as a combination. [6]

As an instance of this, Keeping cites *The Wedding Ghost,* where, in collaboration: 'Leon Garfield writes one story, and I almost illustrate a separate idea . . . a secondary theme'. Again, in his interpretation of Kevin Crossley-Holland's translation of *Beowulf,* he found the crude opposition of good and evil basically unacceptable: 'I tried to present Grendel not so much as a monster but more as a deformed outcast of society . . . and Grendel's mother can't have been absolutely horrid, she must have had some love, because she loved her son enough to come back and avenge his death.'

The 'swinging 'sixties' exercised a fascination for Charles Keeping, then in his own forties; an unforced curiosity into this latest evidence of London's perpetual capacity to renew its colourfulness and spontaneity. This was perhaps echoed in the heightened imagery and colouring of the children's books of the period. Much more recently, in *Sammy Streetsinger,* he tried to send up the pop world gently, without moralising.

A situation of a basically similar kind had arisen slightly earlier, when so much in British art was tending increasingly towards abstraction, in turn creating a dilemma for illustrators who had hitherto regarded themselves as straight draughtsmen. Were they to bury their heads in the sand, or was it necessary to make some effort to keep pace with these new developments? This cannot have been an easy time for Keeping, who admits to a fear of not being part of the world that's going on around him and of falling out of touch. He always knew that he could draw figures in action as well as anyone: 'I could draw them running, jumping, fighting, back-views, forwards, sideways, up, down, – it didn't matter – I'd look down on top of their heads.' And so he allowed experimentation along abstract lines to creep progressively into his own work, almost to the point that he became unsure of his sense of direction. A course of action that he had taken from the best of motives was proving deleterious to his work, and he could see that the road towards abstraction could never be right for him.

It may have been that this apparent crisis (and too much should not in any case be made of it in that many finely illustrated books continued to appear), stemmed from a superabundance of talent and technical facility, and was closely related to his experiences with lithographic printmaking as well:

It must have been in about 1968 that I decided lithography was slipping away, and that I'd do no more at all. I continued to teach, but I didn't want to practise. For ten years I never touched it, my press stood there unused. And then suddenly I felt one day that I might start again, just for my own benefit and to explore ideas, and so I got some plates out and cleaned them up and I started working again . . . and these prints I make all mean something to me. They're mostly concerned with horses, some are comprised of nothing but limitless brick walls with tiny figures. I've got drawers full of them, I'm not interested in showing them, I couldn't care less what anyone thinks of them . . .

15 *Beowulf,* 'Grendel', 1984

Two picture books, *Joseph's Yard* and *Through the Window*, came at the height of his abstract-expressionist phase, with its intense colour, unrestrained pattern-making and tendency towards symbolism. They were thought out equally in terms of colour films for BBC Television, and as books for Oxford. Black and white drawings for *The Christmas Story* had already suggested to him the use of successive levels of plastic overlay as a means of creating an actual, physical depth-of-field to which the camera could respond. The artwork for the colour films was produced as one continuous frieze or mural, 65 feet long in the case of *Joseph's Yard*, but unfortunately the depth and richness of colour which made the films such a triumph could not be reproduced adequately by printing technology and there was a serious loss of quality in the resultant books.

Throughout much of the 1960s the careers of Keeping, Brian Wildsmith and John Burningham had run to some extent in parallel; they were acknowledged as being at the crest of a new wave. Very distinct artistic personalities, they did at the time seem to share a joy in the almost riotous colour possibilities which *they* had unlocked for the picture book. This changed the face of children's publishing and brought wide acclaim; but the external pressure of an international market flooded with camp-followers combined with the artists' own imperative to innovate and develop, in order to bring about a reassessment of individual styles and objectives.

It is difficult to say when and how this occurred for Keeping, and the only reason for enquiry is a real desire to identify and describe fresh qualities that may be present in the middle-period work and which may have eluded critical attention to a degree. Certainly there was no abrupt transition; many individual traits and obsessions with subject matter are life-long immutable matters in any case.

In my view much may be revealed through studying slight changes in the choice of media for a particular task; and in observing the development of a more rigorous selectivity, a heightened delicacy and purity in the use of line. It has already been suggested that the break with lithography may have a bearing, almost as if a musician should sense the need to retreat from working with large orchestral forces for a while to concentrate on the rigorous logic of more intimate forms.

A characteristic that runs through most of Keeping's output is the alternation of two moods; major with minor, apparent ferocity with great tenderness, action with atmosphere. One comes to associate this to some extent with the media in use. Powerful colour or vigorous pen handling in contrast to soft pencilled shadings, diffused sepia or coloured inks staining through from the back of the sheet. All this comes together beautifully in a book like *Wasteground Circus*, where the monochrome riverside wasteland of the endpaper is step by step augmented by subdued colour as the two boys see the circus vans arrive, the preparations for the opening night, and then an incredible colour crescendo as they buy tickets, take their seats and the lights go up – and finally the inevitable return to the endpaper – but with memories.

The Highwayman (1981) may be taken as one final instance in the development of

16 *Classic Ghost Stories,* 'The Canterville Ghost', 1986

17 *Troilus and Criseyde,* jacket drawing, 1984

his many-faceted art for children's books, since it signals a return to straighter draughtsmanship, which also characterises the gentler, poetic mood of much recent work. Nonetheless this is a razor-sharp performance; administering a kick in the pants to Noyes's ultimately soporific metres, and saying to all those children who are asked to close their eyes and imagine – 'Wake up, here's what this story is really about!' This is illustration overtaking literature on the inside; love it or hate it.

A full-length study – which must surely come – would be able to describe all the picture books and show how each sets out to say something different, whilst revealing an underlying symbolic core, in which Keeping's views on the constants of the human condition – life, death, questing, violence, loneliness – find embodiment in the recurrent imagery of cage and embryo, fog and garish lighting, horses and brick walls. At present he will be found to be his own best apologist in the scattered lectures and interviews that have so far been published. One sees the son of a one-time professional boxer at work in these self-assured performances, where skill and contentiousness must have held audiences enthralled. At first he had a tendency to berate teachers, librarians and others for their frequently false prejudgement of the aims of illustration, and then to counter in all honesty and modesty whatever accusations were then current concerning violence or allegedly taboo subject-matter, abstraction or complexity of style, in his own picture books. As the children's book world gradually became more professionalised, more provocative insights on the genesis of work in hand and the purpose of it all are advanced strongly, but with irrepressible good humour. He would be the first to agree that you can't please all the people all the time, but even those who dislike much of his work must concede his immense influence in shaping attitudes to children's books over the past three decades and for the future.[7]

18 *The Lantern Bearers,* jacket drawing, 1959

19 *Barnaby Rudge,* undated pencil study

It is interesting to speculate how Charles Keeping might have handled a commission to illustrate the complete works of Charles Dickens had it come to him earlier in his career. Almost certainly a series of fine, if uneven, drawings would have resulted, and all stops would have been pulled out to exploit the scope of offset lithography whether in black and white or in colour. However, preliminary discussions with the Folio Society opted for letterpress rather than lithographic printing, much to Keeping's disappointment. The limitations this decision imposed were enormous; it placed him back on a parity with Dickens's nineteenth-century illustrators, Cruikshank and 'Phiz', in terms of being restricted to the technical resources of pure, steely line.

He made a start with *Pickwick,* and was well into *Great Expectations,* before he saw proofs of any kind, and then he was astonished to discover that the first proofs had been produced lithographically. During the 1970s it became generally apparent that the age of letterpress was drawing to a close just as surely as that of the steam locomotive had done before it, and amid scenes of comparable partisan nostalgia. Tim Wilkinson, then in charge of design and production for the Folio Society, was determined to continue to use one of the finest surviving letterpress houses – Mackays of Chatham – for as long as possible, but that company had run into a series of crises and changes of ownership to which the letterpress process was to fall swift victim.

The illustrator realised there was no going back at this stage, the series would have to keep its unity, and he must continue to draw without a vestige of tone as though for letterpress, whilst the entire series would gradually be issued lithographically. However painful it may have been for him at the time, I think it may be argued that the enterprise ultimately gained more than it lost thereby. The linear discipline prevented any of the drawings from going 'over the top' in directions that one might have predicted from a high voltage alliance between Keeping and Dickens. Dickens – who left almost as little unillustrated as he left understated – benefits from Keeping's deft and low-key counterpoint. All the volumes stand together amazingly well as the first full edition to be undertaken by a single illustrator. The evocation of a nineteenth-century line characteristic arises naturally from the process described, in a way that no conscious pastiche or nod in that direction – which in any case would have been completely alien to the artist – could possibly have achieved.

But I believe that there is far more to it than that, and that it may be reasonable to adduce the inauguration of a fresh phase in the artist's development through this vast corpus of drawings. Take the fog scene which forms the frontispiece to *Bleak House:* as

20 *Barnaby Rudge,* 1987

a line drawing it is technically formidable. One can't imagine even the conjoined talents of James McNeill Whistler and Paul Klee finding a way round that one, and it is simply one of some 800 drawings in the full edition. In fact there were far more drawings than that, since many were not used, and most of the pen drawings were preceded by an independent pencil study. Those who have seen these frequently prefer the pencil versions to some of the pen and ink ones that were published.

These drawings comprise an important landmark in modern British book illustration, and it may be predicted with confidence that they will come to hold a permanent place alongside those of the greatest masters of the eighteenth and nineteenth centuries. Charles truly believes that there are few books that may not benefit from illustration, and accordingly his work for numerous publishers spans many fields, with the result that each reader associates him only with that part of this range with which they are familiar – children with his picture books and the general reader mainly with the Folio Society publications. Only a full exhibition would reveal the scope and stature of his vision as artist and illustrator.

NOTES

1. Lecture to Children's Literature Association of Canada, reprinted in *ChLA Quarterly* (Winter 1983), 14–19.
2. Quotations, unless otherwise stated, are from an interview recorded at Shortlands, Kent, on 5 February 1986, and subsequent correspondence.
3. Conversation with Nigel Lambourne, recorded at Oakhill, Somerset, on 23 March 1986.
4. Kandinsky, in turn quoting the Russian theatre historian, Nelidoff.
5. G. A. Glaister, *Glaister's Glossary of the Book* (2nd edn, Allen & Unwin, 1979), 383.
6. Charles Keeping, 'Illustration in children's books', *Children's Literature in Education,* 1 (March 1970), 41–54.
7. Awards have included: *Charley, Charlotte and the Golden Canary* (Kate Greenaway Medal, 1968); *Tinker Tailor* (Francis Williams Prize, 1972); *Railway Passage* (Bratislava Biennale Golden Apple Award, 1975); *The Wildman* (Francis Williams Prize, 1977); *The Highwayman* (Kate Greenaway Medal, 1982); *Jack the Treacle Eater* (Emil/Kurt Maschler Award 1987); *Charles Keeping's Classic Tales of the Macabre* (W. H. Smith Illustration Award 1988).

BIBLIOGRAPHY

Note: A few datings, notably those for Heron Books, remain tentative. The illustrations for the Dickens edition were in fact completed ahead of the scheduled rate of issue at two volumes per year.

1953–6
Daily cartoon drawing for the DAILY HERALD

1953
WHY DIE OF HEART DISEASE?
    Ted Kavanagh   Harrap/Clarke, Irwin

1955
HEUTE UND MORGEN, BOOK 2
    M. Freudenberger and M. Kelber   Ginn
MAN MUST MEASURE   Lancelot Hogben
    [ill. with Kenneth Symonds *et al.*]   Rathbone

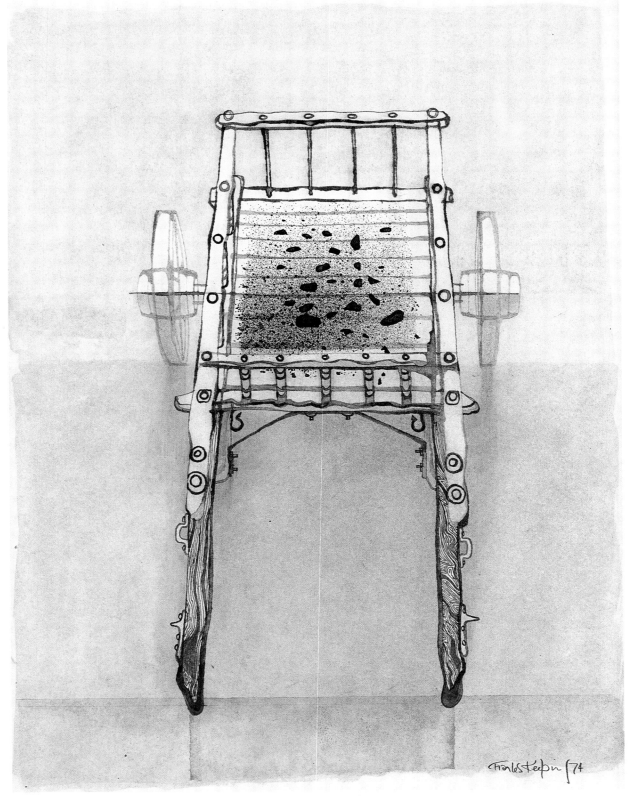

21 *Cockney Ding Dong,* 1975

1956
HEUTE UND MORGEN, BOOK 3
    M. Freudenberger and M. Kelber   Ginn

1957
THE SILVER BRANCH   Rosemary Sutcliff
    OUP/Walck

1958
BRIDGES   John Stewart Murphy   OUP
WARRIOR SCARLET   Rosemary Sutcliff
    OUP/Walck

1959
THE LANTERN BEARERS   Rosemary Sutcliff
    OUP/Walck
MERRILY ON HIGH   Guthrie Foote [ed.]
    OUP
SHIPS   John Stewart Murphy   OUP

1960
KNIGHT'S FEE   Rosemary Sutcliff
    OUP/Walck
RIVERBEND BRICKY   Ira Nesdale   Blackie
ROADS   John Stewart Murphy   OUP
TALES OF PIRATES AND CASTAWAYS
    Kathleen Fidler   Lutterworth

1961
BEOWULF   Rosemary Sutcliff   Bodley Head/
    Dutton [reissued as DRAGON SLAYER by
    Penguin in association with Bodley Head,
    1966]
CANALS   John Stewart Murphy   OUP
DAWN WIND   Rosemary Sutcliff   OUP/Walck
THE HEROES   Charles Kingsley   Hutchinson
KING SOLOMON'S MINES   H. Rider Haggard
    Blackie
'THE QUEEN OF TRENT'   Mitchell Dawson
    Abelard-Schuman
TALES OF THE WEST COUNTRY   Kathleen
    Fidler   Lutterworth

1962
FLOOD WARNING   Paul Berna   Bodley Head/
    Pantheon
THE GOLDEN AGE and DREAM DAYS
    Kenneth Grahame   Bodley Head/Dufour
    1965
LOST JOHN   Barbara Leonie Picard
    OUP/Criterion

THREE TRUMPETS   Ruth Chandler
    Abelard-Schuman
TIPITI THE ROBIN   René Guillot   Bodley
    Head

1963
THE CASTLE AND THE HARP   Philip Rush
    Collins/McGraw-Hill
DAMS   John Stewart Murphy   OUP
HARRIET AND THE CHERRY PIE   Clare
    Compton   Bodley Head
HORNED HELMET   Henry Treece
    Brockhampton/Criterion
THE KNIGHTS OF THE GOLDEN TABLE
    E. M. Almedingen   Bodley Head/Lippincott
THE LATCHKEY CHILDREN   Eric Allen   OUP
THE MOONSTONE   Wilkie Collins   Heron
    [n.d.]
PATRICK KENTIGERN KEENAN   Mollie
    Hunter   Blackie/Funk 1965 [as THE
    SMARTEST MAN IN IRELAND]
REFLECTIONS: AN ENGLISH COURSE FOR
    STUDENTS AGED 14–18   Simon Clements
    et al.   OUP
UNDER GREEK SKIES   S. C. George and
    Brenda Collins   New Zealand Department of
    Education

1964
BRICKY AND THE HOBO   Ira Nesdale
    Blackie
THE CHILDREN'S CRUSADE   Henry Treece
    Longman
THE GROUP APPROACH TO DRAMA, BOOKS
    1–3   D. E. Adland   Longman
JENNY   Joan Tate   Heinemann
THE KELPIE'S PEARLS   Mollie Hunter
    Blackie
THE KING'S CONTEST   James Holding
    Abelard-Schuman
LA CAZA DEL LOBO   B. Mitchell and N. J.
    Margetts   Longman
THE LAST OF THE VIKINGS   Henry Treece
    Brockhampton/Pantheon 1966 [as
    THE LAST VIKING]
MISCELLANY ONE   Edward Blishen [ed.]
    OUP/Watts 1965
THE NEXT-DOORS   Joan Tate   Heinemann
RAILWAYS   John Stewart Murphy   OUP
THE STORY OF EGYPT   Jacoba Tadema-Sporry
    Nelson
THEY TOLD MR HAKLUYT   Frank Knight
    [ed.]   Macmillan

THE TREASURE OF SIEGFRIED
E. M. Almedingen   Bodley Head/Lippincott
1965

WHITSUN WARPATH   Elizabeth Grove   Cape/
Clarke, Irwin

WUTHERING HEIGHTS   Emily Brontë   Folio

YOUR ENGLISH, BOOK 4   Denys Thompson
and R. J. Harris   Heinemann

1965

BENT IS THE BOW   Geoffrey Trease   Nelson

DAMIEN, THE LEPERS' FRIEND   John
Reginald Milsome   Burns & Oates

ELIDOR   Alan Garner   Collins

HEROES AND HISTORY   Rosemary Sutcliff
Batsford/Putnam

KING HORN   Kevin Crossley-Holland
Macmillan/Dutton

THE LIFE OF OUR LORD   Henry Daniel-Rops
Burns & Oates/Hawthorn

THE MARK OF THE HORSE LORD   Rosemary
Sutcliff   OUP

SPLINTERED SWORD   Henry Treece
Brockhampton/Dell

STUMPY   Clifford Carver   OUP

LA VUELTO DEL LOBO   B. Mitchell and N. J.
Margetts   Longman

WELLS   John Stewart Murphy   OUP

1966

ALL QUIET ON THE WESTERN FRONT
Erich Maria Remarque   Folio

BLACK DOLLY   Charles Keeping
Brockhampton/World [as
MOLLY O' THE MOORS: THE STORY
OF A PONY]

CELTIC FOLK AND FAIRY TALES   Eric and
Nancy Protter [eds.]   Meredith [USA]

DOCKS AND HARBOURS   John Stewart
Murphy   OUP

ISLAND OF THE GREAT YELLOW OX
Walter Macken   Macmillan

KOMANTCIA   Harold Keith   OUP

MRS JENNY   Joan Tate   Heinemann

AN OWL FOR HIS BIRTHDAY   Richard
Potts   Lutterworth

RAIN BOAT   Lace Kendall   Hamish Hamilton

THE RED TOWERS OF GRANADA   Geoffrey
Trease   Macmillan/Vanguard

SHAUN AND THE CART-HORSE   Charles
Keeping   OUP/Watts

THE SKY-EATER   James Holding
Abelard-Schuman

1967

BACH   Frederic Westcott   Garnet Miller/Walck

CHAMPION OF CHARLEMAGNE   Marie Butts
Bodley Head

CHARLEY, CHARLOTTE AND THE GOLDEN
CANARY   Charles Keeping   OUP/Watts

THE COLD FLAME   James Reeves   Hamish
Hamilton/Meredith

THE DREAM-TIME   Henry Treece
Brockhampton/Meredith

OF HUMAN BONDAGE   W. Somerset Maugham
Heron [n.d.]

MAINLY IN MOONLIGHT   Nicholas Stuart
Gray   Meredith, [USA]

THE STRANGE CASE OF DR JEKYLL AND
MR HYDE, AND OTHER STORIES
R. L. Stevenson   Heron [n.d.]

SWORDS FROM THE NORTH   Henry Treece
Pantheon [USA]

THOMAS AND THE WARLOCK   Mollie Hunter
Blackie

WITH BOOKS ON HER HEAD   Edna Walker
Chandler   Meredith [USA]

THE WRECKER   R. L. Stevenson   Heron [n.d.]

1968

AFTER MANY A SUMMER   Aldous Huxley
Heron [n.d.]

ALFIE AND THE FERRYBOAT
Charles Keeping   OUP/Watts [as
ALFIE FINDS THE OTHER SIDE OF
THE WORLD]

AN ANTHOLOGY OF FREE VERSE   James
Reeves [ed.]   Blackwell

THE CHRISTMAS STORY, AS TOLD ON
'PLAY SCHOOL'   Charles Keeping
BBC Publications/Watts

THE FLIGHT OF THE DOVES   Walter Macken
Macmillan

GRIMBOLD'S OTHER WORLD   Nicholas Stuart
Gray   Meredith [USA]

THE HAUNTED MINE   Richard Potts
Lutterworth

THE MIXTURE AS BEFORE   W. Somerset
Maugham   Heron

MORE NEW ARABIAN NIGHTS
R. L. Stevenson   Heron [n.d.]

NEW ARABIAN NIGHTS   R. L. Stevenson
Heron [n.d.]

POKO AND THE GOLDEN DEMON   James
Holding   Abelard-Schuman

THE SHADOW LINE   Joseph Conrad   Heron
[n.d.]

THE STORY OF AENEAS Kenneth McLeish
Longman
TIME MUST HAVE A STOP Aldous Huxley
Heron [n.d.]
TINKER TAILOR: FOLK SONG TALES
Charles Keeping [ed.] Brockhampton/World
WITHIN THE TIDES Joseph Conrad Heron
[n.d.]

1969

THE APPLE-STONE Nicholas Stuart Gray
Meredith [USA]
THE 'ILIAD' AND 'ODYSSEY' OF HOMER
[radio plays] Kenneth Cavander,
ill. Swiethlan Kraczyna and Charles Keeping
BBC Publications
JOSEPH'S YARD Charles Keeping
OUP/Watts [also as a television play from his
own story, 1970]

KNIGHTS, BEASTS AND WONDERS
Margaret J. Miller Brockhampton/White
MR BRITLING SEES IT THROUGH
H. G. Wells Heron [n.d.]
RUINED CITY and LANDFALL Neville Shute
Heron
THE TALE OF ANCIENT ISRAEL
Roger Lancelyn Green Dent

22 *Adam and Paradise Island,* 1989

23 *Black Beauty,* 1988

1970

THE ANGRY VALLEY Nigel Grimshaw
    Longman
EARLY ENCOUNTERS John Watts Longman
ENJOY READING! BOOK 4 R. E. Rogerson
    and C. M. Smith [eds.] Chambers
FIVE FABLES FROM FRANCE Lee Cooper
    Abelard-Schuman
THE GOD BENEATH THE SEA Leon Garfield
    and Edward Blishen Longman/Pantheon
ON THE BEACH Neville Shute Heron [n.d.]
OVER THE HILLS TO FABYLON Nicholas
    Stuart Gray Hawthorn [USA]
THROUGH THE WINDOW Charles Keeping
    OUP/Watts [also as a television play from his
    own story, 1970]

1971

ENJOY READING! BOOK 5 R. E. Rogerson
    and C. M. Smith [eds.] Chambers
THE GARDEN SHED Charles Keeping OUP
THE IDIOT Fyodor Dostoyevsky Folio
THE POET'S TALES William Cole [ed.]
    World [USA]
THE VALLEY OF THE FROST GIANTS Mary
    Francis Shura Lothrop [USA]

1972

THE INVADERS Henry Treece
    Brockhampton/Crowell
THE SPIDER'S WEB Charles Keeping
    OUP/Phillips
THE TWELVE LABORS OF HERCULES
    Robert Newman Crowell [USA]/Hutchinson
    1973
WELAND, SMITH OF THE GODS Ursula
    Synge Bodley Head/Phillips
WIZARDS AND WAMPUM Roger Squire
    Abelard-Schuman

1973

THE BIRDS, AND OTHER STORIES Lewis
    Jones [ed.] Longman
THE CAPRICORN BRACELET Rosemary
    Sutcliff OUP/Walck
GHOST STORIES OF M. R. JAMES Nigel
    Kneale [ed.] Folio
THE GOLDEN SHADOW Leon Garfield and
    Edward Blishen Longman/Pantheon
I'LL TELL YOU A TALE Ian Serraillier
    Longman

THE NANNY GOAT AND THE FIERCE DOG
    Charles Keeping Abelard-Schuman/Phillips
RICHARD Charles Keeping OUP
WEIRDIES Helen Hoke Franklin Watts/Watts
    [as WEIRDIES, WEIRDIES, WEIRDIES]
WHEN DARKNESS COMES Robert Swindells
    [jacket and frontispiece only]
    Brockhampton/Morrow

1974

THE MAGIC HORNS Forbes Stuart Abelard
    Schuman/Addison-Wesley
MONSTERS, MONSTERS, MONSTERS Helen
    Hoke Franklin Watts/Watts
RAILWAY PASSAGE Charles Keeping OUP

1975

ABOUT THE SLEEPING BEAUTY Pamela
    Lyndon Travers McGraw-Hill, [USA]/
    Collins 1977
COCKNEY DING DONG Charles Keeping
    [ed.] Kestrel Books with EMI Music
    Publishing [Charles Keeping recorded a
    selection of these songs with his aunts and
    uncles and cousins on the Line Records label,
    no. 2032]
THE LITTLE BOOK OF SYLVANUS David
    Kossoff Collins/St Martins
TERRY ON THE FENCE Bernard Ashley
    OUP/Phillips
TOWER BLOCKS: POEMS OF THE CITY
    Marian Lines Franklin Watts
WASTEGROUND CIRCUS Charles Keeping
    OUP

1976

A BOY AND HIS BIKE Richard Potts
    Dobson
THE CASTLE OF OTRANTO Horace Walpole
    Folio
THE DANCER OF BURTON FAIR Forbes
    Stuart Abelard-Schuman
LES MISÉRABLES Victor Hugo [2 vols.]
    Folio
THE WILDMAN Kevin Crossley-Holland
    Deutsch

1977

BLOOD FEUD Rosemary Sutcliff OUP/Dutton
FOG MAGIC Julia L. Sauer [jacket only]
    Hodder & Stoughton
INTER-CITY Charles Keeping OUP

SPECTRES, SPOOKS AND SHUDDERY
    SHADES Helen Hoke [ed.]
    Franklin Watts/Watts [as
    HAUNTS, HAUNTS, HAUNTS]

1978
MISS EMILY AND THE BIRD OF MAKE-
    BELIEVE Charles Keeping Hutchinson
RIVER Charles Keeping OUP

1979
THE BATSFORD BOOK OF STORIES IN
    VERSE FOR CHILDREN Charles Causley
    [ed.] Batsford
BREAKBACK ALLEY Tony Drake Collins
THE MERMAID'S REVENGE Forbes Stuart
    Abelard-Schuman
THE ROBBERS Nina Bawden Gollancz
THE TALE OF PRINCE IGOR Leonard
    Clark Dobson

1980
BREAK IN THE SUN Bernard Ashley OUP/
    Phillips
WILLIE'S FIRE ENGINE Charles Keeping
    OUP

1981
GODS AND MEN Bailey, MacLeish, Spearman
    [eds.], ill. Collard, Keeping, Roy OUP
GREAT EXPECTATIONS Charles Dickens
    Folio
THE HIGHWAYMAN Alfred Noyes OUP
THE PICKWICK PAPERS Charles Dickens
    Folio

1982
THE BEGINNING OF THE ARMADILLOES
    Rudyard Kipling Macmillan/Bedrick
EDWIN DROOD Charles Dickens Folio
OUR MUTUAL FRIEND Charles Dickens
    Folio
THE SUN, DANCING Charles Causley [ed.]
    Kestrel

1983
DAVID COPPERFIELD Charles Dickens Folio
HARD TIMES Charles Dickens Folio

1984
BEOWULF Kevin Crossley-Holland OUP
DOMBEY AND SON Charles Dickens Folio

OLIVER TWIST Charles Dickens Folio
RIKKI-TIKKI-TAVI AND OTHER ANIMAL
    STORIES Rudyard Kipling Macmillan/
    Bedrick
SAMMY STREETSINGER Charles Keeping
    OUP
TROILUS AND CRISEYDE Geoffrey Chaucer
    [jacket only] Longman

1985
BLEAK HOUSE Charles Dickens Folio
A TALE OF TWO CITIES Charles Dickens
    Folio
THE WEDDING GHOST Leon Garfield OUP

1986
CHARLES KEEPING'S BOOK OF CLASSIC
    GHOST STORIES Blackie/Bedrick
THE LADY OF SHALOTT Alfred Tennyson
    OUP
LITTLE DORRIT Charles Dickens Folio
NICHOLAS NICKLEBY Charles Dickens
    Folio

1987
BARNABY RUDGE Charles Dickens Folio
CHARLES KEEPING'S CLASSIC TALES OF
    THE MACABRE Blackie/Bedrick
JACK THE TREACLE EATER Charles Causley
    Macmillan
THE OLD CURIOSITY SHOP Charles Dickens
    Folio
THE TALE OF SIR GAWAIN Neil Philip
    Lutterworth

1988
BLACK BEAUTY Anna Sewell Gollancz
CHRISTMAS BOOKS Charles Dickens Folio
DRACULA Bram Stoker Blackie/Bedrick
FRANKENSTEIN Mary Shelley
    Blackie/Bedrick
MARTIN CHUZZLEWIT Charles Dickens
    Folio

1989
ADAM AND PARADISE ISLAND
    Charles Keeping OUP

3 · FAITH JAQUES

AGAINST the background of the unremarkable flood of books published for children each year, one spots from time to time a book which breaks new ground — Sendak's *Where the Wild Things Are* — or one which through sheer quality is clearly a classic in the making. The best of Faith Jaques's children's books, from a working span which now approaches four decades, fall into this second category; books which are already being sought out as the true heirs of Greenaway, Rackham and Ardizzone become increasingly apparent to a new generation of collectors.[1] Nostalgia has a large role to play in the recall and re-interpretation of the artist's own childhood world, but there must always be a key for today's child to unlock the door to that world, and a magic beyond that door.

Faith Jaques, who was born in Leicester on 13 December 1923 and spent a conventional childhood there, writes that she has hardly stopped drawing and reading since the age of four, but it was not until she left Leicester that she was to meet people who read and discussed books as much as she did. The writer Frank O'Connor once propounded in a television interview a theory that all cities have a mental age above which they can no longer provide intellectual sustenance for their sons and daughters; hence Cork would have a mental age of thirteen and Dublin one of about eighteen. Faith would probably assign the Leicester of her youth a value of fourteen on the 'O'Connor scale', whilst acknowledging that things may be very different now. Even during her years at the Wyggeston Grammar School, family and friends remained rooted in a social life and interests that were centred on local business and commerce and from which she found herself increasingly alienated. 'I went to a perfectly good school, but truly believe I was educated by Penguin Books, public libraries and the BBC.'[2]

Although at first it cannot have been at all clear how her twin interests in art and literature could be made to work together in career terms, it must have become plain that the eventual answers would only be found against an independent background; a life — and as soon as possible a home — of her own. Independence would make the career possible, but the career in turn must finance that independence entirely.

24 *Tilly's House*, 1979

It will be seen later that single-minded determination and good navigation brought this objective within reach quite quickly, but to have maintained status in a fickle market over a long period of time, as Faith Jaques has done, explains and is explained by much in her character, her actions, and her art. Although she is a splendid conversationalist and a prodigious letter-writer, she has always liked to be alone a lot and actually prefers her own company. This frees time for compulsive but discriminating reading, and she finds cats impeccably adapted to accord with this chosen life-style.

From the beginning Faith Jaques's technique as an illustrator has been based on meticulous research followed up by unremitting hard work. Hers is an art in which

improvisation – the short cut or happy accident – plays little part. How is it that magical or emotional power doesn't fly out of the window on occasion when confronted by such an organised and conscientious practioner? An answer of sorts may be reached by likening her to a theatrical performer for whom preparation and rehearsal must continue until time and place become tangible, and the significance of each word and gesture first nature. Only then can a convincing interpretation take wing.

> I like to have as much knowledge and information as possible, in order to select the important factors and throw out what's unnecessary. It's an imaginative and analytical process all in one. But I need information because I've always hated 'fake' illustrations where the artist botches, or tries to disguise, the things he or she doesn't understand. As a child, in the 1930s, I was always riled by the embroidered tablecloths which practically everyone had brought out when visitors came to tea: they were all embroidered tastefully with ladies in poke bonnets and crinolines standing by hollyhocks. I used to call them 'crinoline ladies with no faces' because the poke bonnets carefully obscured the entire profile of the face; the designer couldn't draw faces, presumably? You can still see these transfers for embroidery even now . . . Decoration and ornament are rife with ignorance of structure or knowledge of period style; haven't we all seen a million examples of fake baroque or rococo, showing no understanding of period? And who (except Rex Whistler) bothers with the differences between medieval gothic, Regency gothic, and Victorian gothic? . . . I like to know how tables and chairs are made, how a building is constructed – perhaps too much so – I've probably got a bit too 'documentary' at times. But I believe you can't simplify, or stylise, unless you understand the underlying principles of the style and period. Eric Fraser, a marvellous stylist, could illustrate a Greek play or a Victorian novel without changing his natural style because he knew what he was doing: no Corinthian capital ever appeared on a Doric column in his drawings!

If, in her own words, 'Information sparks imagination, sound drawing underpins creative flight', then the foundations for this were laid whilst she was a student at the Leicester College of Art for eighteen months in 1941–2. This was at the time of the Board of Education examinations, entailing two years' intensive study for the drawing exam, followed by two years leading to the painting qualification, which was normally undertaken with a view to entry into teaching.

The approach to drawing was severely academic: a thorough grounding in anatomy, perspective, light and shade, drawing from life and cast, classical composition and the study of the histories of architecture, furniture and costume – in fact those disciplines which the art academies had long provided as a background for fine artists, printmakers and illustrators alike.[3]

Her studies at Leicester began as soon as she was able to leave school, but she passed the drawing examination in her brief time there as well as fitting in a lot of painting under the encouragement of D. P. Carrington. Painting exerted an allure without practical prospects, whereas teaching as an end in itself held no attraction. The volition towards book illustration was already present, but the need to break the mould and escape into a wider world must have built towards a crisis at this time. It is possible to see how far she had already travelled, from recollections of some of the earlier influences that were still found to be valid when the time came to map out her true path as an illustrator:

> I think I became an illustrator by way of Rex Whistler and Eric Fraser. Sometime in the 1930s I looked through a copy of Beverley Nichols's *Down the Garden Path* which was lying around the house. I greatly admired Whistler's illustrations, and later, when I saw *Gulliver's Travels* I thought his illustrations were some of the best I had ever seen (and still do). From the age of about ten I used to cut out magazine illustrations that I liked, and many of my favourites were by Eric Fraser, taken from *Radio Times* . . . These two artists still stand as exemplars, to be followed later by Edward Ardizzone.

Faith volunteered to join the WRNS when she was old enough: 'in order to get away from home and from Leicester.' Rapid promotion led to her being stationed at the New Bodleian Library in Oxford, doing useful and fascinating work filing and interpreting topographical photographs of Germany, Occupied Europe and other potential theatres of war. She organised a filing department for more than one million photographs acquired from all sources (of which the family seaside snapshot album was not the least) and was responsible for producing at the drop of a hat everything available on, say, a given point of coastline or the approaches to a village, for inter-Services use as part of the war effort.

During these years at Oxford, despite this exacting occupation, she found a certain amount of time to attend evening classes in life-drawing held at the Oxford School of Art under the tuition of such artists as William Roberts and Bernard Meninsky, and it was there that she finally realised that book illustration was what she wanted to do. Perhaps not surprisingly, her work for the Services spilled over into a private habit of accumulating, classifying and filing visual reference material; and to the beginnings of a very comprehensive reference collection (of some 15,000 pictures to date) covering history of costume, architecture and ornament, trees, transport, the changing environment and telling social detail. She still keeps up this archive and its related library of books on specialised subjects as an invaluable working tool.

Both within and outside the University, Oxford acted as a haven for many who had moved away from London during the war, and so Faith made her first friendships with authors and intellectuals as well as artists and illustrators. Her prolific reading and artistic theorising had long been carried out in isolation and the abstract, and now here

were the people behind it all: approachable, stimulating and amusing. She was introduced to cinema[4] and theatre and to the inter-relatedness of the arts. The role of the interpretative illustrator became more clearly defined:

> Illustration has been called 'an impure art',[5] and being an executant art, rather than the primarily creative one, this may be true, since in the context of narrative illustration the text is normally provided by someone else. But so it is with actors, solo musicians and opera singers . . . we have to serve his text or his music, and search out the style and 'voice' of the creator. One mustn't be subservient and trot along behind like a dog on a lead, but one mustn't knock him out of court either. We need really to understand the author's intentions and his manner of conveying them, and try to enter and extend his characters and incidents – 'the power to slide into another man's soul', said Mervyn Peake . . .

Knowledgeable friends recommended that she should resume her art training at the Central School of Arts and Crafts, since of all the London art schools, the Central had at that time the strongest orientation towards the practical application of art and design in industry and commerce. She longed to settle in London in any case, and so she was able after a relatively short period of training, and instruction from and contact with artists as diverse as John Farleigh, Laurence Scarfe, Ruskin Spear, Roderigo Moynihan, and John Minton among others,[6] to make the necessary transition from art school to starting to earn a living with less anguish than those less talented or organised. (However, material struggle enough there was, and an unpublished recollection is reproduced as an extended note, both for its relevance to underlying themes in her work as well as for its general social historical interest.)[7]

She studied at the Central from 1946–8 and was soon herself engaged as a lecturer, but never for more than two days a week, first at the Guildford School of Art from 1948–53, and later at the Hornsey College of Art from 1960-8. This brought a measure of financial security and continuity during the uphill years of striving to become known and established as one of the select group of professional black and white illustrators. Whilst still at College or shortly after leaving, she had made her début in many of the leading magazines of the day – *Strand, Lilliput, World Review, The Leader, Our Time, Housewife, House and Garden* – journals which then provided an important outlet for illustrators of calibre. From the end of the war until the late 1950s there was a considerable market for skilled line artists:

> . . . So much work available at this period – photography has taken most of it now. Advertising was much more fanciful and imaginative . . . I did decorative menus, borders and ornaments for Shell and ICI; half-page newspaper illustrations for J. Arthur Rank; drawings for the Central Office of Information, the Gas Board, Electricity Board, Milk Board, Cheese Board; full-colour illustrations for Horniman's Tea, decoration for Fortnum & Mason's,

25 *The Orchard Book of Nursery Rhymes,* in preparation

exhibition work, Portmeirion mugs, Post Office posters and – later – commemorative stamps, educational film-strips, and so on . . . I worked for most of the advertising agents of the time, and earned quite a lot.

Many magazine editors and advertising art directors shared an idealistic, enterprising and informed view of the nature and scope of illustration. Standards overall were remarkably high at this time, but the artist's remuneration followed no consistent pattern. One quickly came to hear of the clients who paid handsomely, as well as the many who offered derisory sums and paid tardily. The first of Faith's redoubtable series of battles (from which the more timid as well as the more professional of her colleagues were equally to benefit) must have taken place quite early on. Battles – in which Faith was always ready to field her legal light artillery should need arise – took place against the background of a continuous campaign for educating the client in the realities of the freelance artist's life. In British business circles, despite the calls made on artistic skills and the evident benefits to be derived, a widespread, philistine stereotype persisted: it was that of the artist as someone who actually aspired to dwell in a garret and live on air – and those designers and illustrators who aimed for the highest professional standards in all matters still had a long, hard task ahead of them.

Another important source of commissions for representational black and white illustration was *Radio Times,* to which Faith regularly contributed drawings from 1948 to 1973. More than one book has been devoted to the high aesthetic standards achieved in this publication, notably during the decade 1950–60 when R. D. Usherwood was

26 *On the Eve,* mid 1960s

27 *The Storm,* 1966

editor. In each issue one could expect to find an abundance of fine individual drawings by such eminent artists as Edward Ardizzone, Pearl Falconer, Eric Fraser, David Knight, Lynton Lamb, R. F. Micklewright, Leonard Rosoman, Ronald Searle, Fritz Wegner, as well as by Faith Jaques and a host of others. Faith produced well over 500 drawings for *Radio Times,* illustrating plays and books (generally eighteenth- and nineteenth-century classics) and the extensive reading this involved developed further a fine ear and a fine eye for nuances of period, location and social mores.

The background research for a single *Radio Times* drawing might frequently prove as extensive as that required for the actual illustration of the same text as a whole. The concentration of all this effort into a tiny area frequently resulted in illustrations of great concision and dramatic power. In the years before television became the dominant medium for most households, these small illustrative windows overlooking radio drama served the listener well, and the illustrators had the satisfaction of knowing that no real characters, costumes or settings would appear to conflict with their own visualisation. 'Faith Jaques is a particularly conscientious and thoughtful illustrator. She has clearly studied the character [of Soames Forsyte] and come to a definite view of what he looked like. Her style of drawing has a flavour of the period, but this in itself would be no substitute for an accurate reading of the text.'[8]

In addition to drawings for *Radio Times* and other magazines, there was a constant demand for book jackets, greetings cards and menus, as well as for all the types of

28 *A Likely Lad*, 1971

commission already mentioned. Taken together with lecturing, this must have added up to a very reasonable income for the time.

But, despite this apparent success, what Faith wanted to do most in life still eluded her. After a number of years producing decorations and illustrations for all and sundry, she was still not in sight of being able to devote her time exclusively to the illustration of books in black and white, and for a time it looked as though this could never be economically viable. However, the whole market for illustration was gradually to change, and this combined with her growing reputation within publishing to achieve this ambition by the mid-1960s.

By this time the magazines which had used black and white extensively had either ceased publication or had embraced new tendencies in photo-journalism. Ornament and decoration had become unfashionable as Swiss-inspired theories of typography and page layout gained ground. The revolution in colour printing was harnessed in these fields to successive youth-dominated trends in op and pop culture, advertising and fashion photographics, prefigurations of computer graphics and so forth to the virtual exclusion of more traditional approaches to illustration. This drastic contraction in demand from the magazine, advertising and ephemeral sectors was happily counterbalanced by an unprecedented growth in the market for both black and white and colour attributable to new initiatives in book publishing.

In the past Faith had received sporadic commissions for books on gardening and cookery, educational biographies and abridgements, even pop-up and colouring books, as well as for the splendid series of decorations produced over the years for the *Saturday Book*. She also had a commitment to the four-volume *Hugh Evelyn History of Costume* that then stretched into the future – but that was closely related to a lifelong interest. Once the primary objective of working exclusively for book publishers was within sight, she immediately set another; and that was not to let herself be regarded as

29 *The Faber Book of Greek Legends*, 'Agamemnon', 1973

30 *Charlie and the Great Glass Elevator,* 1973

an all-rounder any longer, but to concentrate on the illustration of imaginative literature, whether for adults or children.

As things turned out there were to be comparatively few adult books. *The Torrents of Spring* for Folio Society proved an uncharacteristic venture for which she was induced to provide two-colour lithographs, not a medium she might normally have chosen to work in. Chinagraph is used deftly to invoke poetic garden or landscape settings, but becomes over-worked in establishing the foreground characters. An engaging early book; but comparison with the black and white 'trailer' drawing for the same novelist's *On the Eve* shows greater dramatic urgency and suggests that her finest drawings to European literature and drama are to be sought in the corpus of work for *Radio Times*. (In recent years Faith has in fact advanced rigorous arguments against the illustration of modern adult fiction.)[9]

By 1967 the successful outcome of this resolve to specialise is apparent from a glance at the bibliography of books illustrated. In the years prior to this her career had taken the strain of frequent visits and absences for family reasons, and it had been necessary to restrict her output and to work overtime in consequence. And during the revolutionary year of 1968, when the Hornsey College became a national centre of student unrest, she said her farewell to teaching with mixed feelings. Any committed teacher must continue to miss the contact and experience long afterwards, but the extra working hours could hardly have come at a better time.

In the presentation of children's fiction, writers and illustrators now came together in a natural alliance, resenting the 'children's' prefix which seemed to imply a diminution of their work as compared to that for the serious or 'adult' market. Mutual respect for the value of each other's contribution increased between collaborators. And so it is not surprising, in view of her highly developed literary sense, to find Faith's name linked with those of writers of merit and distinction (including, among others, Allan Ahlberg, Gillian Avery, Nina Bawden, Helen Cresswell, Roald Dahl, Leon Garfield, Ursula Moray Williams, Philippa Pearce, Margery Sharp and Henry Treece[10]), as well as a natural instinct on the part of publishers to associate her with classic children's writers of the past such as Andrew Lang, John Masefield, E. Nesbit, Arthur Ransome and many more.

Having observed that a new balance was being struck between author and illustrator (as earlier between soloist and accompanist on the concert platform), and sensing that many publishers were slow to acknowledge how much the current children's book boom owed to their efforts, it was natural that Faith should have been drawn once again into the issue of 'illustrators' rights'.[11]

> . . . The artist creates the *visual* image, which is . . . accepted by the reader and often becomes part of popular culture. From Struwwelpeter to Orlando, from the Mad Hatter to Mrs Tiggy-Winkle; Pooh and Piglet, Mary Poppins, William, Paddington Bear, Mr Toad, and Mole, Rat and Badger, not to mention Sherlock Holmes – the list is endless . . . It should also be remembered that often the character is not described [in appearance] in the text at all; the illustrator is doing his job of translating the author's meaning into a visual form.[12]

> . . . 'Alice' is not described in the text at all I believe; our idea of her appearance – still the most familiar, despite new versions by many illustrators – Tenniel's 'Alice', is still the way we think she looked. And Sherlock Holmes' deer-stalker hat is never mentioned in the texts of the stories; we owe the well-known image entirely to the illustrator, Sydney Paget. All the films followed this image, and perhaps it's no surprise that Basil Rathbone seems the 'best' Sherlock Holmes; because he is so like Paget's illustrations?[13]

On the nature of this balance between text and illustration, she would argue that because the arts are interlinked, the analogy with acting may prove to be a valid one. Like an actor, the illustrator must regard the author's script as sacrosanct. It forms the starting point and must be interpreted with fidelity. On the other hand the actor/illustrator has to bring an individual approach to the task, and not merely underline points which the author has already established consummately within the text. In this sense, too, any film or television adaptation of a literary classic *becomes* illustration.

31 *The War of the Birds and the Beasts,* 1984

For a decade or more Faith Jaques worked intensively as a black and white illustrator with some of the finest writers of fiction, an activity which has continued on a slightly reduced scale to the present. The 1960s and early 1970s were vintage years for the illustrated novel and anthology for older children. Towards the end of this period, Faith, like a seismograph, began to register misgivings. In conversation with other artists, she proved capable of questioning whether narrative illustration could have any real future. In part this reflected her current preoccupation with the lines along which her own work might need to develop, but it was also a sober assessment of a changing scene. In her view only a handful of illustrators with either the technical ability or motivation necessary for this work remained, and it was also open to question whether publishers would continue to commission black and white illustration to the same extent as hitherto. Over recent years and for economic reasons, the age group for which the trade publisher would consider having a children's novel illustrated had continued to drop until it levelled out at a reading age of about ten.

Faith's analysis may have been largely borne out by subsequent events; certainly fewer and fewer novels are illustrated; if they are important ones they go to the established handful. The names of several artists spring to mind who moved on into other activities after initial acclaim, and little fresh talent of note appeared on this particular scene, although there have been encouraging recent signs. A fallow period is often needed until conditions change sufficiently to make room for new thinking and approaches. So Faith Jaques may have sensed, without any disillusionment with the

32 *The Old Nursery Stories*, 1975

black and white medium as such, that its best days might soon be over for the illustration of children's fiction, at least for the time being.

Throughout the intensive period of black and white illustration to imaginative literature, it does seem that Faith Jaques was deliberately holding the full-scale deployment of colour in reserve for the future. It must of course have been a bonus to see her full-colour jacket artwork for these titles benefit from advances in colour printing, but she appears to have had no wish to be drawn into picture books for younger children until she was quite ready. To have attempted to work at both levels concurrently would have been an impossibility for an artist with such single-minded devotion to excellence in her own, or for that matter anyone else's, professional work. Some remarks of the time may shed light on a kind of barrier that may have been set up to defend her time and concentration for the work in hand:

> I find black-and-white illustration to a high quality text much more demanding than a picture book. It requires a different attitude . . . Why do the Greenaway and Caldecott prizes always go to picture books? Any artist ought to be able to do something decent in that area where you've got colour and freedom. Whereas illustrating a really good text requires knowledge and understanding and draughtsmanship and design and a million other things. [14]

This dismissive attitude towards the picture book was to undergo modification as her thoughts turned in that direction in the mid-1970s. Her re-interpretation of the *Peter Piper's Alphabet* rhymes of 1813 as *A Peck of Pepper* had appeared as early as 1974, and it remains an enchanting book. She may have been persuaded to tackle it because the period was familiar territory, and line and colour wash the only appropriate medium. A glance at this book is enough to tell that the illustrator enjoyed doing it and saw that it was going well. In addition, she had overall control of the design and no living author to consider. And so it may be reasonable to assign to the experience of working on this title the beginnings of the two quite different types of colour project which ensued: the cut-out models which augment the tradition of the early chapbooks and Pollock's Toy Theatre, and her own picture books.

It was earlier suggested that Faith had tended to regard the typical picture book as a free ride for the self-indulgent colourist, based on a tricksy or a vacuous story line. Things looked different once she could visualise the direction her own picture books might take. She had always longed to write, and so set to work on *Tilly's House*, in secret. There is much of herself in this first book, and at one level it sets forth the values and virtues by which Faith Jaques has always set store: 'It was an awful long time before I got a house, but in 1964 I bought my pretty house in Uxbridge Street, which gave me great joy for sixteen years. *Tilly's House* is built around all these early feelings, as you probably realise.'

The significance of this first book was instantly recognized by Judith Elliott, then

33 *Tales of Little Brown Mouse,* 1984

editorial director of Heinemann Young Books, who published it in 1979. Faith had embarked upon a further phase in her career and she was soon to write a sequel, *Tilly's Rescue,* as well as *Kidnap in Willowbank Wood.* Long before, in material and professional terms, Faith had realised Tilly's own ambition, where she says: 'I've got to find a place where I can be free and decide things for myself.' Her success as a writer brought the fulfilment of a dream older even than the wish to become an illustrator.

Faith left London in 1987 to live and to continue to work in Bath, where she has since concentrated almost exclusively on her colour illustrations for *The Orchard Book of Nursery Rhymes,* two of which are reproduced here prior to publication. These drawings capture the detail, atmosphere and colouration of late eighteenth-century classicism (the period in which these rhymes first found their way into print) quite delightfully. Her output as a leading illustrator throughout practically the whole of these exciting post-war years proceeds – taking a love of early children's books and a joy in drawing the past as a starting point – to evoke a secure and credibly imagined world for the most modern reader to inhabit and recall.

NOTES

1. Some of this material first appeared in Douglas Martin, 'The book illustrations of Faith Jaques', *The Private Library,* 3rd series, 7/4 (Winter 1984), 150–70; and acknowledgment is made to the editor, David Chambers, for kind permission to base this expanded essay on that article.

2. Except where otherwise stated, quotations are from correspondence and discussions with the artist over a number of years, and in particular from extensive notes on illustration which she kindly set down between 25 and 29 December 1985.

3. The neglect or abandonment of this curriculum in various schools at different times since the 1950s can be seen as a direct cause of depressingly low levels of draughtsmanship in narrative illustration; but equally it may have fostered the emergence of positive new trends in picture books for younger children.

4 'My great Oxford experience was joining the University Film Society . . . I've always been fascinated by the film, as a visual medium for telling the story, and of course the medium allows *anything* to be possible – and not lost in reproduction either . . . In recent converse with an American colleague, who is also an illustrator, we agreed that if we had our time over again we'd probably have gone in to film or television – and we're far from being the only illustrators who are fascinated by film.' Letter to author, Bath, 4 April 1987.

5. 'It is of course an ''impure'' art, mixing literature with painting – but no more impure than opera which mixes literature with music.' David Bland, *A History of Book Illustration* (2nd edn, Faber, 1969), 16.

6. Other starry names on the part-time staff of the Central at the time included Robert Buhler, Mervyn Peake, Eduardo Paolozzi and Clarke Hutton; and also Jesse Collins, whom Faith recalls as one of the finest teachers she ever had. Edward Bawden and Eric Fraser were the strongest external influences on her early work, although she was soon to fall under the spell of Edward Ardizzone. He seemed to her the modern link to the Victorian illustrators she had always loved, and she still finds much common ground with his attitudes to illustration.

7. 'I was demobbed from the WRNS in Dec. '46 with a gratuity of £30 – worth probably £100 now? I had been accepted at the Central School of Arts & Crafts, with a grant for 4 terms only. I'd made several trips to London in search of somewhere to live; but London at the end of the War was pretty desperate; I couldn't find even the most meagre bed-sitter, which was all I could hope for. So when I arrived in London early in Jan. to start my first term I had to live at a Salvation Army Hostel, & stayed there for 6 months. My grant was for £4 a week (male students got £4 10s. I spent a lot of time later

34 *The Strawberry Ice,* early 1960s

writing to the Board of Education, & my MP, about this: the only answer I ever got was that women were expected to go home during vacations, men were not. Thus feminism is born!)

I hung on to my precious £30 as long as I could, but it got whittled away in that first term because the Grant didn't actually arrive for 2 months. The Hostel was cheap, but I had to eat, pay for fares, &, worst of all, materials, & I was nearly penniless by the time the Grant started, & had to walk everywhere to avoid bus fares. Clothes were a big problem. Apart from 18 months at Leicester College of Art, I had been in uniform practically all my life; clothes rationing started just after the War began & continued till the 1950s. I had some coupons but no money, & very few civilian clothes. I had no overcoat of any kind, & soon wished I'd kept my Petty Officer's greatcoat – the winter of 1947 was the worst since the 17th century, when an ox was roasted on the frozen Thames.

Eventually my Grant arrived, collected at the Central every Friday. The following term I managed to find a bed-sitter, 6 ft square with divan bed, chest of drawers, chair, cupboard, & a gas-ring. This cost 30 shillings a week, leaving £2 10 shillings with which to pay bus fares, & clothe & feed myself, & buy materials. Of course the money was worth much more then, but it was a great struggle. The Grant was back-dated, but I had to spend most of that on a saucepan, a kettle, a frying-pan, 2 plates & a cup & saucer, knife, fork, spoon, & various other necessities. By Friday each week I was spent out, I had to walk from Earls Court to Southampton Row as nothing was left for a bus fare. I brought work home every w/end & worked every day & most nights – I couldn't afford to do anything else. People think students lead a riotous 'Bohemian' life – it certainly wasn't like that after the War, & I suspect is still pretty tough.

This may sound a grim picture, & I shudder when I look back on it now. But in fact I was reasonably happy all the time: I had new friends, enjoyed the work & felt I was improving quite fast, & loved London (walking is the best way to get to know a new city). Everything I saw was new & interesting, & thanks to Public Libraries, could read as much as I wished. Money was certainly a problem, but there was plenty to compensate for the lack of it. But I've met few people since who were as poor as I was for those 20 months. Not surprisingly, though, my mind was fixed on earning money as soon as possible, so in my last 2 terms at the Central I assembled a portfolio and took it around to several magazines, with some success. I also investigated part-time Art School teaching, & was lucky enough to land 2 days a week as a Visiting Lecturer at Guildford School of Art. I started there straight away after I left the Central; I think the pay was about £12 a week plus fares, – a fortune! Thanks to this I had security, with 5 days of each week clear to continue forging a free-lance career. On the whole I think being poor for a while when young is quite a good thing. It gives you a challenge to overcome, & teaches you to sort out the things that matter most in life.' Letter dated Bath, 4 April 1987.

8. R. D. Usherwood, *Drawing for Radio Times* (Bodley Head, 1961), 74.

9. ' . . . Modern adult novels are rarely illustrated now, except by book clubs and private presses. The best modern writing doesn't need it' . . . 'I always think Jane Austen is better not illustrated – the characters exist more satisfactorily in one's own imagination' . . . 'I cannot see any point in illustrating such modern writers as V. S. Naipaul, Salman Rushdie, Martin Amis, Julian Barnes, Borges, Vonnegut, Iris Murdoch, Márquez, to name but a few. Putting aside the impossibility of production costs, I would say illustrated modern novels are against the feel of the times, and I doubt if this sort of book will ever return.' . . . 'I believe the modern form of ''illustration'' is best done in the theatre, film and television. I make this statement unwillingly (thankful, since one has to earn a living, that books for small children are best handled by artists) . . .' Notes to author, Bath, 25–29 December 1985.

10. 'Have just been through the drawings [for *The Windswept City*] by Faith Jaques. She is a sheer bloody genius. Not only can she draw like a *maestra,* she sees the angle-shot I make in the concept that lies *behind the words.* That angle that a writer sees inside himself, but gives up trying to tell to anyone outside. She sees that and puts it down. Now that is what illustrating really is in my book. That is a creative partnership. What two artists are for. (I've worked with all sorts – some who are wayward and want to draw their own great Art; some who tell me to change my text; some who just draw alongside the words and put no feeling into it. But she is great. Could you tell her this, in your nice way? Not my primitive way!) . . .' Letter from Henry Treece dated 8 June 1966 – two days before his death – to Richard Hough of Hamish Hamilton.

35 *The Windswept City,* endpiece, 1967

11. In fact no other individual can have achieved more on behalf of the professional community in matters such as establishing the artist's ownership of original drawings, the right to sell them after an agreed period, and the right to a continuing interest in the

ongoing commercial success of an edition to which they had made a substantial contribution. In recent years Faith Jaques has been an active member of the Society of Authors, both in the negotiations to establish equitable shares between author and illustrator, and to clarify the illustrators' entitlement under Public Lending Right.

12. Faith Jaques, 'The illustrator is also worthy of his hire', *The Bookseller,* 18 June 1977, 2834-6.

13. Unpublished notes, expanding the article cited above.

14. From notes about her work for: L. Kingman, G. A. Hogarth and H. Quimby (compilers) *Illustrators of Children's Books* 1967-1976 (Boston: The Horn Book, 1978), 131.

36 *The Forsyte Saga,* 1960 or earlier

BIBLIOGRAPHY

Note: The novelty books from the 1950s are sometimes difficult to trace beyond the artist's records – although some have already become Museum of Childhood items – but it is fascinating to be able to detect, in these early pop-ups and similar products, prefigurations of the cut-out model books of the 1980s.

c.1950

ALICE IN WONDERLAND [unattributed text, a novelty book with a small record of the Mock Turtle's Song attached] Adprint [Publicity Products]

CINDERELLA [unattributed text, with record] Adprint

THE FOOTBALL ASSOCIATION BOOK FOR BOYS 1950 – 51 Naldrett Press

GOLDILOCKS [unattributed text, with record] Adprint

LITTLE WOMEN Louisa M. Alcott Contact Publications

THE YOUNG CRICKETER John St John [ed.] Naldrett Press

c.1951

LISTEN WITH MOTHER, Nos. 1 & 2 Jean Sutcliffe [ed.] Adprint

c.1952

THE CIRCUS BOOK George Buckett Adprint

THE MOUSE CALLED DORA [copy untraced, a 'shaped' book] Adprint

THE THREE BEARS [untraced, but distinct from GOLDILOCKS, 1950] Adprint

1953

THE SATURDAY BOOK 13 John Hadfield [ed.] [FJ in all cases as contributor to this anthology] Hutchinson

c.1954

THE FARMYARD [pop-up book] Adprint

RAG, TAG AND BOBTAIL AND THE MUSHROOMS [a 'jump-up' book] Adprint

RHYMES FOR MIDDLE YEARS Dorothy Wellesley James Barrie

THE SATURDAY BOOK 14 John Hadfield [ed.] Hutchinson

1955

LISTEN WITH MOTHER, Nos. 4 & 5 Jean Sutcliffe [ed.] [FJ with Kathleen Dance] Adprint

THE SATURDAY BOOK 15 John Hadfield [ed.] Hutchinson

TAG TAKES A TRIP L. Cochrane and S. and E. Williams Adprint

1956

BAMBI [pop-up book] Adprint
MISS HONEYBUN'S HAT [copy untraced]
Univ. London Press
THE SATURDAY BOOK 16 John Hadfield [ed.]
Hutchinson

1957

A PORTRAIT OF BACH Jo Manton
Methuen/Abelard-Schuman
SIR LANCELOT [a colouring book] Adprint
THE TWELVE DAYS OF CHRISTMAS
[pictorama version – i.e. 12 pictorial cards
which can be arranged in any order, but
always make a continuous scene of figures
and landscape] Hugh Evelyn

1958

A GOLDEN LAND James Reeves [ed.]
[drawings as contributor] Constable/
Hastings House
IVANHOE Sir Walter Scott [abridged] Ginn
WATCH WITH MOTHER TALES Freda
Lingstrom [ed.] Adprint

1959

THE WHITE SHADOW René Guillot OUP

1960

THE BOOK OF KNOWLEDGE [drawings as
contributor] Amalgamated Press
A DOG FOR RICHARD [copy untraced]
Univ. London Press
LOIS THE WITCH Elizabeth Gaskell
Methuen

1961

THE FISHERMAN'S FIRESIDE BOOK Clive
Gammon Heinemann
KIRSTI COMES HOME Aili Konttinen
Methuen
THE STORY OF MRS PANKHURST Josephine
Kamm Methuen

1962

A CHILD'S BOOK OF COMPOSERS [author
un-named] Novello
CHILDREN'S COOKERY BOOK [copy
untraced] Longman

1963

RESCUE IN THE SNOW Isobel Knight Univ.
London Press
THE TRUE STORY OF JUMBO THE
ELEPHANT Eric Mathieson Hamish
Hamilton

1964

DRAWING IN PEN AND INK Faith Jaques
Studio Vista/Watson-Guptill

1965 –

1966

THE HUGH EVELYN HISTORY OF COSTUME,
VOL. I, 1800 – 1900 Margaret Stavridi [ed.]
Hugh Evelyn
THE ROAD BOOK [drawings as contributor]
Reader's Digest

1967

ANTHOLOGY [copy untraced – drawings as
contributor] Odhams Press
BALMORAL [title-pages and maps to
guidebook; similarly for SANDRINGHAM]
Hazell, Watson & Viney for H.M. the Queen
THE HUGH EVELYN HISTORY OF COSTUME,
VOL. II, 1660 – 1800 Margaret Stavridi [ed.]
Hugh Evelyn
JOSEPH PAXTON AND THE CRYSTAL
PALACE Josephine Kamm Methuen
LORNA DOONE R. D. Blackmore Heron
THE TORRENTS OF SPRING Ivan Turgenev
Folio
TREASURE ISLAND R. L. Stevenson Heron
THE TURN OF THE SCREW Henry James
[abridged] Longman
THE WAY OF ALL FLESH Samuel Butler
Heron
THE WINDSWEPT CITY Henry Treece
Hamish Hamilton/Meredith

1968

CHARLIE AND THE CHOCOLATE FACTORY
Roald Dahl Allen & Unwin
THE HUGH EVELYN HISTORY OF COSTUME,
VOL. III, 1500 – 1660 Margaret Stavridi
[ed.] Hugh Evelyn
THE HUMBUGS Mary Treadgold Hamish
Hamilton
THE SMALL HOUSE AT ALLINGTON
Anthony Trollope Heron

1969

CUSTOMS AND FESTIVALS   David Smith and
   Derek Newton   Blackie
THE MAGIC FISH-BONE   Charles Dickens
   Oliver & Boyd/Harvey House
MOG   Ursula Moray Williams   Allen & Unwin
A SEASONING OF MENUS   Georgina Infield
   Heinemann

1970

THE HUGH EVELYN HISTORY OF COSTUME,
   VOL. IV, BC-AD 1500   Margaret Stavridi
   [ed.]   Hugh Evelyn
THE GREAT FIRE   Monica Dickens   Kaye &
   Ward
THE ISLAND OF THE NINE WHIRLPOOLS
   E. Nesbit   Kaye & Ward
JOHNNIE GOLIGHTLY AND THE
   CROCODILE   Ursula Moray Williams
   Oliver & Boyd/Harvey House
THE MOUSE AND THE MAGICIAN   Eric
   Houghton   Deutsch/Lippincott

1971

DAVID COPPERFIELD   Charles Dickens
   Everyweek
THE GIANT WHO STOLE THE WORLD   John
   Cunliffe   Deutsch
A LIKELY LAD   Gillian Avery   Collins/Holt,
   Rinehart
NICHOLAS AND THE DRAGON   Euan
   Cooper-Willis   Blackie
OLD PETER'S RUSSIAN TALES   Arthur
   Ransome   Nelson

1972

A FIRST LOOK AT COSTUME   Margaret
   Crush   Franklin Watts
A PICNIC WITH THE AUNTS   Ursula Moray
   Williams   Chatto & Windus
THE GIANT WHO SWALLOWED THE WIND
   John Cunliffe   Deutsch
THE GLORY HOUSE   Charlotte Morrow
   Chatto & Windus
THE HALF SISTERS   Natalie Savage Carlson
   Blackie
THE LONELY DRAGON   Margaret Howell
   Longman
WHAT THE NEIGHBOURS DID, AND OTHER
   STORIES   Philippa Pearce   Longman/
   Crowell

1973

BEYOND THE BLUE HILLS   Hilary Seton
   Heinemann
CARRIE'S WAR   Nina Bawden   Gollancz
CHARLIE AND THE GREAT GLASS
   ELEVATOR   Roald Dahl   Allen & Unwin
A DAY NO PIGS WOULD DIE   Robert
   Newton Peck   Hutchinson
THE FABER BOOK OF GREEK LEGENDS
   Kathleen Lines [ed.]   Faber
JOE AND THE CATERPILLAR   Sheila Glen
   Bishop   Heinemann
JOURNEYS   Margery Fisher [ed.]
   [FJ contributed jacket and a suite of part-title
   drawings for this anthology]   Brockhampton
THE KING'S BIRTHDAY CAKE   John Cunliffe
   Deutsch
PERSUASION   Jane Austen [abridged]
   Longman

1974

FALTER TOM AND THE WATER BOY
   Maurice Duggan   Kestrel
THE GOLDEN CRUCIFIX   John Rae
   Brockhampton
GRANDPAPA'S FOLLY AND THE
   WOODWORM-BOOKWORM   Ursula Moray
   Williams   Chatto & Windus
GREAT BRITISH SHORT STORIES   [drawings
   contributed]   Reader's Digest
HENRY   Elizabeth Yandell   Bodley Head
A LION IN THE GARDEN   Hilary Seton
   Heinemann
LIZZIE DRIPPING   [*Lizzie Dripping Again,
   Lizzie Dripping and the Little Angel, Lizzie
   Dripping by the Sea, More Lizzie Dripping*]
   Helen Cresswell   BBC Publications
THE MAGICAL COCKATOO   Margery Sharp
   Heinemann
THE MILL ON THE FLOSS   George Eliot
   [abridged]   Collins
A PECK OF PEPPER   Faith Jaques   Chatto &
   Windus
SMITH   Leon Garfield [abridged]   Longman

1975

FIELD AND FOREST   Barbara Willard [ed.]
   Kestrel
A GIANT CAN DO ANYTHING   Eric
   Houghton   Deutsch
THE OLD NURSERY STORIES   E. Nesbit
   Hodder & Stoughton
THE TREASURE OF WESTMINSTER ABBEY
   John Rae   Hodder & Stoughton

1976

THE APPRENTICES [*Moss and Blister, The Cloak*] Leon Garfield Heinemann

BERNARD THE BRAVE Margery Sharp Heinemann

CHRISTMAS IS COMING John Rae Hodder & Stoughton

THE MOUSE AND THE MAGICIAN Eric Houghton [originally published in 1970, with different illustrations by FJ] Deutsch

THE RED FAIRY BOOK Andrew Lang Kestrel

1977

THE APPRENTICES [*The Valentine, Labour in Vain*] Leon Garfield Heinemann

A TRAVELLER IN TIME Alison Uttley Puffin

1978

THE APPRENTICES [*The Fool, Rosy Starling, The Dumb Cake, Tom Titmarsh's Devil, The Filthy Beast, The Enemy*] Leon Garfield Heinemann

MOULDY'S ORPHAN Gillian Avery Collins

PRIVATE – KEEP OUT! Gwen Grant Heinemann

1979

TILLY'S HOUSE Faith Jaques Heinemann/ Atheneum

1980

THE ORDINARY PRINCESS M. M. Kaye Kestrel

TALES OF LITTLE GREY RABBIT Alison Uttley Heinemann

TILLY'S RESCUE Faith Jaques Heinemann/ Atheneum

1981

FRANK AND POLLY MUIR'S BIG DIPPER [FJ contributed a story called *Tilly's Day Out*] Heinemann

MR BUZZ THE BEEMAN Allan Ahlberg Kestrel/Golden Press

MR TICK THE TEACHER Allan Ahlberg Kestrel/Golden Press

37 *The Orchard Book of Nursery Rhymes,* in preparation

1982

KIDNAP IN WILLOWBANK WOOD   Faith Jaques   Heinemann
LITTLE GREY RABBIT'S HOUSE   Alison Uttley [a cut-out model devised and painted by Faith Jaques]   Heinemann/Philomel

1983

OUR VILLAGE SHOP   [a cut-out model devised and painted by Faith Jaques]   Heinemann/Philomel
THE RAILWAY CHILDREN   E. Nesbit   Puffin

1984

THE BOX OF DELIGHTS   John Masefield   Heinemann/Dell
ONE WAY ONLY   Gwen Grant   Heinemann
TALES OF LITTLE BROWN MOUSE   Alison Uttley   Heinemann
THE WAR OF THE BIRDS AND THE BEASTS, AND OTHER RUSSIAN TALES   Arthur Ransome   Cape

1985

THE RETURN OF THE ANTELOPE   Mary Hoffman and Faith Jaques   Heinemann

1986

THE CHRISTMAS PARTY   [a cut-out model devised and painted by Faith Jaques]   Orchard/Philomel

1987

GOLDILOCKS IN THE HOUSE OF THE THREE BEARS   [a cut-out model devised and painted by Faith Jaques]   Heinemann/Philomel
GOOD GIRL GRANNIE   Pat Thompson   Gollancz

1988

MISS DOSE THE DOCTORS' DAUGHTER   Allan Ahlberg   Viking Kestrel

in preparation

THE ORCHARD BOOK OF NURSERY RHYMES   Faith Jaques   Orchard/Orchard New York [as THE ORCHARD BOOK OF MOTHER GOOSE]

38   *The Apprentices*, 'The Filthy Beast', 1978

4 · VICTOR AMBRUS

VICTOR G. AMBRUS was born in 1935 in Budapest, but since 1956 has lived and worked in England. He mediates, as one of nature's diplomats, between these two cultures which he has inherited 'in the accidental turning of the world'.

Although his family came originally from the east of Hungary, his entire childhood and student years were spent in the capital, except for summer holidays when he fell completely under the influence of the countryside:

> My childhood was full of horses in a strange way. My uncles and relatives lived in very 'horsey' areas, as it were. When I was about seven or eight I remember travelling a lot in open carriages which were drawn by two horses, as fast as lightning! It was routine, no-one thought anything of it, and even up until fairly recently horse-drawn carts provided the natural mode of transport in the country. Another memorable thing was that I actually used to see them in the wild – horses and cattle were all driven out in the morning – and they would come stampeding back through the village at dusk.[1]

From his earliest childhood he recalls drawing away happily; but it was his step-grandfather who inspired him to work at it non-stop. The young Victor Ambrus was absolutely fascinated and bewildered by the speed with which this man, the headmaster of a small school, could sketch-in charging horses and knew he wouldn't rest until he could learn to draw horses as well. His father also gave him enormous encouragement to draw from about the age of nine, although, as a scientist and knowing little enough about drawing as such, he may have been faintly disappointed that his son chose eventually not to become a painter.

Besides the images of Hungarian rural life evoked perhaps nowhere more potently than in his picture-book *A Country Wedding,* there are many other aspects of national history and culture which he absorbed early and which still find new forms of expression through his work. Nostalgia for the Austro-Hungarian Dual Monarchy is a case in point; this was a reality under which he grew up, and which he was to re-explore

in his book, *Under the Double Eagle,* [2] which appeared in 1980. Whereas Austria became a socialist republic after 1918, Hungary remained a kingdom and the military traditions of the Habsburgs survived there to a greater extent in consequence.

It is interesting to reflect that the Second World War would have been in mid-course at the time of these childhood recollections:

39 *Under the Double Eagle,* 1980

. . . There was a nostalgia for the Monarchy as well, a lot of pictures of the last King and Queen about the place, and a big volume called *The Coronation Album* which my mother had. It had belonged to my grandfather, and I used to spend hours looking at that . . . The militaria was tremendously picturesque, and visually it was very impressive. I also had a lot of uncles who were in the army and they used to come home with their swords and shakos and things. I can remember my mother telling my uncle Lajos when I was seven that he'd have to put his sword on top of the wardrobe so that it would be out of reach.

Nineteenth-century illustrated books surrounded him at home, and at the time he was enormously influenced by an artist little known in the rest of Europe called Zichy,[3] who had illustrated volumes of poetry, drama, Shakespeare and endless classical subjects. There were of course all the usual children's books as well; of the English ones, he used to adore *Winnie-the-Pooh* and Shepard's illustrations, and Ursula Moray Williams's *Adventures of the Little Wooden Horse* with its illustrations by Joyce Lankester Brisley (a story which he would like to illustrate again).

In the years before career decisions had to be thought about, he spent a lot of time at exhibitions and saw a great many paintings, – deriving stimulation from nineteenth-century historical canvases in particular – the vaster the better. Paintings were at that stage as important, if not more so, than the books he grew up with. Before following a natural inclination to go to art school, other occupations that were socially useful as well as potentially remunerative were considered, and for a time his father planned for him to study architecture at university. However, the hazards likely to attend the practical application of his shaky mathematics in that field were foreseen in good time, and at eighteen he applied to enter the Hungarian Academy of Fine Arts in Budapest.

This nineteenth-century establishment was steeped in classically based drawing, but in the final year all painting students were expected to go to Paris and return with a copy of a Rembrandt or other set piece. His first impression of the school was that the whole building was hung with these copies of old masters which over the years had acquired a lot of grime and patina so that they looked absolutely fantastic and authentic. To a certain extent, if a non-Hungarian may be permitted such a comment, it would seem that time had stood still in the art academy as it had for the army; but Victor Ambrus has a respect for the professors who insisted on sound drawing and administered massive doses of anatomy, and maintains that in the interaction between Budapest classicism and the more liberated atmosphere of the Royal College in London he had the best of both worlds.

In Budapest he gravitated towards the printmaking course since this would further his growing interest in illustration. The technique of etching contributed to the evolution of his distinctive line technique, in fact in his first black and white drawings he found it difficult to forget that he was not using an etching needle. In discussing the characteristic qualities of line and hatching in the early black and white drawings recently, he had this to say:

> . . . the hatching came in because once again we're looking back to this intensive training in printmaking, the countless etchings I did at that time. We were very much trained on Rembrandt, he was the ultimate, and I was so involved in this technique that I used an awful lot of hatching. This you can do very well in etching, because you could have a subtly-etched line so that you get such a very fine grey tint over a grey tint that you almost have a half-tone. But it doesn't work that way when it comes to line illustration where it comes up much heavier, and gradually over a period of years I tried to get rid of that.

And then, into this gradual development, came the events of Autumn 1956 in Hungary:

> My art training came to an abrupt end with the outbreak of the 1956 Uprising. With the city in ruins and friends killed there seemed to be little hope of normal life. After weeks of heavy street fighting, Budapest lay in rubble. It felt like the end of the last war. Like thousands of Hungarians, I headed for the Austrian border, hoping for a better life. [4]

In the longer term, the West was to benefit from a major creative presence, whilst Hungarian culture retained a distinguished honorary ambassador.

Thoughts of art college and career were far from his mind at that time of national trauma; as the year drew to a close the school building had been ransacked and was largely shut up, and he had to abandon his studies in the third year of a four-year course. He reached Austria at the very beginning of December, and was flown into England just before Christmas. A number of students were congregated at Crookham Army Camp, understandably enough in varying states of psychological depression or shock. At first Victor Ambrus couldn't even see himself drawing again really seriously; but sitting about with nothing to do it was a natural instinct to drift towards the nearest art school, which happened to be at Farnham where two of his friends were already starting to do some work. As soon as he was allowed in, he found that he was only able to produce a series of terribly depressing lithographs and etchings reflecting his experiences. It took a long time to work through that phase, and he believes that it was not until he reached the Royal College of Art that he was able to think again purposefully in terms of illustration and printmaking.

However, the two terms spent at Farnham were valuable for the life-drawing classes in particular, and for the opportunity to engage in straight drawing that didn't call for any particular comment. His fellow-Hungarians shared his total lack of English, and the language gulf was augmented by a culture gap between the teaching staff and themselves – not without good-natured amusement on both sides – caused by their very classical way of drawing; techniques of draughtsmanship which would have been

instantly comprehended in Renaissance Florence did not go down too well in Farnham. Nevertheless the Principal decided that, since they couldn't readily be fitted into any existing courses and were much older than the average art student, their work should be submitted to the Royal College of Art. Victor Ambrus's work spoke for him at interview and he was taken on for a three-year course in graphic design and printmaking.

In terms of art training the Royal College helped to loosen up the rigid and classical approach which had been inculcated in Hungary, and to widen his intellectual horizons in general. During those years (1957 – 60) the College was already afflicted to a degree by the trendiness which was later to undermine its credibility in some quarters; action painting was rife and already the first bicycles were being ridden over canvases. Many of the tutors in printmaking were pushing out into abstraction just then, indeed very many artists with very different backgrounds and approaches have described a feeling in the air at the time of the need or duty to venture beyond the insular limitations and sterile conventions of post-war British art and design. In retrospect it can be seen that abstraction was to provide an answer for very few, and that the majority swiftly recanted. Victor Ambrus had a go at one or two abstract prints but admitted to himself that they were meaningless, that he was doing them for no apparent reason, and so he soon abandoned that line of enquiry.

In his final year he married Glenys Chapman, also a student of the College, and latterly an illustrator of colourful and decorative picture books for younger children. At this juncture he was ready to set out on his professional career as a book illustrator, but was keenly aware of another and less attractive feature of the College's establishment, its anti-commercialism: 'I was in my last year when the first book I illustrated was commissioned, and they were very unhappy about it. The climate at the time was that commercial commissions were very much frowned upon, so they almost penalised you for it. It was altogether inadvisable to put such work into the diploma show.'

By some strange chance the first commission he received had to do with horses: it was for black and white line drawings and a full colour jacket to a story by Alan C. Jenkins entitled *White Horses and Black Bulls.* The publisher was Blackie, from whom he felt he received a lot of help and encouragement in bridging the gap between printmaking and book illustration, and for whom he was to illustrate a number of interesting titles over the next few years.

Looking back at these early books for Blackie and other publishers he admits that there are just one or two which he would prefer to forget about altogether, attributing this to a conflict between the freer style of drawing which by then came naturally to him, and a tendency to go to the other extreme and perhaps overwork things, 'for the sake of publishing or being channelled into a tighter medium'.

However, his first published drawings were well received, and that formidable talent-spotter Mabel George was as ever quick off the mark, with the result that the first titles he illustrated for Oxford University Press appeared in the following year.

40 *A Country Wedding,* 1973

41   *White Horses and Black Bulls*, 1960

At that time she was primarily concerned with building a quality list of historical and other fiction for older children, and had recruited a fine 'stable' of artists which included Charles Keeping and Brian Wildsmith as well as Victor Ambrus, who recalls:

> Mabel George, who I thought always picked a very good story, had excellent authors and so there was tremendous potential in each commission. Drawings always reflect the quality of a text in a way, so if you have a story that's uninspiring it's difficult to make much out of it. I did a lot of Hester Burton's historical books, K. M. Peyton's and others, and even now I look back on those and wish I could do some more like that, because I so enjoyed doing that type of black and white line which has largely disappeared now.

The harsh economics of diminishing print runs decimated the black and white line-illustrated novel for older children, but new economic perspectives made possible the colour printing revolution of the early 1960s. Victor Ambrus continues:

I think of Brian Wildsmith's *Tales from The Arabian Nights* [1961] as a big turning point, where suddenly there was a book of stories which was printed with full-colour illustrations inside, and from then on it seemed that good quality colour printing became widely available. Mabel George still held a theory, in common with many of her contemporaries, that you had to graduate through numerous black and white books before you could be let loose with colour; which is a curious principle because you either had colour or you hadn't!

Victor Ambrus is a brilliant colourist, though not in a painterly sense, since wherever one looks closely into the colour, irrespective of how it has been applied, it will be found to be informed and underpinned by sound draughtsmanship in line. He admits: 'I mixed the media quite a lot, in all kinds of phases which I don't think I could repeat now even if I tried.' As early as 1964, one critic noted: 'Mr Ambrus uses colour with a particular, and highly characteristic, verve and dramatic sense, as can be seen in

42 *Living in a Castle,* 1971

his many jacket designs with their blotted darks and exciting sweeps of colour, but he thinks of himself essentially as a line man.'[5]

The marvellous thing about Mabel George's commissions to her artists as soon as she deemed that they were 'ready for colour' is that they were all given full responsibility in creating their own picture-book world. Since they were to be virtually in charge of the design of the book as a whole, illustration could be visualised together with story-line, the spatial spread of illustrations and disposition of copy brought into balance, and everything thought out down to such details as endpaper treatment. Of course Oxford was not alone in evolving what was later to become an accepted procedure, but at the time it was still commonplace for a sacrosanct manuscript of a few dozen words from an eminent pen to go the rounds in search of a complaisant illustrator.

Of the picture books written and illustrated by Victor Ambrus for Oxford between 1965 and 1975, four remain particular favourites: *Hot Water for Boris, The Sultan's Bath, Mishka* (where the Ringmaster is almost the Ur-Dracula), and *A Country Wedding:* 'I've tremendous nostalgia about these books because they are deeply rooted in childhood – the colours, the feeling of the country, the buildings, even the sense of humour – I know the stories I heard as a child and thought funny and I'd wanted to see if drawings came across.'

After *Mishka* in 1975, there were to be no more picture books until *Dracula* five years later, but two projects dear to his heart came about though Oxford: *Horses in Battle* in the same year as *Mishka,* and *Under the Double Eagle* in 1980.

At the beginning of his career he foresaw the danger of being type-cast as a 'horse specialist', a fate that Imre Hofbauer, his distinguished compatriot of an earlier generation, had to some extent suffered. 'Although he has been widely praised for his drawings of horses, he says firmly that he prefers people to animals, "and I do not consider the horse the most interesting of all animals either – it is just that I *know* the horse".'[6]

His approach to research for illustration is exemplified by *Horses in Battle*. There is a basic insistence that historical fact should be presented in a way that is physically and functionally plausible, and not merely accurate in matters of decorative detail. His researches in this instance were by chance overlooked from the nearby motorway by travellers who reported the strangely-clad apparitions riding about the countryside at night to the press:

> The first few drawings were seriously wrong, in that the figures were not sitting on their horses properly. So we took it into our heads that we'd go riding, and it made all the difference being on horseback, riding in a group and observing the horse in front. This provided direct evidence; at first the horse was driven berserk by having a sword slapping at its side and giving the impression that it was being urged to go along ever faster, and secondly it was

difficult to wield a sword avoiding the horse's head to one side or the other because it was right in front of you. This deteriorated to the level of taking out a sword and testing it against different sabre-cuts, and it was then that we must have been spotted.

Another glimpse into working method is provided through his collaboration with Bernard Miles over the illustrations for *Favourite Tales from Shakespeare*. These retellings have an individual flavour, and the texts stand in their own right in relation to those of the original plays. The author has very positive views on how some characters should look, but then so must any illustrator have who is going to do justice to such transcendent subject-matter. Differences of this kind have to be reconciled, and it is evident from the book that this was achieved to great creative effect. The artist recalls their meetings in terms that make one long to have been a fly on the wall: 'The great thing about him of course is that he has been acting Shakespeare from his earliest days, and so you get an impromptu performance every time we talk about different characters.'

It was to be many years before Bernard Miles came to write his second collection, *Well Loved Tales from Shakespeare*, for Hamlyn, a publisher for whom the illustrator has produced a run of interesting books. In the course of working on this later Shakespeare, Victor Ambrus discussed an interesting problem, the treatment of the

44 *Horses in Battle*, 1975

45 *Kate Rider,* 1974

great moment of Caesar's murder. Normally the choice of subject-matter for an illustration – the timing and camera-angle aspect – are instinctive for him: 'I could close my eyes and see how the characters act.' Here a whole sequence of pencil roughs was needed to reach the optimum solution from the range of possibilities in the seconds which elapse from the particular moment where Brutus plunges the dagger into Caesar and his realisation of what he has done.

Although Victor Ambrus continued to illustrate a number of books with various editors for Oxford after Mabel George's retirement, it was not until Ron Heapy's appointment that he felt confident that the essential creative rapport had been re-established:

> I think it is because he has this enormous sense of fun, and feels that books should be fun, that he encourages me to go towards this direction. I've always had a streak in me which enjoys cartoons and all kinds of crazy goings-on, and

it was a terrific outlet to be able to pour all this into the *Dracula* books. I think that the initial *Dracula* title sold more in its first year than all my picture books put together; and one rewarding thing about it is that children who wouldn't normally be reading books will go and read those, so they're 'Grade A' for reluctant readers.

Fresh from perpetrating a pop-up version of *A Christmas Carol* ('. . . it had to come' – *The Bookseller*), when we discussed it he was full of enthusiasm for the paper engineers, whom he had found marvellous collaborators. Most illustrators have difficulty working out their drawings in other than two dimensions, whereas these people work as animators from the outset. Dickens's crowded tableaux presented them with slightly more complex problems than they would have encountered in the straightforward animation of a single figure or motif: 'If one was not careful, limbs would be found to move at other than their proper joints.'

In recent years he has been involved with a number of challenging projects that are not strictly to do with books, such as stamp design for the Post Office, and work for *Reader's Digest*. He has enjoyed teaching and working with students of illustration for many years now. Printmaking no longer holds such an appeal as it did earlier, and he has transferred his interest to drawing from life again, and painting, 'with varying degrees of success'. Enthusiasm for historical topics remains as strong as ever; he recalls with evident pleasure his involvement with such projects as *The Story of Britain* and *The Heritage of Britain* and would like to do more history books and books for the adult market in the future. Work in progress at the time of interview included *Pinocchio* in direct translation from the Italian, *El Cid*, and *The Canterbury Tales*.

Victor Ambrus has illustrated some 300 titles to date, and it would appear to be a formidable task to attempt to evaluate such a prodigious output. But in examining, reading and handling many of his illustrated books once again in connection with this essay, the first impression is of the freshness and durability of the majority of the drawings within their respective contexts. This is after all work produced over the time-span of a quarter century, and at a steady rate of one book a month, and – in view of the short life-expectation of most books – the number of new impressions and reissues, and the general level of library stocks, provide evidence of the value that even certain of the earliest titles continue to yield.[7]

The categories into which this vast output falls may be summarised as follows: classics and stories for older children, historical novels for older children, and then – in broadly similar numbers – collections of tales and various anthologies, educational resource books, and his own picture books for younger children and other books that he has written. There is a tiny residue of religious titles, Christmas books and oddments. Naturally enough, considerable overlapping is to be found, in that historical, military and equine subject-matter figure largely in several of these fields;

46 *Stories from Chaucer*, 1984

but it is interesting to raise the question of how and to what extent the graphic style is adapted or modulated across a spectrum, from, say, a book with educational purpose such as *The Story of Britain*, to *Dracula* as unadulterated entertainment. The answer must be that no-one could mistake a Victor Ambrus drawing for anyone else's, but that the choice of media and the handling of the drawing will be conditioned by his response to each specific brief.

It has been noted that the artist feels that his style has loosened up in a number of ways since the early days, and this can certainly be seen to be so. The improved standards of offset printing, in monochrome as well as in colour, have helped to restore control over the subtlety of line quality. It may be softened, greyed, or allowed to spread on dampened paper, and this can be retained by the skilled use of a fine half-tone dot as in the case of *The Traitor Within*, in a way that was never possible with the letterpress line blocks used for most of the early novels, and their unspeakable paperback reprintings from rubber or plastic plates.

Whereas resource material for historical studies from primary school upwards has improved immensely in overall design and typographic presentation in recent years, very little drawing approaches the level set by such illustrators as Alan Sorrell, Christine Price and Victor Ambrus in the field. Weaknesses – both in drawing and intellectual vision in much current educational illustration – are quickly exposed on a comparative basis, and it may simply be that much of this publishing area has become too specialised or restrictive to attract the best all-round creative talent. Victor Ambrus fears that losses may occur as the educational presentation of history changes, and unquestionably he has done as much as anyone to make history visually accessible to the child in library and classroom.

'I'm very much aware of the *responsibility* for illustrating a book,' observes Victor Ambrus; and this may be taken to apply to almost everything he does, because it follows logically from his maxim that 'I remember the illustrations as much as I remember the story of each individual book.'

47 'Long John Silver', 1984

NOTES

1. Quotations are from conversations recorded at Farnham, Surrey, on 11 March 1986.
2. *Under the Double Eagle* is a neglected book, in which Ambrus imaginatively recalls his Habsburg homeland; and from which it is not unrealistic to envisage the successful historical painter he might readily have become in former times.
3. Mihaly von Zichy (b. Zala 1827 – d. St Petersburg 1906).
4. Letter dated 4 June 1987.
5. M. R. Hodgkin, 'Introducing illustrators: Victor G. Ambrus', *The Junior Bookshelf,* 28/2 (March 1964), 80–5.
6. *Ibid.,* p82.
7. His signal contribution to the illustration of children's books is recorded in the history of the Kate Greenaway Medal: commended in 1963 for *The Royal Navy* and *Time of Trial,* and in 1964 for his work in general, he received the Medal in 1966 for *The Three Poor Tailors* and *The Royal Air Force,* and in 1975 for *Mishka* and *Horses in Battle.*

BIBLIOGRAPHY

Note: In common with many illustrators, Victor Ambrus has kept no record of the books which he has illustrated; additional titles continued to come to light in the course of compiling this present list which, although balanced and representative, has to be regarded as provisional; jacket commissions and lightly-illustrated titles have generally been left out.

1960

WHITE HORSES AND BLACK BULLS   Alan C. Jenkins   Blackie/Norton 1963

1961

THE CHANGELING   William Mayne   OUP/Dutton 1963
THE GREEN LINNET   Gwyneth Vacher   Blackie
JUNGLE FOSTER CHILD   Florence and Richard Agnew   Blackie
LOOKING FOR ORLANDO   Frances Williams Browin   OUP/Criterion
MASTER OF THE ELEPHANTS   René Guillot   OUP/Criterion [as FOFANA]
THE PRISONER OF ZENDA   Anthony Hope   Blackie
SCHOOLBOY JIM   Joan M. Goldman   Blackie/ Ryerson

1962

CASTORS AWAY!   Hester Burton   OUP/World
THE COSSACKS   Barbara Bartos-Höppner   OUP/Walck
THE HERON RIDE   Mary Treadgold   Cape

HILLS AND HOLLOWS   Sheena Porter   OUP
MALIK AND AMINA   Franz Baumann   OUP/ Bobbs-Merrill
SON OF THE SAHARA   Kelman Dalgety Frost   Hutchinson/Roy
WINDFALL   K. M. Peyton   OUP/World [as SEA FEVER]

1963

ARRIPAY   Rosemary Manning   Constable/ Farrar, Straus
BARCHESTER TOWERS   Anthony Trollope   Longman
CAMERONS ON THE HILLS   Jane Duncan   Macmillan/St Martin's
CAMERONS ON THE TRAIN   Jane Duncan   Macmillan/St Martin's
CARAVAN AT COONABURA   Margaret Moran   New Zealand Department of Education
CLUNIE   Hugo Charteris   Heinemann
AN ELIZABETHAN SAILOR   Elspeth J. Boog-Watson [ed.]   OUP
GULLIVER'S TRAVELS   Jonathan Swift [ed. Michael West]   Longman
THE HOUND OF ULSTER   Rosemary Sutcliff   Bodley Head/Dutton
JACOB'S LADDER   Sheena Porter   OUP
JUMPER   Nicholas Kalashnikoff   OUP
KINGDOM OF THE ELEPHANTS   Alan C. Jenkins   Blackie/Follett 1966
RETURN TO THE HERO   Mary Treadgold   Cape
THE ROYAL NAVY   Peter Dawlish   OUP
SAVE THE KHAN   Barbara Bartos-Höppner   OUP/Walck

A SEAMAN AT THE TIME OF TRAFALGAR Hester Burton OUP
A SERAPH IN A BOX Robina Beckles Willson Hart-Davis
TALES FROM THE ARABIAN NIGHTS Michael West [ed.] Longman
TIME OF TRIAL Hester Burton OUP/World
THE WILD HEART Helen Griffiths Hutchinson/Doubleday
THE YOUNGEST TAYLOR Griselda Gifford Bodley Head

1964

THE BRITISH ARMY Edward Fitzgerald OUP
CAMERONS AT THE CASTLE Jane Duncan Macmillan/St Martin's
CARNIVAL IN TRINIDAD Samuel Selvon New Zealand Department of Education
THE GREYHOUND Helen Griffiths Hutchinson/Doubleday
THE HAMISH HAMILTON BOOK OF KINGS Eleanor Farjeon and William Mayne [eds.] Hamish Hamilton/Walck [as A CAVALCADE OF KINGS]
HIGH AND HAUNTED ISLAND Nan Chauncy OUP/Norton
THE MAPLIN BIRD K. M. Peyton OUP/World
THE MEREDITHS OF MAPPINS Irene Byers Oliver & Boyd/Scribner 1966 [as MYSTERY AT MAPPINS]
MISCELLANY ONE Edward Blishen [ed.] OUP
NORTH OF NOWHERE Barbara Sleigh [ed.] Collins/Coward 1966
PASANG THE SHERPA Peter Webster New Zealand Department of Education/ Wheaton 1970
PINEAPPLE PALACE Robina Beckles Willson Hart-Davis
PRIVATE BEACH Richard Parker Harrap/ Duell
THE RED KING AND THE WITCH Ruth Manning-Sanders OUP/Roy
RIDE A NORTHBOUND HORSE Richard Wormser OUP/Morrow
THE THREE BROTHERS OF UR J. G. Fyson OUP/Coward 1967
WATCH FOR THE MORNING Jane Oliver Macmillan/St Martins

1965

BILBERRY SUMMER Maribel Edwin Collins
BRUMBY FOAL Mary Patchett Lutterworth
THE BUSHBABIES William Stevenson Houghton [USA]/Hutchinson 1966
THE CAT THAT WALKED A WEEK Meindert DeJong Lutterworth
DAVID IN SILENCE Veronica Robinson Deutsch/Lippincott
FLORENCE NIGHTINGALE AND MARIE CURIE Odwen MacLeod New Zealand Department of Education
THE GREY APPLE TREE Vera Cumberlege Deutsch
THE HAMISH HAMILTON BOOK OF QUEENS Eleanor Farjeon and William Mayne [eds.] Hamish Hamilton/Walck [as A CAVALCADE OF QUEENS]
HANDS FOR PABLO PICASSO Helen Kay Abelard-Schuman [USA]/Abelard-Schuman 1966 [as HENRI'S HANDS FOR PABLO PICASSO]
IN PLACE OF KATIA Mara Kay Hart-Davis
THE JOURNEY OF THE ELDEST SON J. G. Fyson OUP/Coward
ONE IS ONE Barbara Leonie Picard OUP/Holt
THE PLAN FOR BIRDSMARSH K. M. Peyton OUP/World
THE ROYAL AIR FORCE John W. R. Taylor OUP
THAILAND Martyn Sanderson New Zealand Department of Education
THE THREE POOR TAILORS Victor G. Ambrus OUP/Harcourt, Brace
THE THREE SORROWFUL TALES OF ERIN Frances M. Pilkington BodleyHead/Walck
A TURKISH VILLAGE Mary Gough and Victor G. Ambrus OUP

1966

CAMERONS CALLING Jane Duncan Macmillan/St Martin's
THE CHALLENGE OF THE GREEN KNIGHT Ian Serraillier OUP/Walck
DEERFOLD Sheena Porter OUP
THE DOG CRUSOE Robert M. Ballantyne Dent/Dutton
LITTLE KATIA E. M. Almedingen OUP/Farrar, Straus 1967
THE MERCHANT NAVY Peter Dawlish OUP

48 *Under the Double Eagle*, 1980

NO BEAT OF DRUM   Hester Burton   OUP/
World

STORM OVER THE BLUE HILLS   Alan C.
Jenkins   Oliver & Boyd/Norton

THUNDER IN THE SKY   K. M. Peyton   OUP/
World

THE WILD HORSE OF SANTANDER   Helen
Griffiths   Hutchinson/Doubleday

THE YOUNG PRETENDERS   Barbara Leonie
Picard   Edmund Ward/Criterion

1967

BRAVE SOLDIER JANOSH   Victor G. Ambrus
OUP/Harcourt

THE CHIEF'S DAUGHTER   Rosemary Sutcliff
Hamish Hamilton

FLAMBARDS   K. M. Peyton   OUP/World

THE HOUSE OF THE SPECKLED BROWNS
Irene Byers   Oliver & Boyd

HUSKY OF THE MOUNTIES   Francis Dickie
Dent

KNIGHTS OF GOD   Patricia Lynch   Bodley
Head

LEÓN   Helen Griffiths   Hutchinson/Doubleday

MATHINNA'S PEOPLE   Nan Chauncy   OUP

PAULINE   Margaret Storey   Doubleday [USA]

THE PIECES OF HOME   Miska Miles   Little,
Brown [USA]

PRISONERS IN THE SNOW   Arthur Catherall
Dent/Lothrop

ROBIN IN THE GREENWOOD   Ian Serraillier
OUP/Walck

A SAPPHIRE FOR SEPTEMBER
H. F. Brinsmead   OUP

SNOW CLOUD, STALLION   Gerald Raftery
Longman

VENDETTA   Shirley Deane   Viking [USA]

YOUNG MARK   E. M. Almedingen   OUP/
Farrar, Straus

1968

CAMERONS AHOY!   Jane Duncan
Macmillan/St Martin's

A CIRCLET OF OAK LEAVES   Rosemary
Sutcliff   Hamish Hamilton

FOLK TALES FROM THE NORTH   Winifred
Finlay [ed.]   Kaye & Ward/Watts

THE GLASS MAN AND THE GOLDEN BIRD
Ruth Manning-Sanders   OUP/Roy

A GLIMPSE OF EDEN   Evelyn Ames   Collins

THE GREAT BOW   Reginald Maddock
Collins/Rand McNally [USA]

HAKI THE SHETLAND PONY   Kathlen Fidler
Lutterworth/Rand McNally 1970

THE HORSE   Siegfried Stander   Gollancz/
World

IN SPITE OF ALL TERROR   Hester Burton
OUP/World

KIDNAPPED BY ACCIDENT   Arthur Catherall
Dent/Lothrop

THE LITTLE COCKEREL   Victor G. Ambrus
OUP/Harcourt Brace

ROBINSON CRUSOE   Daniel Defoe   [copy
untraced]   Longman

SHANNON   Barbara J. Berry   Follett [USA]

STALLION OF THE SANDS Helen Griffiths
Hutchinson/Lothrop 1970

STRANGER IN THE HILLS Madeleine
Polland Doubleday/Hutchinson 1969

TWICE SEVEN TALES Barbara Leonie
Picard Kaye & Ward

WHEN JAYS FLY TO BÁRBMO Margaret
Balderson OUP/World

1969

BEYOND THE WEIR BRIDGE Hester Burton
Crowell [USA]

BIG BEN David Walker Houghton Mifflin
[USA]/Collins 1970

THE CHILDREN OF THE CAVE Zvi Livne
OUP

THE COURAGE OF ANDY ROBSON
Frederick Grice OUP

THE DIVERTING HISTORY OF JOHN GILPIN
William Cowper Abelard-Schuman

THE EDGE OF THE CLOUD K. M. Peyton
OUP/World

THE FAMILY ON THE WATERFRONT
Natalie Savage Carlson Blackie

FLAMBARDS IN SUMMER K. M. Peyton
OUP/World

FOLK TALES FROM MOOR AND MOUNTAIN
Winifred Finlay [ed.] Kaye & Ward/Roy

FOREVER ENGLAND Lavinia Russ [ed.]
Harcourt, Brace [USA]

GAWAIN AND THE GREEN KNIGHT [a play]
Nicholas Stuart Gray Dobson

IN THE BEGINNING Zvi Livne OUP

JONNIKIN AND THE FLYING BASKET Ruth
Manning-Sanders OUP/Dutton

KNIGHTS OF GOD: TALES AND LEGENDS
OF THE IRISH SAINTS Patricia Lynch
Holt, Rinehart [USA]/Penguin 1971

THE LIGHTHOUSE KEEPER'S SON Nan
Chauncy OUP

THE MYSTERY OF STONEHENGE Franklyn
M. Branley Crowell [USA]/David & Charles
1972

RED SEA RESCUE Arthur Catherall Dent/
Lothrop

ROBIN AND HIS MERRY MEN Ian Serraillier
OUP/Walck

THE SEVEN SKINNY GOATS Victor G.
Ambrus OUP

SLAVE OF THE HUNS Géza Gárdonyi Dent/
Bobbs-Merrill

THE STORY OF BRITAIN R. J. Unstead
A & C Black/Nelson [as 4 vols, Transworld
1971]

THOMAS Hester Burton OUP/Crowell [as
BEYOND THE WEIR BRIDGE]

1970

CELTIC FAIRY TALES Joseph Jacobs Bodley
Head/World

THE HENCHMANS AT HOME Hester Burton
OUP/Crowell

THE SAGA OF SASSOUN Mischa Kudian
Kaye & Ward

WHITEY Ernest Claes OUP

1971

CAPTAIN WHACKAMORE Michael Mason
Deutsch

CLAYMORE & KILT Sorche Nic Leodhas
Bodley Head

FOLK TALES FROM THE WEST Eileen
Molony Kaye & Ward

THE GALLEON Ronald Welch OUP

DER GOLDENE MÄRCHENSCHATZ
Ueberreuter [Vienna]

LIGHT HORSE TO DAMASCUS Elyne
Mitchell Hutchinson

LIVING IN A CASTLE R. J. Unstead A & C
Black/Addison-Wesley

LIVING IN A CRUSADER LAND R. J.
Unstead A & C Black/Addison-Wesley

THE NIGHT OF THE WILD HORSES
Gregory Harrison OUP

THE REBEL Hester Burton OUP/Crowell

THE SULTAN'S BATH Victor G. Ambrus
OUP/Harcourt Brace

THE TRAITOR WITHIN Alexander Cordell
Brockhampton/Nelson 1973

TRISTAN AND ISEULT Rosemary Sutcliff
Bodley Head/Dutton

THE TRUCE OF THE GAMES Rosemary
Sutcliff Hamish Hamilton

WEST OF WIDDERSHINS Barbara Sleigh
Collins/Bobbs-Merrill [as
STIRABOUT STORIES]

1972

A CHRISTMAS FANTASY Carolyn Haywood,
pictures by Glenys and Victor Ambrus
Morrow[USA]/Brockhampton 1973

HEATHER, OAK, AND OLIVE: THREE
STORIES Rosemary Sutcliff Dutton [USA]

HOT WATER FOR BORIS Victor G. Ambrus
OUP
THE LIFE AND TIMES OF CORNELIUS
PLUM Kay King Abelard-Schuman
MARKO'S WEDDING Ian Serraillier Deutsch
RIDERS OF THE STORM Hester Burton
OUP/Crowell
SNOW-LION James MacDonald Marks OUP
STRANGER IN THE STORM Charles Paul May
Abelard-Schuman
TALES OF ANCIENT PERSIA Barbara Leonie
Picard OUP/Walck
TANK COMMANDER Ronald Welch
OUP/Nelson 1974

1973
A COUNTRY WEDDING Victor G. Ambrus
OUP/Addison-Wesley 1975
THE HAMISH HAMILTON BOOK OF
MAGICIANS Roger Lancelyn Green [ed.]
Hamish Hamilton/Walck [as A CAVALCADE
OF MAGICIANS]
IT'S THE SAME OLD EARTH Elsie Locke
New Zealand Department of Education
HUNTED IN THEIR OWN LAND Nan
Chauncy Seabury [USA]
THE KINGDOM AND THE CAVE Joan Aiken
Abelard-Schuman/Doubleday
KODI'S MARE Bonnie Highsmith Abelard-
Schuman [USA]
THE LADY FROM THE SEA Michael West
Longman
RUSSIAN BLUE Helen Griffiths Hutchinson/
Holiday House
SILVER BRUMBY WHIRLWIND Elyne
Mitchell Hutchinson
TRUE STORIES OF EXPLORATION Frank
Knight Benn
TRUE STORIES OF THE SEA Frank Knight
Benn
THE YEAR OF THE WOLVES
Willi Fährmann OUP

1974
CAP O' RUSHES, AND OTHER FOLK TALES
Winifred Finlay [ed.] Kaye & Ward/Hale
THE CHANGELING Rosemary Sutcliff
Hamish Hamilton
THE GLASS KNIFE John Tulley Methuen

THE GOLDEN FUTURE Thorsteinn Stefansson
OUP
THE GREEN AND THE WHITE Diana
Moorhead Brockhampton
IN THE SHADOW OF THE FALCON Ewan
Clarkson Hutchinson
THE JOURNEY OF THE ELDEST SON
J. G. Fyson OUP
JUST A DOG Helen Griffiths Hutchinson/
Holiday House
KATE RIDER Hester Burton OUP/Crowell
[as KATE RYDER]
KIDNAPPED Robert Louis Stevenson OUP
LIVING IN THE ELIZABETHAN COURT
R. J. Unstead A & C Black
LIVING IN THE TIME OF THE PILGRIM
FATHERS Glenys Ambrus A & C Black
MADATAN Peter Carter OUP
SIX DAYS IN THE LIFE OF CORNELIUS
PLUM Kay King Abelard-Schuman
THE SPUDDY Lillian Beckwith Hutchinson

1975
THE BATTLE OF LEIPZIG Per-Eric Jannson
Almark
CHANCE, LUCK AND DESTINY Peter
Dickinson, illustrated by Victor Ambrus and
David Smee Gollancz
THE COLT AT TAPAROO Elyne Mitchell
Hutchinson [Australia]/Hutchinson [UK] 1976
HORSES IN BATTLE Victor G. Ambrus OUP
MISHKA Victor G. Ambrus OUP/Warne 1978
TRUE STORIES OF ESCAPES Moyra
Hamilton Benn
TRUE STORIES OF SPYING Frank Knight
Benn
THE WHITE CAT John Tulley Methuen
WITCH FEAR Helen Griffiths Hutchinson/
Holiday House [as THE MYSTERIOUS
APPEARANCE OF AGNES]

1976
THE BOOK OF MAGICAL HORSES Margaret
Mayo Kaye & Ward/Hastings House
ENSIGN CAREY Ronald Welch OUP
THE FARTHEST-AWAY MOUNTAIN Lynne
Reid Banks Abelard-Schuman/Doubleday
THE HAMISH HAMILTON BOOK OF OTHER
WORLDS Roger Lancelyn Green [ed.]
Hamilton

HUNTER OF HARTER FELL   Joseph E.
Chipperfield   Hutchinson
FAVOURITE TALES FROM SHAKESPEARE
Bernard Miles   Hamlyn/Rand McNally
MELANIE IN ENGLAND   Kay King   Abelard-
Schuman
TO RAVENSRIGG   Hester Burton   OUP/
Crowell
SON OF THE WHIRLWIND   Elyne Mitchell
Hutchinson [Australia]/Hutchinson [UK]
STORIES FOR 10 YEAR OLDS AND OVER
Sara and Stephen Corrin [eds.]
Faber/Merrimack
A VALENTINE FANTASY   Carolyn Haywood,
pictures by Glenys and Victor Ambrus
Morrow [USA]
VOYAGE TO VALHALLA   Robert Swindells
Hodder & Stoughton
THE WORLD OF DINOSAURS   Richard Moody
Hamlyn/Grosset & Dunlap

1977
THE ANATOMY OF COSTUME   Robert Selbie
Mills & Boon
CHASING THE GOBLINS AWAY   Tobi Tobias
Warne [USA]
PABLO   Helen Griffiths   Hutchinson/Holiday
House [as RUNNING WILD]
THE RIGHT-HAND MAN   K. M. Peyton   OUP
ROBIN HOOD   Antonia Fraser   Sidgwick &
Jackson
TIM AT THE FUR FORT   Hester Burton
Hamish Hamilton
THE VERY SPECIAL BABY   Robert Swindells
Hodder & Stoughton/Prentice-Hall
THE YEAR THE RAIDERS CAME   M. A. Wood
Andersen Press

1978
MONKEY'S PERFECT   Nora Rock   Andersen
Press/State Mutual Book, 1981
WHEN THE BEACONS BLAZED   Hester Burton
Hamish Hamilton

1979
THE COLT FROM SNOWY RIVER   Elyne
Mitchell   Hutchinson [Australia]/
Hutchinson [UK] 1980
THE FOLK DRESS OF EUROPE   James
Snowden   Mills & Boon
THE LAST SUMMER: SPAIN 1936   Helen
Griffiths   Hutchinson/Holiday House

MASTER DEOR'S APPRENTICE   M. A. Wood
Andersen Press
OXFORD JUNIOR READERS,   Green series I &
III   Roderick Hunt [ed.]   OUP
ROBIN HOOD: HIS LIFE AND TIMES
Bernard Miles   Hamlyn/Rand McNally [as
ROBIN HOOD: HIS LIFE AND LEGEND]
TALES FROM THE BORDERS
Winifred Finlay [ed.]   Kaye & Ward

1980
BLACKFACE STALLION   Helen Griffiths
Hutchinson/Holiday House
BUZZ BOMB   Freda Kelsall   Macmillan
DEUTSCHE HELDENSAGEN   Martin Beheim-
Schwarzbach   Ueberreuter [Vienna]
DEUTSCHE RITTENSAGEN   Martin Beheim-
Schwarzbach   Ueberreuter [Vienna]
DRACULA: EVERYTHING YOU ALWAYS
WANTED TO KNOW BUT WERE TOO
AFRAID TO ASK   Victor G. Ambrus   OUP
THE KING'S MONSTER   Caroline Haywood
Morrow [USA]
OXFORD JUNIOR READERS,   Green series IV
Roderick Hunt [ed.]   OUP
ROPE AROUND THE WIND   Nora Rock
Andersen Press/State Mutual Book
SNOWY RIVER BRUMBY   Elyne Mitchell
Hutchinson [Australia]/Hutchinson [UK] 1981
UNDER THE DOUBLE EAGLE   Victor G.
Ambrus and Donald Lindsay   OUP
THE VALIANT LITTLE TAILOR   Victor G.
Ambrus   OUP
WHITE FEATHER   Freda Kelsall   Macmillan

1981
BRUMBY RACER   Elyne Mitchell   Hutchinson
[Australia]/Hutchinson [UK] 1981
THE CHILDHOOD OF JESUS   Christopher
Rawson and R. H. Lloyd   Usborne
DRACULA'S BEDTIME STORYBOOK   Victor G.
Ambrus   OUP
EAGLE'S EGG   Rosemary Sutcliff   Hamish
Hamilton
THE EASTER STORY   Christopher Rawson and
R. H. Lloyd   Usborne
ENCYCLOPEDIA OF LEGENDARY CREATURES
Tom McGowen [ed.]   Rand McNally
[USA]/Hamlyn 1982 [as THE HAMLYN BOOK
OF LEGENDARY CREATURES]
HINTER DEM NORDWIND   George Macdonald
Annette Betz Verlag [Munich & Vienna]

THE MIRACLES OF JESUS   Christopher Rawson and R. H. Lloyd   Usborne

MY LITTLE BOOK OF JESUS   Norman J. Bull   Hamlyn

MY SILVER STORYBOOK   illustrated by Victor Ambrus *et al.*   Hamlyn

OXFORD JUNIOR READERS,   Green series V   Roderick Hunt [ed.]   OUP

OXFORD JUNIOR READERS,   Red series II, IV and VI   Roderick Hunt [ed.]   OUP

STORIES JESUS TOLD   Christopher Rawson and R. H. Lloyd   Usborne

TALES OF FANTASY AND FEAR   Winifred Finlay [ed.]   Kaye & Ward

1982

BILLY BUNTER COMES FOR CHRISTMAS   Frank Richards [ed. Kay King]   Quiller Press

BILLY BUNTER OF GREYFRIARS SCHOOL   Frank Richards [ed. Kay King]   Quiller Press

BILLY BUNTER'S DOUBLE   Frank Richards [ed. Kay King]   Quiller Press

BLACKBEARD: THE PIRATE   Victor G. Ambrus   OUP

GRANDMA, FELIX, AND MUSTAPHA BISCUIT   Victor G. Ambrus   Morrow [USA]/OUP 1984

JUST SO STORIES   Rudyard Kipling   Rand McNally [USA]

TALES OF KING ARTHUR   James Riordan [ed.]   Hamlyn/Rand McNally

1983

BILLY BUNTER DOES HIS BEST   Frank Richards [ed. Kay King]   Quiller Press

BILLY BUNTER'S BENEFIT   Frank Richards [ed. Kay King]   Quiller Press

BILLY BUNTER'S POSTAL ORDER   Frank Richards [ed. Kay King]   Quiller Press

LA FANTÔME FÂCHÉ   Graham Sedgley   Nelson

JEENO, HELÖISE AND IGAMOR, THE LONG LONG HORSE   Michael de Larrabeiti   Pelham/Merrimack

SANTA CLAUS FOREVER!   Carolyn Haywood, pictures by Glenys and Victor Ambrus   Morrow [USA]/OUP 1984

TALES FROM THE ARABIAN NIGHTS   James Riordan [ed.]   Hamlyn/Rand McNally 1985

1984

STORIES FROM CHAUCER   Geoffrey Chaucer [ed. Geraldine McCaughrean]   OUP/Macmillan [as THE CANTERBURY TALES]

THE LEGEND OF THE FOURTH WISE MAN   R. H. Lloyd   Mowbray

STORIES OF THE BALLET   James Riordan   Hodder & Stoughton/Rand McNally [as FAVORITE STORIES OF THE BALLET]

1985

HOW THE FIRST LETTER WAS WRITTEN   Rudyard Kipling   Macmillan/Bedrick

A MEDICAL NOBODY   Reader's Digest

1986

A CHRISTMAS CAROL   Charles Dickens [pop-up book]   Methuen/Rand McNally

CHRISTMAS STICKER BOOK   Susannah Bradley   Purnell

JAMES HERRIOT'S DOG STORIES   James Herriot   Michael Joseph

FATHER CHRISTMAS AND HIS SLEIGH   Carolyn Haywood   Morrow [USA]/OUP [as HOW THE REINDEER SAVED SANTA]

FRANKENSTEIN   Mary Shelley   Heinemann Educational

KING DICKY BIRD AND THE BOSSY PRINCESS   Dorothy Edwards   Methuen

PETER AND THE WOLF   James Riordan   OUP

SON OF DRACULA   Victor G. Ambrus   OUP

WELL LOVED TALES FROM SHAKESPEARE   Bernard Miles   Hamlyn

1987

BLACK BEAUTY   Anna Sewell [ed. D. K. Swan]   Longman

THE CANTERBURY TALES   Geoffrey Chaucer [ed. M. West]   Longman

AN ILLUSTRATED TREASURY OF MYTHS AND LEGENDS   Hamlyn

THE JUNGLE BOOK   Rudyard Kipling [pop-up book]   Macdonald

1988

PINOCCHIO   Carlo Collodi   OUP

5 · NIGEL LAMBOURNE

30 MAY 1919 – 12 DECEMBER 1988*

NIGEL LAMBOURNE is one of the supreme draughtsmen of our time.[1] He is best known as a book illustrator through the cycle of books produced at roughly three-yearly intervals for the Folio Society between 1949 and 1983. At the outset, let it be conceded that Lambourne is to some degree a reclusive and enigmatic figure, but an influential presence in the field of illustration despite a relatively low published output. Little published work apart from that for Folio really matters; but his unpublished drawings to literary texts and themes tell another story, and one which will eventually deserve to be recounted and catalogued in full.

This present enquiry falls into three sections: the assembly of a factual background to his career; discussion of the published books; and an examination of those aspects of his unpublished work and thinking which relate to the topic of book illustration.[2] Subscribing to the theory that an ounce of contemporary observation is worth a ton of speculative archaeology (the contemporary art historian, H. M. Wingler, once remarked: 'It's like detective work, one has to be round at the studio as soon as the crime has been committed, before the paint dries.'), it is disconcerting to find how indistinct and incomplete the past record can be in the case of an artist still in his creative and intellectual prime. Work dispersed, letters undated, gallery archives destroyed, early commissions undocketed: '. . . another skeletal fragment I am very much afraid. And, as usual, some dates are indeed very movable feasts.'[3]

Nigel Lambourne was born on 30 May 1919, of part-Irish descent in Croydon. His father had been shot down and invalided out of the Royal Flying Corps, and subsequently lectured in chemistry at Nottingham University for a time before the family returned to Croydon. Nigel attended Selhurst Grammar School until his vocation became apparent and he was able to enrol at the Regent Street Polytechnic School of Art under Bernard Meninsky and W. P. Robins, and at the Central School of

---

*This essay had been written and discussed with Nigel Lambourne prior to his death, and it is printed in unchanged form.

49 *Moll Flanders,* 1954

Arts and Crafts in the evenings for etching (1934–37). He went on to the Royal College of Art, and studied with John Nash, Robert Austin and Malcolm Osborne (1937–39).

The outbreak of war found him in France – a country he has always loved and which surely would have rendered him greater recognition and honour as an artist – but he immediately enlisted and served in the British Army for six and a half years. In circumstances where he could draw little, he observed deeply; but will only talk – and then rarely – about the closing months before demobilisation during which some sort of inventory could be made within occupied Germany.

He married Barbara Ward Standen in 1943 and their only son, Martyn, was born in 1945. After the war, Lambourne returned to the RCA to complete his degree course in some four to five terms, being awarded the Medal for Draughtsmanship in addition to the Engraver and Lithographers Diploma.

To become established in the post-war London art world was a difficult task, and the primary aim for most was to get together enough freelance work and teaching for basic survival. Nigel Lambourne organized this efficiently enough, teaching life classes at the Isleworth Evening Institute whilst still at College. From 1947 his first press and editorial illustrations started to appear in *Lilliput* and *The Leader,* followed shortly afterwards by freelance work for the J. Walter Thompson Agency and children's book illustration for Elek, Dobson and Oxford. In 1948 he began to teach illustration and engraving part-time at both the Regent Street Polytechnic and St Martin's Schools of Art. In 1950–51 he joined a team including F. H. K. Henrion, Jock Kinnear and James

Holland attached to the Central Office of Information, for which his own main contribution was to be a series of drawings of Victorian scientists that appeared in the 'Dome of Discovery', a centrepiece of the Festival of Britain South Bank Exhibition.

This record of achievement is impressive enough in itself, but has to take a back seat to Lambourne's commitment as an artist and printmaker; his energies were primarily engaged in these years in producing work for a succession of major London exhibitions.

His first one-man show of drawings took place in the Spring of 1949 at the Kensington Gallery. In 1950 he shared an exhibition with Lionel Bulmer and Edward Bawden at the Leicester Gallery, and another with Clifford Hall and John Buckland Wright at Colnaghi in the following year. One-man shows were held at the Wilton Gallery in 1951 and again in 1952, and at the Zwemmer Gallery in 1954, 1956 and 1959. His work was included in the important 1954 exhibition at the Leger Gallery, 'The New Realism in English Art'. Prints had been shown in travelling exhibitions to Chicago, New York and San Francisco in 1950, 1952 and 1953, and he was well represented in the Zwemmer 'New Edition Prints' exhibitions in 1957 and 1958. This decade of exhibitions was greeted with critical acclaim,[4] many works were purchased for public collections, and it is still keenly recalled by many, whether or not they are aware that Lambourne's artistic odyssey is still in progress, although hidden from view by a long-standing reluctance to exhibit and an indifference to public or critical response. He considers this deliberately chosen isolation almost as a precondition for the development of his art. Teaching, however, remained a self-imposed and intermittently rewarding obligation for many years after he had effectively withdrawn from London's formal art circuits.

Many schools in the history of art – religious, historical or narrative – have been illustrative in that they took for granted a familiarity with the stories or events depicted, and frequently referred the spectator back to specific texts. Ruskin's dictum that one should look at a picture as if it were the only thing of its kind in the world has proved devastatingly easy to follow, to the neglect of work which is firmly rooted in a literary frame of reference or explores relationships between the arts through the medium of drawing. But some drawings linked to books can continue to resonate in the mind, just as notable stagings in the theatre may remain susceptible to almost total recall.

In common with most illustrators, Lambourne asks such questions as 'Why illustration?', and 'How illustration?', but more frequently than most he reaches reasoned conclusions as to why a particular title should not be illustrated, least of all by him. This stems from a long-standing enquiry into *how* pictures are related to text in the conventional format of the book. *Why* should an illustrator interpose himself between author and adult reader; what good or harm will it do any of them? And if the traditional juxtaposition of text and illustration on the page will not serve in a given situation, what alternatives are available? He has often pursued the design possibilities

50 *The Informer*, 1961

of printing a suite of illustrations at the end of a text in a trade edition, but has never found a publisher to take him up. Thereby no offence would be offered to the author; the reader could take or leave the visual interpretation presented; and it might prove innovative publishing to bring within general reach a concept that has hitherto been confined to *éditions de luxe.*

Had Lambourne been French, then, with certain reservations, it is probable that he would have felt at home with the *livre d'artiste.* [5] The British private press tradition has engaged his attention only fleetingly; from time to time he has been approached but generally finds himself out of sympathy with the text or treatment proposed. And so Lambourne ventures what can best be described as 'literary illustration without benefit of publisher' – which forms the subject matter for the final pages of this chapter.

To return to the outline of his career: it has to be faced that at the end of the 1950s a certain change in his attitude took place towards the art establishment. He saw lucidly the direction his work should take, and recognised the pendulum swing between those extremes of his range – from life drawing to the frontiers of abstract draughtsmanship and technical experiment in printmaking – within which any fruitful development would have to take place. For gallery owners and pundits to have advanced alternative scenarios for adapting to the emergent trends of the 1960s in order to stay in the commercial limelight was an act of presumption that completely failed to take into account Lambourne's integrity, and which precipitated him into estrangement from that particular market-place.

He taught graphics and printmaking at the Guildford College of Art from 1950–56, concurrently with freelancing for the Ogilvie-Mather, Wasey, and Colman-Prentice-Varley agencies. At this time a number of children's books and standard classics were illustrated for the Department of Education & Science in Wellington, New Zealand. In 1959 he went to lecture part-time in illustration at the Leicester College of Art (later Leicester Polytechnic), where he was shortly joined by his wife, who accepted a full-time appointment within the Faculty of Fashion & Textiles which she held until her retirement in 1984. They discovered a late Georgian house with rambling terrain that almost promised to cut them off from one of Leicestershire's more hideously developed industrial villages. Lambourne set up studio there, with a small photographic darkroom attached, in which the photogrammes for *The Trial* were later to be devised. An old outbuilding close to the kitchen – more French than English – overlooked a garden which was part wilderness, part inventiveness, with pockets of practical cultivation. For a few days in a good year, the illusion of a Mediterranean lifestyle was sustained late into the evening, fuelled by the blackest of red wines, olives and cigarettes.

Escape from the English climate and the teaching environment for weeks at a time has always been a priority; for many years Marseilles used to be almost a second home where the Lambournes could pass for locals. He drew in the cafés and bars there, single-figure drawings of almost monumental presence. He relished the settings, but was rarely enthused to draw the cityscape, and so there is no *Nigel Lambourne's Marseilles* to set against the travel books of Topolski, Hogarth, Gentleman and others: his city must be seen through its inhabitants.

As Marseilles fell victim to post-war development and despoilation, they moved further afield; overland by mobile caravan, to quieter parts of the South of France, or to Turkey or the Spanish interior. Although Nigel Lambourne is neither painter nor landscapist, the illustrations to *The Georgics* stem more directly from these travels than from his staple winter readings in Loeb's Classical Library. The Lambournes' present home in Somerset was selected as much for its proximity to the Channel ports as for its other merits. Lambourne resigned from the Leicester Polytechnic in 1972. The experiment in the Graphic Design Faculty under G. B. Karo had been brave but unstable. The idea had been to assemble an unparalleled cabinet of visiting talent. Edward Bawden, George Him, Barbara Jones, Paul Peter Piech, Peter Morter and Ferelith Eccles-Williams among others were at one time, together with Nigel Lambourne, in attendance in the area of illustration alone. Lambourne must always have been superb as a teacher. He was unfailingly courteous, hyper-alert, deploying every resource to stimulate awareness and response; and yet just below the surface lay a hidden rage at any lack of vocation or refusal to think.

The case for Lambourne's eminence as a book illustrator must largely rest on the ten titles commissioned by the Folio Society. By temperament he has never claimed an affinity with books for children, and in the present context it would be pointless to extend the strict bibliographical record further. Whilst superb illustrations to major literary themes remain unpublished, why list in full occasional work that held little significance for him even at the time?

Nigel Lambourne's first book for the Folio Society, Sterne's *A Sentimental Journey* (1949), was only the fourteenth volume to be issued by the Society. At this date, not surprisingly, typography and use of colour had more to do with the persistence of pre-war tastes than with the mature and recognisable idiom which Charles Ede was shortly to evolve. At the same time the project was forward-looking in being the first printed book to make use of Plastocowell (a new material of considerable importance to several major artists at the time – see p. 42). Like Charles Keeping, Lambourne also recalls the mystery surrounding the subsequent processing and proofing of these intractable sheets of grained plastic on which the artist had chalked, inked and scratched. During the interval necessary for this work he was wined and dined by the printers with the object of keeping him away from the shop-floor and the secrets of the new process. Something of the heady uncertainty of the experiment – for the illustrations were to be printed in no fewer than three colours – communicated itself to the publisher, and in December 1948 Charles Ede wrote to Lambourne: 'Do make the colours a kind of tint; quite aleatory, since we have no idea of exactly how it will emerge.'

51 Maupassant's *Short Stories,* 'The Sign', 1959

'And how bloody right!', Lambourne was later to observe. Sensibly and predictably, he saw to it that nothing of the intrinsic drawing should escape the black plate. The supporting colours (a blue and a pink) are followed through in Barbara Ward Lambourne's binding design. As if fearing the impact that the voltage of his current graphic language might have on Sterne's tone of voice, it is possible that certain styles in eighteenth-century French engraved book illustration may have come to his aid. Certainly the artist seems to have been prepared to go along – short of pastiche – with the slightly mannered approach adopted by the publisher, and on those terms has produced a result which accords well with the text. There is precision and vitality in plenty to be found in the black drawing, but not as yet the confident energy that was to break out in the masterly sequence of drawings to *Moll Flanders* (1954).

Moll Flanders was an astonishing book to have come from an English illustrator in the early 1950s. It was a marvellous text for Lambourne to have been offered, since themes and preoccupations within this commission converge as only rarely before or since for him. At about this time he published a three-part article, 'Drawing for the love of it', which affords glimpses into his working method; how he progresses from drawing from life to analysis and composition, whether for a finished drawing or a book illustration. [6]

The difference in approach between *Moll Flanders* and *Short Stories by Guy de Maupassant* (1959) is striking. *Moll* has a raw energy linked to the German expressionist tradition – Beckmann in particular comes to mind – whereas the later drawings are lighter yet more complex in handling. This may follow from the notorious difficulties that the full-page use of the zinco (or letterpress line block) presented to many illustrators during the comparatively short life-span of that reproductive method. If a book illustrated in this way is to retain integrity of style, one constraint is that the margins and weight of the opposing text page have to be considered, another that the pictorial image must normally be designed to share the paper and the degree of inking and impression that is right for the typeface in question. In this instance a special attempt was made to establish a harmony between illustrations and facing text pages by means of a fairly elaborate incorporation of mechanical tints (i.e. dry-transfer texture sheets primarily intended for use by commercial artists) into these drawings. Although not without experimental interest, and incidental details which pay off as a direct outcome of this treatment, the effect is to give a static and slightly dated cast in places to otherwise fine drawing.

An unpublished drawing has survived as a preliminary idea for the story 'Paul's Mistress' which displays a purer technique by virtue of remaining unencumbered by the direct-transfer texture patented as 'Zipatone'. It was presumably to this drawing that Brian Rawson, then editorial director of the Folio Society, referred when he wrote to the artist: 'This is utterly against the grain, textually. And, at the same time, has an explicit sensuality, which (whilst admirable in the abstract) is without relevance in my jaundiced view, to the idiom of the story. Of course, I *am* thinking of our members, as if you didn't know!' [7] The wrap-round drawing printed direct on to cloth may be regarded as one of the most successful forerunners of the many binding designs of its type essayed by this publisher.

In contrast to the slightly contrived impression which is left by the overall design of the Maupassant volume, *The Informer* (1961) by Liam O'Flaherty is a fluent and compelling performance. Through a production gaffe, according to the publisher: 'The text was set up in page before the artist began work, and the passages to be illustrated were selected only from the first and last pages of each section – a fierce discipline from which Lambourne emerged with flying colours.' [8] The grounds for success are surely to be found in the appositeness of both lithographic technique and social observation (in the manner of Daumier) to the Irish situation so graphically recounted by the author of this uneven book. Now and then the story attains a taut, almost hypnotic credibility which the lithographs are able to match, notably in the magnificent draughtsmanship and humanity of the drawing reproduced. This is unusually direct, closer to the naturalism of the life-class, as if the artist had deliberately cut out some of the compositional procedures which were customary for him at the time.

The Brothers Karamazov (1964) is arguably the most impressive in scale and profundity of all the books which Nigel Lambourne has illustrated to date for the Folio Society. It was not without its problems in gestation, for Lambourne felt there were large expanses, notably Father Zossima's narration, where illustration would be impossible, even ridiculous. His basic response to the vastness and Russianness of the book was to decide that when an illustration did appear after endless pages of snow-filled text, it would be a massive close-up in rich black – so black that it would have to be printed separately from the text for technical reasons.

Edward Ardizzone always held that the proscenium-arch decorum of the half-page drawing should be respected, and that to essay close-up portraits of the characters one had to be either mad or asking for trouble. The drawing from *Karamazov* reproduced here is one of several fine examples in the book which demonstrate the fallacy of golden rules of this type, and show that illustrators can approach their craft successfully from diametrically opposed directions.

A dynamic rhythmic energy runs through *Karamazov*, although there is scarcely a continuous unbroken line to be found. The whole is built up of short, jabbing dots, that may be likened to the jabs of a reed pen in a late Van Gogh drawing, reinforced with sweeps of 'Instantex' dry-transfer textures, which preserve the integrity of the dot convention without dissipating the vigour of the design as hand-drawn dot techniques would have tended to do. Since dot techniques were also prevalent at this time in the work of such illustrators as Leonard Rosoman, Robert Micklewright and Robin Jacques, it is interesting to compare Lambourne's broader use and the different ends he has in view.

The next two volumes which Lambourne illustrated for the Folio Society were Kafka's *The Trial* and Virgil's *The Georgics*. It is not surprising that the prospect of illustrating Kafka should rocket any illustrator's thoughts well into the realms of abstraction, and it follows that Nigel Lambourne should quickly decide that no conceivable figurative approach could be other than absurd when he was invited to produce *The Trial* for publication in 1967. Instead he proposed to revive the photogramme[9] – pioneered duing Kafka's lifetime by Man Ray and Laszlo Moholy-Nagy – because he saw in it an hallucinatory power to evoke cerebral concepts through abstract, depersonalised means. This must have been a journey into unfamiliar territory for the artist, but he returned with material which more than vindicated his theoretical standpoint: photogrammes rich in tonal and kinetic depth, probing and illuminating the hidden recesses of a dark imagination. The pity is that the resultant book fails to do itself justice in terms of appropriate format and presentation (a production decision to reduce the page size was made without the artist's sanction),

52 *The Brothers Karamazov*, 1964

so that what might have been one of the milestones in modern book design and illustration remains only an interesting experiment.

By its nature, *The Georgics* (1969) is lacking in any sustained figurative interest. The solitary worker appearing in three of the five soft-ground etchings is only sketchily indicated and perhaps it is possible to detect, in the plate reproduced, a reminiscence of the ploughman in Bruegel's *Landscape with the Fall of Icarus*. Whilst this is a gentle, wise and classical book, informed by a backward glance at the pastoral tradition in European culture in general, the artist's preoccupation with the medium comes across strongly. He was offered a rare opportunity to fathom the technical possibilities opened up by working directly on the plate for a gravure press normally reserved for security printing. The sheer range of depths of ink-film imparted to paper by this direct-plate intaglio process operated by Kultura, Budapest, has to be seen – if not felt – to be believed, and each illustration is an original print of great tactile presence.

When the eight aquatints to Chekhov's *Short Stories* were commissioned by the Society for publication in its 1974 programme, a decade had elapsed since the last appearance of a *figurative* cycle of illustrations from Nigel Lambourne. Where such intervals of time are involved it is a challenge to look for evidence of shifts in emphasis or stylistic development, and it does seem possible to detect a fresh preoccupation with effects of spatial recession. Devices such as the way characters face into or out from the picture-plane, sometimes involving the use of mirrors, have long featured in Lambourne's work as a means of engaging or repelling the onlooker. Here people and objects inhabit a gradated series of tonal planes within each interior, and conduct their dialogue – or more commonly fail to connect – in a way that is true to Chekhov's own techniques of theatre. Lambourne reads and researches his authors extensively, and so in illustrating these short stories it is likely that he had the plays also in mind.

At a technical level, successive stopping-out procedures in the aquatint process facilitate the creation of this sequence of receding planes. The full bled-off page area takes a light grey ground and this provides a field of action undisturbed by any interplay between illustration and surrounding margin; similarly there is no acknowledgment of the facing type area. The eye is funnelled into direct engagement with the image which correspondingly hints at spatial extensions beyond the strict format of the page. Foreground close-ups, door-frames and mirrors have as vital a role to play here as in the interiors of the Dutch masters of the seventeenth century, and the viewer's leisurely involvement is comparable.

Ralph Rashleigh (1977) is a harrowing account of convict life in Australia from 1820 onwards, and consequently the contemporary visual record is likely to have proved too sparse to yield a solution. For any illustrator without special knowledge of the country such an assignment must pose many problems, and it is to Nigel Lambourne's credit that he has managed to provide a valid commentary. His responsiveness to historical atmosphere is so unerring that, intentionally or otherwise, certain kinds of line drawings that popularised the exploits of the British Empire in newspapers and later

53 Virgil's *Georgics*, trial soft-ground etching, 1969

through boy's magazines and adventure stories are brought to mind here and there. It is as if he is prepared to let his own voice be replaced by a more anonymous one and to produce some drawings which it would be difficult to date or assign out of context.

Disraeli's *Sybil* (1983) caused the illustrator some anguish, because he could neither whip up much enthusiasm for the text, nor see for a time how illustration could supply more than the kind of trite underlining he so despises. He found an answer through sheer effort of will, first by concentrating to an unusual degree on costume and social minutiae so that the age could be evoked in drawings of considerable elegance, and then by inventing a range of characterisation and expression so that the protagonists should at least have a convincing visual presence on the page.

That Lambourne should have turned in polished and professional solutions on occasion to books for which his natural response was one of indifference, if not antipathy, is remarkable. That he should not have done so more frequently, particularly in areas such as children's fiction with which he has never really been able to connect temperamentally, is understandable. That so many other promising ventures were abandoned through no fault of his is naturally a matter for regret.

Anyone who has had the opportunity to examine a fair sample from the wealth of unpublished prints and drawings will find that they cluster about themes and titles without overmuch regard for the chronology of dates of commission, completion or curtailment. The artist's internal clock is not synchronised with any external one, so that a decision taken not to publish a certain book rarely leads to a cancellation of his interest or work for it, which may be continued sporadically over many years.

A high proportion of projects are of particular interest for the very reason that they are self-starters, whether or not there was an interested publisher in the background at the time. In one or two of these cases there would be few problems in designing a book belatedly around the extant illustrations. If it were possible to reassemble the great early cycle of bullfighting drawings with an appropriate text, the result would be an impressive book and not – as might be thought – an exhibition catalogue.

Literary motifs or allusive starting points have been present throughout his graphic output, and he frequently returns to key themes at intervals over many years. Subjects are not drawn exclusively from imaginative literature, for there is also evidence of wide and systematic reading – in the social anthropology of myth and sexuality, for example – which informs the thematic structure of certain major cycles of drawings.

The titles briefly considered below have been selected to try to represent the extent and variety of this unpublished material, and some of the ways in which it came about.

Lambourne had been encouraged to start making drawings for James Joyce's *Ulysses* in 1968 and it soon became apparent, in more senses than one, that he had set to work on no ordinary book. Exhilaration alternated with bile as negotiations over the legal feasibility of an illustrated edition of *Ulysses* in Britain and the United States dragged on. Against this background of uncertainty two issues became increasingly clear: a harsh coming to terms and a deliberate calling on his own residual Irishness in order to confront the problem of how to illustrate the unillustratable; and a growing regard for the abilities of Brian Rawson, who as editor must have shown great idealism in the pursuit of what would surely – had it been published – have proved to be the Folio Society's most enterprising and courageous book. The continuing impasse with the Joyce estate, and Brian Rawson's untimely death, led sadly to the eventual shelving of the project several years later. Six drawings had been completed by then, but the dialogue with the text still continues.

Ovid's *Amores,* from which a revised woodcut dated 1977 is reproduced, proved yet another abortive project. This begins by nodding respectfully in the direction of Aristide Maillol's classical woodcut illustrations, whilst promising something equally fine. Life compositions, of which this represents an economically stated subject,

54 Ovid's *Amores,* unpublished woodcut, 1977

frequently undergo a set of variations – almost scientific tests – in which they progress from their origin as line drawings, to lino- or woodcut, and also to copper-engraved versions. Time frequently elapses between these stages, but when the results are brought together, the changes wrought within a clearly thought-out composition by passage through these distinct disciplines are always fascinating to compare.

During preparations for the Leipzig Internationale Buchkunst-Ausstellung 1971, Lambourne was invited to propose a classic of English literature which he would like to illustrate with a view to publication by the Leipziger Presse. There were distinguished precedents in the involvement of such illustrators as HAP Grieshaber (West Germany) and Anatoli Kaplan (USSR) in bibliophile editions from this house, and always a possibility that a publisher might be found to take an edition with the original language text restored. Lambourne nominated Marlowe's *Dr Faustus.*

Two of the Faustus drawings were exhibited in Leipzig in 1971, and soon thereafter trial lithographic proofs were received in England. It seemed that a truly remarkable book might be in the making, but once again hopes were to be dashed. Since the Leipziger Presse was only empowered to produce two or three titles a year, and had recently undertaken both parts of Goethe's *Faust* with illustrations by Josef Hegenbarth, it deemed it best not to proceed with a title with such obvious, if superficial, similarities.

Once again, the breakdown of plans for publication did not affect Lambourne's commitment to his theme in the least, for he continued to work on it for many years without any evidence of shift in style or slackening of concentration. Faustus represented a close personal involvement for the artist, yet at the same time it stood at several removes from the usual exigencies of publication; so it is no surprise to find few concessions made in these drawings to the accepted conventions and supposed limitations for illustration within the current framework of book production.

It is as if the very incompleteness of Marlowe's text, and conjecture as to how it may have been elaborated on the stage, had set a precedent for the graphic artist to approach the work in a spirit of collaboration. The task was to show the play in the process of 'becoming' in the author's mind as well as to imply possible stagings, metamorphoses, outcomes. Beyond the figurative treatment, there is the barest economy of means; here and there the scene is set or a few lines of speech are noted as if in the handwriting of a set or costume designer; at times there is a compelling sense of movement along the boards or a magnificent realisation of the potential for transformation in the blackness of the theatre. Perhaps the scope which the play offers for such an existential perspective goes some way to elucidating the artist's own opinion that: 'whereas Goethe's *Faust* is impossible for the illustrator, that of Marlowe is not'.[10]

A further stage in the process of withdrawal from the expectation of publication, and the consequent shift into a higher stratum of artistic freedom, can be seen in his obsession with *Hundejahre*. This, the third and arguably greatest novel by Günter Grass, had appeared in this country as *Dog Years* in Ralph Manheim's translation in 1965. It set in train in Lambourne's eye a sequence of scarecrow images: these culminated in 1968 in some monumental versions which achieve the archetypal status of the 'Icarus' theme in the hands of Michael Ayrton or the 'Birdman' of Leonard Baskin; yet Lambourne was actively producing further variations at least as recently as 1981.[11] Again he writes, in 1985: 'I am grinding on, *still* and yet, with the bloody von Kleist *Über das Marionettentheater* ideas for illustration. Very slow!' – and that was at least 15 years after Kleist's celebrated essay had first engaged his attention.

By this point it should have become apparent that illustration as understood in relation to practical exigencies and any normal time-scale no longer appears to be under consideration. But Lambourne is still calling it illustration. He views himself and wishes to be regarded as an illustrator, and *not* as a fine artist and printmaker who happens to have illustrated a few books.

55 *Dr Faustus,* unpublished lithograph, 1971

56/57 *Ulysses,* preliminary Conté pencil drawing, late 1960s   *Ulysses:* Conté pencil drawing

If for a moment the field of illustration is seen, like mathematics, to have a pure as well as an applied aspect, then Lambourne's place in the scheme of things becomes clearer. He chooses to pursue both aspects and to study them in interaction. In consequence he disregards subject-matter that will not further his researches, and in turn does not claim attention for his findings. This brief account can only attempt to fill in some of the gaps concerning an illustrator who deliberately shuns publicity almost to the point of avoiding publication; and to celebrate the magnitude of his achievement.

NOTES

1. 'I admired his work and how my mind boggled at the time at a group of bullfight drawings that he exhibited in those days with Michael Chase at the old Zwemmer Gallery': Charles Keeping, letter to author, 8 August 1986.

58 *Ulysses:* unfinished pen drawing

59 *Ulysses:* unpublished drawing

2. This chapter is intended to supplement rather than supplant an earlier account given in Douglas Martin, 'Nigel Lambourne', *The Private Library,* 3rd series, 5/1 (Spring 1982), 2-24. However, some overlap is unavoidable, and acknowledgment is made for kind permission to quote from that article.
3. Quotations, unless otherwise stated, are from conversations and correspondence with the author.
4. The following extracts from contemporary reviews are intended both to corroborate the high claims advanced, and to define characteristics which may be recognised in free drawings and published illustrations alike: ,

'Lambourne's forms are constructed as a cage of fine taut lines . . . He has a close affinity with the unisonant drum-tight volumes of Henry Moore, but he has evolved a style, which, although sculptural in feeling and rendering, is completely his own . . . His efforts to revive the drawing as a work of art are meeting with success, and his leadership may prove strong enough to turn the tide of English graphic art.' Albert Garrett, reviewing the 1950 Zwemmer show for *The Studio.*

'Mr. Nigel Lambourne . . . sets [his forms] in a high wind, throws a net round them and pulls it tight . . . His drawing has, in fact, a splendid tension . . . and – a rare quality – Mr. Lambourne does not cheat. There is firmness, and not merely the look of firmness, in his drawing.' John Russell, *Daily Telegraph,* 1950.

' ''Line and guts, that is what you want in drawing, not all this delicate fiddling nonsense.'' [Meninsky] . . . Nigel Lambourne is truly a draughtsman of the twentieth century. He is a student and master of line, vigour his characteristic; like all men of his generation, time is divided not by years but in pre-war, war, and post-war periods, and for them guts was the essential to survival. In the aftermath this fiddling nonsense had no meaning . . . Few English draughtsmen are as convincing, none more economical.' Eric Newton, *Art News & Review,* 1954.

5. cf. the standard works: W. J. Strachan, *The Artist and the Book in France* (Peter Owen, 1969) and its useful up-date provided by *Le Livre d'Artiste: A Catalogue of the W. J. Strachan Gift to the Taylor Institution* (Ashmolean Museum, 1987).

6. Nigel Lambourne, 'Drawing for the love of it', *(The Artist,* 1969), 5–6, 34–5, 54–5. This is recommended reading in its entirety; the drawing called *The Corset* is followed through from preliminary drawing stage to a discussion of the process of selective analysis from which the following extract is taken: '. . . Little more was drawn from the subject herself, instead notes of such details as the number of major folds in the tension and slack of the skirt and the mechanics of the corset itself were made. These were then transcribed and selected for use in the final stages not of elaboration, but of reassessment and drawing together of the rhythm of arms to back and skirt tensions, to the simple, suave rolling of the shoulders. In my view, to have attempted such a study entirely from life would have meant seeing too much: seeing flesh without body shape, taut folds without the big sense of the skirt itself, and thus bearing out my belief that, to complete a picture (of any appreciable size) from Nature is tempting disaster. In this instance (as with others cited previously) the most logical approach was, first, through the senses; the impact of the whole impression was noted down and then a careful selection

and rejection of causes towards the total effect. Not *all* the causes, because they are infinite and are there in profusion in the living subject, but much rather aim towards the distillation of the sum of the whole.'

7. There are many Lambourne drawings which may disconcert some people by their explicit treatment of sexual thematic material; but basic qualities of draughtsmanship, humanity and scientific detachment ensure that no single drawing could reasonably be deemed to be obscene. It is a bizarre sidelight on our culture that a recent exhibition catalogue should have had to be reprinted with plate substitutions prior to issue, because a gallery owner feared a re-run of the D. H. Lawrence affair only slightly less than any affront which might conceivably be offered to his established clientèle.

8. *Folio 21,* 134.

9. Images produced directly on to photographic paper during successive phases of dark-room exposure; no camera or negative is involved, natural objects placed on the paper or interposed between enlarger lens and paper enable the desired tonal result to be fashioned under controlled experimental conditions.

10. 'I continue with *Faust* – Marlowe that is – because I still have a hang-up on the thing. Even years ago – now – when I began a series, the stage version is visible in every sense that Goethe obviously cannot be . . . But, the series continues because there is no where else to go. Other than ON – I mean . . .' (letter of 17 July 1986).

11. Although Grass's own graphic background and preoccupations were known, little had been seen in this country save the jackets for his books, and it was not possible to form an assessment until his first London exhibition in 1974 at Patrick Seale Prints. There was a certain fascination in discovering surface affinities – a similarity in appproach to historical qualities of line and subject matter within a German tradition – between Lambourne and Grass.

BIBLIOGRAPHY

Note: Numbers in square brackets are those assigned to volumes in the Folio Society's own bibliographies and checklists.

1949
A SENTIMENTAL JOURNEY   Laurence Sterne
    [16 lithographs in 3 colours]   Folio [14]

1950−53 −

1954
MOLL FLANDERS   Daniel Defoe   [19 line
    drawings]   Folio [65]

1955−58 −

1959
SHORT STORIES   Guy de Maupassant   [14
    drawings]   Folio [130]

1960 −

1961
DRAWING PEOPLE IN ACTION   [with
    illustrations]   Nigel Lambourne [ed. Mervyn
    Levy]   Studio Books/Watson-Guptill
THE INFORMER   Liam O'Flaherty −
    [8 lithographs]   Folio [155]

1962 −

1963
THE BOREAS ADVENTURE   Peter Knight
    Nelson
BRAESIDE: A SCOTTISH FARM   Lavinia
    Derwent   New Zealand Department of
    Education
FARMING IN ENGLAND   Elsie Locke and
    Ralph Whitlock   New Zealand Department
    of Education
THE ROAD TO ANKARA   S. C. George
    New Zealand Department of Education

1964
THE BROTHERS KARAMAZOV   Feodor
    Dostoyevsky   [24 drawings]   Folio [194]
HENNY AND CRISPIES   Naomi Mitchison
    New Zealand Department of Education
I WILL ADVENTURE   Elizabeth Gray   Oliver
    & Boyd

1965−66 −

1967
LEFT HAND WOOD   George Furnell   Oliver &
    Boyd/Follett 1970
THE TRIAL   Franz Kafka   [41
    photogrammes]   Folio [234]

1968 −

1969
THE GEORGICS   Publius Vergilius Maro
    [5 soft-ground etchings by direct-plate
    process]   Folio [266]

1970−71 −

1972
10 WAR POEMS   Wilfred Owen   illustrated by
    Nigel Lambourne and Paul Peter
    Piech   Taurus Press

1973 −

1974
SHORT STORIES   Anton Chekhov
    [8 aquatints]   Folio [354]

1975−76 −

1977
RALPH RASHLEIGH   James Tucker   [16 line
    drawings]   Folio [424]

1978−82 −

1983
SYBIL   Benjamin Disraeli   [17 line drawings]
    Folio [509]

6 · BRIAN WILDSMITH

BRIAN WILDSMITH is a painter, and painterly values underpin and permeate his work as an illustrator. He says that during the first thirty years of making a living from his books he had time only to *think* about painting, but for over eight years now he has been able to give it some priority over his many other artistic interests. And so the challenge in writing this essay is to relate his published work for children to a growing body of painting, much of which went on show for the first time in New York, San Francisco and Tokyo in 1988. In this way a fascinating creative personality can be glimpsed at work in contrasting disciplines, but ones in which the same rules must apply for some of the time, and between which startling parallels can spring up on occasion.

It is a drawback that few of Wildsmith's paintings or picture books reproduce well in black and white and at a scale reduced from that intended, and so those reproductions that do appear here should be viewed simply as *aides-mémoire*. Whereas it is always possible to return from a children's bookshop or library with an armful of his books, unfortunately the paintings are not yet represented in public collections in the British Isles. [1]

Brian Wildsmith hates it when the sun isn't shining. He has few other hates. In childhood he hated it every time his miner father had to go down the pit. He hates man's inhumanity to man. He reviles exploitation, and is intolerant of incompetence and spuriousness in the arts. [2]

His loves are for people as individuals, children especially, although he has a great need for solitude in his work. Then there are his three dominant passions: for art, for engineering (which his father – himself an amateur painter and skilled mechanic – imparted), and for music.

Heredity and upbringing, in a talented family with two younger brothers and a sister, appear to have allowed his mature personality to emerge naturally at an early age and without turmoil. He and his wife also had four children, three daughters and a son, all talented and now grown up.

60 *High Sang the Sword,* 1959

He was born in the village of Penistone on 22 January 1930, and retains a fierce and typical love for Yorkshire. Had the West Riding been blessed with endless hours of warm sunshine, no doubt he would have been perfectly content to remain there. Chemistry was his favourite study at school – he would read it for pleasure; and he was awarded a scholarship to the De La Salle College for Boys at Sheffield. He remembers walking along a corridor to a chemistry class, when clear questions formulated themselves in his mind in response to which he decided that this was *not* what he wanted to do for the rest of his life, and that he must find something creative. So he turned on his heels, went to see the headmaster, and told him that he was leaving to go to art school.

He had been torn between training for a career as a concert pianist or as a painter. The former ambition was abandoned as soon as the strain that it would have imposed on the family finances became apparent; but both musical and scientific modes of thought have continued to have a considerable bearing throughout his artistic career. [3]

He attended Barnsley School of Art for the intermediate examination from the age of seventeen, between the years 1946 and 1949:

There was a mélange of about ten students, if that – an Academician who painted watercolours – and some needleworkers. At first the classes were held in a couple of big rooms above Barnsley Municipal Canteen which contained a table-tennis table, a litho press and little else. It seemed uninspiring at the time, but, when I think back, it offered the most wonderful entry into art education.[4]

In 1949 he won a scholarship to the Slade School of Fine Art, where he drew and painted from then until 1952. He retains a personal respect for the late Sir William Coldstream as teacher and administrator – and producer of one of the pitiably small handful of paintings of substance or significance in the Royal Academy's 1987 'British Art' retrospective.

Giotto, Piero della Francesca, Michelangelo, Rembrandt and Goya he came to know through the British Museum and National Gallery print rooms during lunchtimes from the Slade, when a student could still find a portfolio of original Michelangelo drawings placed in his hands. Formal art history at the Slade consisted mainly in looking at slides of works of art. His broad Yorkshire dialect and the equally broad Viennese accent of Rudolf Wittkower found little common ground together. The last thing the teaching staff thought about was helping individual talent to find its own individual course, as distinct from working to a standard academic syllabus and talking about their own work. The business of how an artist might set about making a living was none of their concern.

When Wildsmith left the Slade he served his call-up in the army, and had plenty of time to think about the problem of how one supports oneself as an artist without private means. He produced 150 fabric designs and sold two. So, on demobilisation, he decided to teach for a while in order to survive until the way ahead became clear. Whilst teaching at Selhurst Grammar School (1955-57), he read somewhere that 29,000 book titles were published each year, most requiring jacket designs: ' . . . and so I taught myself to letter and so forth, and every day I was first out of school at 4.00, and onto my Lambretta scooter doing the rounds of London publishers' offices before they closed.'

The first book wrapper commission was from John Murray and others quickly followed, and soon he was also being asked to undertake the line illustration of children's books for a number of publishers, including Faber, Penguin and Oxford. His work as a line draughtsman (which can roughly be contained between the years 1957 and 1964), is not very well known today, and he has never returned to the medium. These early drawings in their own way rank with the very best of contemporaneous work, but for obvious and related reasons he was glad to make a break with that particular field. Together with his day a week teaching at Maidstone College of Art from 1960 to 1965, it was a necessary means of supporting his growing family until his personal breakthrough came. He did not see himself continuing long in a situation

61 *Mother Goose*, 'Tom, Tom, the piper's son', 1964

where the author carried the success of the book, and the illustrator as accompanist received a depressed flat-rate fee. Above all he was a painter, with a drive to express books in paint.

The way in which this ambition was to be realised resulted from his approach to Oxford University Press and his first meeting in 1957 with their children's book editor, Mabel George, who was to play such a major part in the development of his career as a creator of picture books in the years ahead. Since the virtual rebirth of the picture book in recent times can be regarded as an Oxford 'first', it is best to quote from Mabel George's own account:

> It is true that I was then concentrating on the novel for older readers, but at the same time it had been my intention ever since taking over the Oxford list for children in 1956 or thereabouts to widen its range to include more non-fiction, and also particularly to develop the younger end with picture books at least equal in quality to the novels that we were producing. It was clear to me that in order to attract artists and illustrators of genuine talent and calibre the quality of colour reproduction and printing in the picture book would have to be improved. It was while searching for a printer who would co-operate with me in taking this branch of publishing seriously at a cost within the range of the project, that I brought into my list through their black and white illustrations the three artists who are the subject of your essays [Ambrus, Keeping, Wildsmith], and others besides. The day on which I established contact with an Austrian fine art printer [Brüder Rosenbaum] was a breakthrough for us.
>
> He was sympathetic to my plan for the picture book: he was used to reproducing and printing to the high standards demanded by museums and artists in the fine art world, and he had private knowledge of ink making that transformed printing results even when limited to the four-colour process which was all our picture book programme could afford. So, as an experiment, I commissioned the *Arabian Nights* colour plates by Brian Wildsmith, and sent the paintings to the printer for reproduction. The result was highly satisfactory, pleasing the artist, most of the public and me. The fact that the work received criticism as well as praise was in itself encouraging. At last the artwork in a children's book was being noticed and judged for its own sake. I felt that the moment had come to launch our first picture-book, and Brian Wildsmith with his daring sense of colour, was to be the artist.[5]

Wildsmith's *ABC*, awarded the Kate Greenaway Medal for 1962, was the outcome. It continues to reprint and to record sales and library issues, as do nearly all his picture books, with a mathematical regularity congruent with the fact that he and his editor had put the child first, and – since children don't change much from one three-year readership generation to the next – had succeeded in redefining the fundamentals.[6]

Wildsmith is a natural educator in the spirit of Comenius:

> From the beginning, what I wanted to do above all for children's literature
> was to try and span the whole spectrum from an ABC to counting – through
> puzzles, myths, nursery rhymes and stories – and stories which dealt with
> those fundamental aspects of human nature which are crucial to a child's
> development; like honesty, like trickery, like good neighbourliness, like
> kindness and understanding: and to take these aspects and treat them in the
> form of the picture book as a vehicle which could express them.

The latter part of this aim is shared with La Fontaine, several of whose fables were
to provide a basis for the individual picture books which consolidated the success of
ABC. Animals relate to landscape in his work as memorably and inevitably as in the
paintings of Le Douanier Rousseau, although ends and means naturally differ.
Wildsmith has always found animal-anthropomorphism, sentimentality, and the
condescension of *childish* as opposed to *childlike*[7] drawing alien to his art; and yet the
habitat he creates for young minds has room for wonder and *joie de vivre,* laughter and
occasional pathos.

When it came, inevitably, to relating the human figure to a setting, new solutions
had to be sought to avoid a mundane, modern-dress naturalism. In place of pattern and
texture arising from the natural world, there is a heightened use of pattern springing
from folk art and costume (*Mother Goose,* an early instance), or pattern expressive of
mankind's intellectual preoccupations (more recently in *Professor Noah's Spaceship*).

Naturally enough he has personal favourites among his many picture books, and
these include *Mother Goose* and *The Owl and the Woodpecker.* Some books have fantastic
stories behind them which he relishes in retrospect, none more so than Maeterlinck's
The Blue Bird. This began with a telegram from the film director, George Cukor,
inviting him to design sets and costumes for what was to be the first US-Soviet co-
production, to be shot in Leningrad with fabulous casting and music. Despite political
intrigue, bad faith and sheer bungling, and the bizarre alternation of lavishness and
parsimony, he appears to have enjoyed the experience of a lifetime and to have got on
well with everyone.

> I conceived a set for the Palace of Night – this extraordinary palace on a cloud
> – and $500,000 was spent in making this one set. After all the scenes on it had
> been shot, it was destroyed to make room for another; but one of the main
> actors fell seriously ill and had to be replaced. All the scenes in which the
> previous actor appeared had to be done again. There was no way they could
> spend another $500,000, so they spent $50, and it looks like it! Disaster
> followed disaster in this way.

At the end of the day it proved a flawed and mediocre film, but the picture book
survives.

62 [above] *Birds,* 1967

A school of butterfly fish

A stare of owls

63 [below] *Fishes,* 1968

64　*The Bonny Pit Laddie,* 1960

Wildsmith is captivated by films, theatre and ballet; and would like to do more work in all of these fields. When this was written he was about to start work on some rehearsal tapes accompanying a commission for a San Francisco ballet group, and looking for a composer for his own most recent story, *Carousel,* which has scope for expansion into an opera for children.

Having been launched and sustained in his publishing career through an initial flash of editorial insight, he has continued to need and appreciate good editors; and considers himself fortunate in the creative working relationships established with Mabel George's successors; for a time with Antony Kamm,[8] and for a number of years now with the present managing editor, Ron Heapy – 'a wonderful person to work with'. When they were in New York together in 1981, and Wildsmith was enthusing about the sheer exhilaration and excitement of the place, Heapy suggested how weird it would be if one of Wildsmith's animals were to be let loose there: the resultant book was *Bear's Adventure.* The idea of using the split-page book technique also came from Heapy in 1983, and so far three books have been produced which exploit this intricate format (see plates 71/2).[9]

His loyalty to Oxford has been outstanding; they quickly became and have remained his exclusive publishers in England. He met Helen Hoke Watts at the time of the publication of his first picture book, and struck up a lasting friendship with her and her husband, so that Franklin Watts were to remain his American publishers for the next fifteen years.[10] His motto might well be 'Loyalties and Royalties', since attempts by other publishers to secure his services invariably founder on both counts. The steady pace of a book a year on a royalty basis has enabled him to put his best thought, time and skill into the work, without the manic pressure to over-produce in order to maintain an income on a flat-rate basis: 'If you're good enough you earn your royalties, if you're not you don't deserve them.'

The vividly orchestrated colour and excitingly devised texture and surface decoration typical of early Wildsmith has recently been labelled as a phenomenon of the 1960s by several writers on children's books. This is true insofar as the first books burst like bombsells during that decade, unprecedented and influential. Successive shock waves of innovation have since reached us from all points of the globe, and there is nothing surprising in that. To have led the field for a while, and to have seemingly been overtaken, has the disadvantage that the inference may be drawn in some quarters that one has dropped out of the race; but it is staying power in the longer term which counts.

What Wyndham Lewis called 'the demon of progress in the arts' has to be resisted: superficial, derivative or fashion-chasing work is likely to prove short-lived, whereas that grounded on true structural and artistic principles ought to survive. This is demonstrated by the incidental fact that the sales graph for most of Brian Wildsmith's 46 picture books in print would resemble a steady horizontal line, with those from the 1960s still making steady box office after a dozen or more evenly spaced impressions. It is fascinating that the artist's evaluation of his own intentions and achievements in the picture book field could equally be represented by a straight line.

Many illustrators view their career in terms of successes and failures, breakthroughs and blocks, stylistic developments and changes in direction. But not so Wildsmith. The 'grand design' became apparent to him at the outset, it is still incomplete, but neither does it progress according to a static formula:

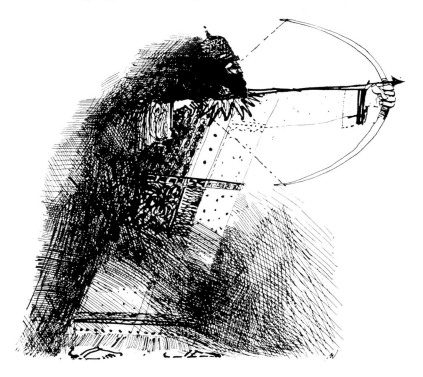

65 *Oxford Illustrated Old Testament,* Joshua 10, 1968

66 'Hill Village', oil on plaster relief with acrylic surround, 1984

67 *Professor Noah's Spaceship*, 1980

My view of illustration is that it is an operation of interpretation, it is like a pianist performing Bach or Chopin or Schubert or Mendelssohn – to each new idea he gives a different interpretation – although it's the same man playing. So a book of big imagery like the *ABC* or *123* is expressed differently from telling a story like *Goat's Trail* for example . . .

Brian Wildsmith was first in the field in establishing new conventions for the picture book. Together with artists such as Ambrus, Burningham and Keeping among others, he set boundaries in certain areas some twenty-five years ago which have not been greatly extended in the past twenty years or so. These boundaries concern points of communication with children *en masse* through this particular medium, and do not relate to questions of artistic originality or excellence as such: 'You make a statement, and it has to be what it says it is, incapable of being taken for anything else. Within this constraint, the style of expression, however naturalistic or abstract, is up to you.'

Beyond this and similar constraints, lies only painting: a land where virtually anything is permissible; where the capacity for self-delusion is an ever-present danger; and where the most clear-sighted attempt to communicate is liable to be met with incomprehension by adults, most of whom will have lost the visual sense they enjoyed as children.

Although Brian Wildsmith's books for children will continue to appear, he now spends seven or eight months each year painting, frequently for up to ten hours a day. He has fought hard for the material freedom to do this, and to opt for what for him are the ideal environmental conditions in which to live and work.

A constant quest for the sun led him with his wife, Aurélie,[11] through the various regions of France (as holidays could be afforded from 1955 onwards) to a flat in Spain for a time, and finally to a private hill village between Cannes and Grasse where the family has lived since 1971:

> Castellaras is a small paradise, built in a domain of 160 acres, comprising approximately 90 houses. It was designed by the architect Jacques Couelle, a formidable ecologist who managed to build the entire village in an olive grove, keeping all its trees, except for one. Almost all the houses are joined together forming a spiral terrace but conceived so ingeniously that each house enjoys total privacy. Couelle called it the village of collective solitude and indeed it lives up to its name.
>
> From my work room, I can look out onto hills covered in pine, olive, and mimosa trees that roll towards the sea; stare at the magnificent sunsets that light up the sky at nightfall; relish the spectacular view that on a clear day allows one to see Corsica, sixty miles away. I have found my ideal home: a place where I can work (busy, social atmospheres stifling me, I need solitude in order to create) and enjoy the basic pleasures that feed my body and regenerate my mind such as national and regional French cuisine and wines (the area is cluttered with restaurants that vary in size, price and choice of dish, from small one-menu bistros to some of the finest tables the country has to offer), and the sun: so much so that I still get depressed when I spot a cloud approaching.[12]

This sensationally beautiful landscape is nowhere directly present in Brian Wildsmith's paintings, and yet it is possible they could not have found their precise identities outside it. Their calm is that of Castellaras.

> I've thirty years of ideas tumbling round in my head. I should really have started painting twenty years ago, but I had a wife and family, and I fell in love with children's books anyway.

How to describe these paintings, of which the artist has repeatedly said that they are totally unconnected with his approach to illustration? Both surely emanate from the same creative personality, the same hands; both are expressive of an individual's concern with the same concepts and values, but at the apparent polarities of communication with the child as set against adult artistic perception. I believe that it is possible to make certain parallel comparisons – for example where the theme of the frontispiece to *Professor Noah's Spaceship* is taken up for treatment (in an admittedly untypical painting), as a plaster relief on canvas, white on white, with the Einstein-like blackboard formulae pencilled in. But it is necessary to respect the artist's words when he says that the mental processes involved are for him so different that it is as if they were from two different lives. The primary field to which his artistic endeavours relate is best explained in his own words:

> I came to various conclusions about modern painting, and, exciting as it is, I feel that recently it has made some very grave wrong turnings, and a lot of it has become doom-laden and 'socially-conscious'. I don't believe that in 200 years time anyone will give a hoot about social conditions in the twentieth century, because that's not the key issue. This will prove to be the enormous explosion in scientific and engineering knowledge, and a new environmental awareness. Very little artistry – and art is always an expression of the times in which it is made – reflects this. Science and engineering have always interested me, and to find new imagery for the expression of what I consider to be relevant has taken me all these years.

He sits on the terrace with the occasional glass of wine, sometimes for two or three days at a time, contemplating the landscape, but at the same time striving to bring a given image into the sharpest intellectual and technical focus before work in the studio can begin:

> A problem I believe many painters encounter is that of changing vision. When you start the image is quite clear, but when you come back to it the idea can shift, sometimes resulting in a complex end-product, but more often just a mess. What you should do is to finish the first image, and then do a second painting of the second image, and so on. (I don't have this problem with my books, it's all perfectly thought out before I start.) But with the paintings, I couldn't get beyond this point for a time, until I had worked out a procedure which wouldn't permit the image to be changed.
>
> Once I have settled on the image, its colours, shapes, and disposition on the canvas; I put on my overalls and with a pot of strong glue in one hand and piles of sand and plaster next to me, I make a moulded shape, a relief structure on the canvas, before applying colour. In that way I cannot change the image without destroying the canvas!

It is not surprising that an artist of Wildsmith's sensitivity and experience should have produced a corpus of paintings that has a claim to the highest international critical evaluation. For the present and future he is painting with assurance, work that is positive in both physical and atmospheric presence, and free from *Angst*, facility, pretentiousness, obscurantism or artificial dogmatic additives. Difficult to describe,[13] it is there to be enjoyed, but not to be underestimated in terms of its intellectual content. These paintings inhabit a world totally different from that of his children's book illustrations; but a benign, humanitarian and deeply thoughtful one nevertheless. The distance which separates them could only be experienced if it were possible to see a show of his paintings and a selection of the picture books in the same day;[14] without prior knowledge of their common authorship, it would be impossible to make the association. But what a day one would have had; since it would have been spent in the company of an artist who has given, and continues to have so much to give, in both spheres.

68 *Circus*, 1970

69 'Dancers by Moonlight', acrylic on linen and paper relief, 1987

NOTES

1. I am confident that there are enough progressive buyers for this situation to change, and for his Mediterranean colour vision to be allowed to brighten up some of our major regional collections.
2. For a recent interview which captures his personality well, see also Stephanie Nettell, 'Crossing barriers: an interview with Brian Wildsmith', *Children's Book Supplement to British Book News,* (March 1987), 2–5. An earlier interview, with Edna Edwards, can be heard on *Focus on Brian Wildsmith* (1 cassette,

duration 50 minutes, no.34199: North Hollywood, Cal., Centre for Cassette Studies, 1975).
3. 'I was not surprised to find that the artist who created such beautiful books, illustrations and posters was very musical, and a good pianist. His work springs from living with children, as well as from a deep conviction that it is a worthwhile aim to make beauty and harmony accessible to the modern child, and to me this makes his books especially valuable; it requires some

courage to live in accordance with such principles these days.' Bettina Hürlimann, *Seven Houses: My Life with Books* (Bodley Head, 1976), 133–4.

4. Except where stated, extracts are from conversations held at Castellaras, Alpes-Maritimes, on 9 and 10 January, and in London on 8 September 1988.

5. Extract from a letter from Mabel George to the author, dated Hythe, 18 January 1988.

6. ' . . . I hope I am making it clear that our interest in the picture book was not centred upon the artist so much as upon the child . . . With the picture book the artist was speaking direct out of his own talent to the child. Not every artist had a natural sympathy with this age group, many could not simplify either composition or colour to a point where they were attractive and comprehensible to the youngest children . . . In fact, over the course of time we found that the picture books struck a similar chord with children in many different countries.' Further extracts from the letter cited in note 5.

7. He defines *childlike* in this context as 'to paint and draw with the freedom and emotional naturalness of a child'.

8. Editor-in-Chief, Brockhampton Press, 1960–72; and Managing Editor (Children's Books), Oxford University Press, 1976–79. Wildsmith, in common with many other illustrators and designers, found him 'a wonderfully sympathetic and encouraging editor'.

9. Alternate leaves throughout the book are only half the page width. Therefore on opening each spread the story reads with the half-page to the right; it is then flapped over to create a new scene and the story continues. This demands hairline precision from the artist and binder alike.

10. i.e., until control of the company changed hands. He recalls that this first book, the *ABC,* was ruled by the US Customs to be a toy and not a book as it had no text; and as such $1 a copy had to be levied. Franklin Watts took legal action, and lost. It was only when a few lines of text explaining its purpose were added that it became a book once more.

11. 'We met when I was 17 years of age and she a mere 14. I had heard that Wentworth Woodhouse, a magnificent place built over a submerged lake, contained some ancient Grecian-style statues worthy of study and had received permission to go there and draw them. As I was busy sketching, a mischievous, freckled face with the most startling green eyes peered over my shoulder, curious to see what I had drawn. She introduced herself as the chef's youngest daughter and nodded with approval having flicked through my pad. I fell in love there and then. I returned to the big house many a time, at first with the excuse that had initially led me there, later at Aurélie's request. We married in 1955.' From an unpaginated proof of *Brian Wildsmith (1930-): A Short Autobiography* (Gale Research Co., Detroit, 1988). Autobiographical writings by modern illustrators are few indeed, but as such this piece is essential reading for a life and times engagingly told.

12. *Ibid.*

13. The following notes set out to describe some of the general features of the works prepared for the 1988 New York show. In the very limited space available, they attempt to give an impression of some of the broad categories into which the paintings may be grouped by similarities in technical procedure.

The action takes place on unframed canvases, 6 ft x 5 ft:
(a) Arrays of hundreds of little triangular woodblocks are angled into the plaster ground, and the whole painted white, so that the tangible physical effect is determined by the active and passive modulations of light.
(b) A complex 3-D fusilage of several thousand painted wooden 'spillikins' and tiny offcuts thrusts out diagonally from the picture plane to a height of several inches.
(c) The field is relatively flat, and an equilateral triangle – perhaps infilled with a bonded aggregate of miniature beads and coloured fragments – is held in repose through the interaction of free horizontal bands, of which one by virtue of general colouration and texture might be taken to evoke the wooded summit of a hill – at most a symbolic reminiscence of landscape, among other possible interpretations.

(d) The heaviest impasto, of colours juxtaposed straight from giant tubes, trails across a delimited area of the ground – possibly painted in summer when the risk of forest fires is at its greatest; and so possibly an ecological content is embedded at some level?

The gallery for the 1988 New York show was so designed as to permit only ten or eleven paintings of this scale to be hung in the central area, side galleries inviting a smaller 3 ft x 2 ft format. The ideas for the larger canvases resisted transposition, and so fresh technical developments ensued:

(e) Circular-section dowels are used instead of triangular wooden wedges, and graduated colour replaces the action of light in controlling the effect in paintings with connotations of scientific enquiry.

(f) The boundaries of this smaller format are delimited by a gilt-plaster 'mock frame', and there is sometimes a faint reminiscence of illustration, of a story being told in the distance.

(g) With the use of gold as an overall ground, the imagery becomes more wide-ranging, less formal, and often altogether magical.

14. By coincidence, shortly after this was written, arrangements were confirmed for the paintings and the illustrations to be exhibited in separate rooms at the 871 Gallery, San Francisco, from 13 November 1988 to 5 January 1989.

BIBLIOGRAPHY

Note: The American editions of all Brian Wildsmith's books except those where Franklin Watts still hold the rights (and new picture-books published by Pantheon/Knopf), are now published in the USA by OUP New York. The imprints given here are taken from the first published edition.

1956
THE BRAVE PAGE   R. C. Scriven   Arnold

1957 –

1958
THE BARON'S SWORD   Kenneth Rudge
    Hamish Hamilton
THE BOY ON TWO WHEELS   Kenneth Rudge
    Hamish Hamilton
INDIAN DELIGHT   R. J. MacGregor
    Dolphin Books
PRINCE OF THE JUNGLE   René Guillot
    OUP/Criterion

1959
THE CALL OF THE BUSH   Mary Patchett
    Lutterworth
THE DAFFODIL BIRD   Ruth Tomalin
    Faber/Barnes

HIGH SANG THE SWORD   Eileen O'Faoláin
    OUP
THE MCNEILLS AT RATHCAPPLE   Meta
    Mayne Reid   Faber
THE STORY OF JESUS   Eleanor Graham
    Penguin

1960
THE BONNY PIT LADDIE   Frederick Grice
    OUP/Watts [as OUT OF THE MINES: THE
    STORY OF A PIT BOY]
THE SAGA OF ASGARD   Roger Lancelyn
    Green   Penguin [reissued as
    MYTHS OF THE NORSEMEN]
TANGARA: 'LET US SET OFF AGAIN'
    Nan Chauncy   OUP/Watts [as
    THE SECRET FRIEND]

1961
THE KNIGHTS OF KING MIDAS   Paul Berna
    Bodley Head/Pantheon
LANDSLIDE!   Véronique Day   Bodley Head
TALES FROM THE ARABIAN NIGHTS
    E. O. Lorimer [ed.]   OUP/Walck
THE TOWN ACROSS THE WATER   Madeleine
    Polland   Constable

70 *Carousel*, 1988

1962

ABC Brian Wildsmith OUP/Watts [as
  BRIAN WILDSMITH'S ABC]
A BRIAN WILDSMITH PORTFOLIO eight
  colour plates in envelope Watts USA [a
  further two portfolios of prints suitable for
  framing appeared c.1962−6, and a number of
  colour posters including one for each month
  of the year appeared in the USA, UK and
  Japan about 1970]
THE WARRIOR'S TREASURE R. J. MacGregor
  Dolphin Books

1963

FOLLOW MY BLACK PLUME Geoffrey
  Trease Macmillan/Vanguard
HAPPILY EVER AFTER: POEMS FOR
  CHILDREN Ian Serraillier OUP
THE LION AND THE RAT Jean de La
  Fontaine OUP/Watts

THE OXFORD BOOK OF POETRY FOR
  CHILDREN Edward Blishen [ed.]
  OUP/Watts
THE WATCHERS Charlotte Morrow
  Hutchinson

1964

HAVELOCK THE DANE Kevin Crossley-
  Holland Macmillan/Dutton
MOTHER GOOSE: A COLLECTION OF
  NURSERY RHYMES Brian Wildsmith
  OUP/Watts [as BRIAN WILDSMITH'S
  MOTHER GOOSE]
THE NORTH WIND AND THE SUN Jean de
  La Fontaine OUP/Watts
A THOUSAND FOR SICILY Geoffrey
  Trease Macmillan

TWITCH, TWITCH
went her nose outside the
butcher's shop. In she went,
and out she ran with another
bone, bigger and better than
the first one.

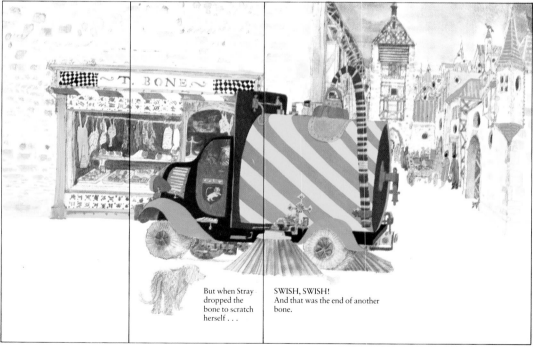

But when Stray
dropped the
bone to scratch
herself . . .

SWISH, SWISH!
And that was the end of another
bone.

71/72 *Give a Dog a Bone,* 1985

1965
1 2 3 Brian Wildsmith   OUP/Watts
[as BRIAN WILDSMITH'S 1 2 3]
THE RICH MAN AND THE SHOEMAKER
Jean de La Fontaine   OUP/Watts

1966
A CHILD'S GARDEN OF VERSES
R. L. Stevenson   OUP/Watts
THE HARE AND THE TORTOISE   Jean de La
Fontaine   OUP/Watts

1967
BIRDS   Brian Wildsmith   OUP/Watts [as
BRIAN WILDSMITH'S BIRDS]
WILD ANIMALS   Brian Wildsmith
OUP/Watts [as BRIAN WILDSMITH'S
WILD ANIMALS]

1968
THE BIBLE STORY   Philip Turner   OUP/Watts
[as BRIAN WILDSMITH'S ILLUSTRATED
BIBLE STORIES]
FISHES   Brian Wildsmith   OUP/Watts [as
BRIAN WILDSMITH'S FISHES]
THE OXFORD ILLUSTRATED OLD
TESTAMENT: WITH DRAWINGS BY
CONTEMPORARY ARTISTS [Brian
Wildsmith contributed 16 line drawings for
Joshua 9–24, and 11 for 1 Esdras] 5 vols,
OUP 1968–9

1969
AHMED, PRINCE OF ASHIRA   Alan Wildsmith
Deutsch
THE MILLER, THE BOY AND THE DONKEY
Jean de La Fontaine   OUP/Watts

1970
THE CIRCUS   Brian Wildsmith   OUP/Watts
[as BRIAN WILDSMITH'S CIRCUS]
PUZZLES   Brian Wildsmith   OUP/Watts [as
BRIAN WILDSMITH'S PUZZLES]

1971
THE OWL AND THE WOODPECKER   Brian
Wildsmith   OUP/Watts

1972
THE LITTLE WOOD DUCK   Brian Wildsmith
OUP/Watts
THE TWELVE DAYS OF CHRISTMAS   Brian
Wildsmith   OUP/Watts [as
BRIAN WILDSMITH'S TWELVE DAYS OF
CHRISTMAS]

1973
THE LAZY BEAR   Brian Wildsmith
OUP/Watts

1974
PYTHON'S PARTY   Brian Wildsmith
OUP/Watts
SQUIRRELS   Brian Wildsmith   OUP/Watts

1975 –

1976
MAURICE MAETERLINCK'S 'BLUE BIRD'
Brian Wildsmith   OUP/Watts

1977
THE TRUE CROSS   Brian Wildsmith   OUP/
OUP New York

1978
WHAT THE MOON SAW   Brian Wildsmith
OUP/OUP New York

1979
HUNTER AND HIS DOG   Brian Wildsmith
OUP/OUPNew York

1980
ANIMAL GAMES   Brian Wildsmith   OUP/
OUP New York
ANIMAL HOMES   Brian Wildsmith   OUP/
OUP New York
ANIMAL SHAPES   Brian Wildsmith   OUP/
OUP New York
ANIMAL TRICKS   Brian Wildsmith   OUP/
OUP New York
PROFESSOR NOAH'S SPACESHIP   Brian
Wildsmith   OUP/OUP New York
SEASONS   Brian Wildsmith   OUP/OUP
New York

1981

BEAR'S ADVENTURE   Brian Wildsmith   OUP/
Pantheon

1982

CAT ON THE MAT   Brian Wildsmith   OUP/
OUP New York
PELICAN   Brian Wildsmith   OUP/Pantheon
THE TRUNK   Brian Wildsmith   OUP/OUP
New York

1983

ALL FALL DOWN   Brian Wildsmith   OUP/
OUP New York
THE APPLE BIRD   Brian Wildsmith   OUP/
OUP New York
THE ISLAND   Brian Wildsmith   OUP/OUP
New York
THE NEST   Brian Wildsmith   OUP/OUP
New York

1984

DAISY   Brian Wildsmith   OUP/Pantheon
TOOT, TOOT   Brian Wildsmith   OUP/OUP
New York
WHOSE SHOES?   Brian Wildsmith   OUP/OUP
New York

1985

GIVE A DOG A BONE   Brian Wildsmith
OUP/Pantheon

1986

GOAT'S TRAIL   Brian Wildsmith   OUP/Knopf
MY DREAM   Brian Wildsmith   OUP/OUP
New York
WHAT A TALE   Brian Wildsmith   OUP/OUP
New York

1987

GIDDY UP   Brian Wildsmith   OUP/OUP
New York
IF I WERE YOU   Brian Wildsmith   OUP/OUP
New York

1988

CAROUSEL   Brian Wildsmith   OUP/OUP
New York

in preparation

A CHRISTMAS STORY   Brian Wildsmith
OUP/OUP New York

73 *The Oxford Illustrated Old Testament,* Joshua 10, 1968

7 · SHIRLEY HUGHES

THE MAINSPRING of Shirley Hughes's success and continuing popularity with children is that it always looks as if she is drawing directly from life – even when, as frequently happens, she is not. Her inimitable sketchbook manner has offered a perfect foil to a wide range of narrative fiction from the early 1950s down to the last few years, when her wealth of experience (she long ago lost count of the number of titles by other authors which she had illustrated) led her to concentrate on her own picture books to the virtual exclusion of interpretative illustration. Through sketching, observing and working with children, she has become both an innovator and a respected theorist in the picture book field without losing any of the spontaneity and dash characteristic of her earlier work. [1]

Shirley Hughes was born in 1927 in Hoylake, near Liverpool, and spent her childhood in nearby West Kirby. There was a very good supply of books in her home, including those illustrated by her abiding favourites: Arthur Rackham and William Heath Robinson. Comics and annuals are also keenly recalled – notably the trail of American comics left by the GIs – although it was to take a great time for the elements of strip cartoon to re-surface creatively in her own work with the appearance of *Up and Up*, to be followed after an interval by *Chips and Jessie*.

As a child, she was always drawing, or writing stories or scripting and acting plays with her two sisters, with an almost Brontë family intensity: 'There were acres of leisure time, in wartime and with few modern diversions, so we kept this going longer than would be probable today'. [2]

It was natural enough for any adventurous spirit to seek out alternatives to bourgeois Liverpool (where her father owned a department store) and to the seaside suburbia of West Kirby, and so, on completing her studies at West Kirby High School and a course in drawing and costume design at Liverpool College of Art, she spent a short time painting sets and pinning costumes at Birmingham Repertory Theatre. This sufficed to dispel any personal ambitions to tread the boards or build a career in the theatre; but proved invaluable when she became an illustrator, since (as Ardizzone had propounded) the interpretative illustrator's purpose is to work from a text, to group the figures imaginatively, to light them, and to make gesture expressive in order to reinforce the narrative – though as Shirley Hughes has moved increasingly into the picture book area, she has come to find film analogies more apt than theatrical ones: 'You think the images and the story all at the same time; the planning and conception are much closer to shooting a film.'

With the theatre out of the reckoning she decided to retrace her steps towards basic drawing, not knowing at the time that for her this would lead on to illustration. Career considerations at that stage took second place to broadening horizons. Oxford seemed the ideal place to be, intellectually, artistically and not least socially, and she was to remain at the Ruskin School of Drawing there for over three years.

No illustrator has ever expressed regret at being made to work from the life model, and this was a strength of the Ruskin under Albert Rutherston's direction. Jack Townend lectured in printmaking, but through his own illustrative experience was in a position to recognise latent talent and encouraged Shirley Hughes to work on dummies for picture books and to undertake a series of two-colour lithographic illustrations to *Lady Windermere's Fan* among other assignments. Despite this valuable practical experience, she has never felt that she belonged to the lithographic tradition: 'I was interested, and always have been, in drawing for hot-metal reproduction. I have gone on drawing as though we were still working for letterpress; that is to say you create your tones by an arrangement of lines.'

Childhood favourites attained classic status as her vocation became more apparent: the work of C. E. and H. M. Brock, and of H. R. Millar (in his illustrations for E. Nesbit), held pride of place. Ardizzone was also regarded as a true descendant of that school. And then came the excitement of seeing her first Anthony Gross drawing – and others by Leonard Rosoman and Ronald Searle – all culled and conserved from the pages of *Radio Times*.

Barnett Freedman was one of the visiting lecturers: 'I was terrified of him and hardly dared to show him my work. He gave a deliberate impression of having little time for the Ruskin School of Drawing. He thought that we were a whole lot of dilettante girls who were there for the May Balls, and he was dead right!' But that was an early impression of Freedman, who really helped when it came to the assessment of her final folder:

> He pounced on it and offered to give some addresses in London. He was
> enormously kind, and actually hand-wrote valuable letters of introduction to a
> number of editors, amongst whom was Patsy Cohen at Collins who offered me
> my first commission – for a pony book – inevitably. This didn't work out, but
> a capacity to draw children was diagnosed, and a manuscript substituted
> which offered endless scope to show children romping about on Scottish
> hillsides.

In the late 1950s and early 1960s children's book illustrators and their art editors led a curious existence. Undoubtedly there were a few exceptions, but both shared the paradoxical experience, whether salaried or freelance, of being in a relative poverty trap at a time when great changes were in the air. The staple market requirement in Britain then centred on skills in drawing horses, children, historical and religious subject matter, and so forth. Beyond that, creative boundaries were in flux and the modern picture book was about to be born. Shirley Hughes met an ever-present need by being able to draw children convincingly, and her work was soon in great demand. Her children were naturalistic from the outset; and their realism, even scruffiness, provided a valuable corrective to current stereotypes for classroom and bookshelf. It could be argued that the directness of her style prefigured later shifts in emphasis, notably towards books designed for a pre-primary school readership, and the lessening of the largely artificial distinction between reading matter for the school and for the home.

On more than one occasion she has volunteered the opinion that her career was held in check by the sheer volume of drawings of and for young children produced at the very time when her own role as mother was most central,[3] and that much early work in consequence was a response to the existing market rather than a considered approach as to how it might be changed for the better. She did have portfolio samples exhibiting a more original and sophisticated approach to colour and jacket design, but could make little headway against prevailing market trends. The ultimate measure of her contribution as an educationist must be that she should have emerged after years of such prodigious and sustained output with undiminished enthusiasm, and then have gone on to break new ground within the strip cartoon idiom and in her books for the very youngest children.

A clue to this vitality may be found in her unpublished *Umbrian Journals,* which reflect frequent family stays in the region. This rich storehouse of drawings runs the gamut from classical landscape studies to astute and impromptu observation:

75 *Stories for 7 year olds,* 1964

76 *Make Hay While the Sun Shines,* 'A cat may look at a king', 1977

I spotted this elderly chap texturing stone with chisel and mallet. He's hitting away at the stone and has these two enormous plastic bottles of wine with him up at the top of the scaffolding. He was working quite hard, but there was a fair bit of swigging as well, and every time a good-looking girl went past he would swing right round and straight back to work. One simply has to pick up whatever's in the handbag at the time – felt-pen or carbon pencil – and draw like lightning . . . One just goes on drawing like this all the time . . .

All narrative illustration has to follow from an interest in human behaviour and conduct, unless it is to be confined to anthropomorphic animals and so forth. If you're not going to sit about endlessly watching people in bars, cafés, parks and restaurants; if you've no interest in getting these people down, how they sit when they are talking, how they edge nearer to each other when they are getting matey and how they withdraw from each other when they are getting not so matey; as well as children hopping, skipping and jumping – which is a whole study in itself – if you're not interested in these things, then how can you become an illustrator?[4]

Although she shares in the widespread wonderment at how the sketchbook quickie or rough can capture qualities that may fail to survive in the two-day working-out of the finished drawing, Shirley Hughes is insistent that this is the only way for her. She believes that children of any age merit a firmly realised picture of the world, to be interpreted at a variety of imaginative levels – though this is not, of course, to imply that other artists might not have similar gifts for conveying their response to different authors through apparent spontaneity, and it must surely be that such brilliant illustrators as Quentin Blake and Richard Kennedy work equally hard to deploy those techniques which enable them to communicate precisely within their respective terms of reference.

For Shirley Hughes, tonality and colour need to be reconciled with line, in order to fix the final nature of the pictorial impression which she is creating for the child. Tonality is essentially a question of adding space and substance to an image, but it is also the means by which colour effect is introduced and consolidated.

Like many superlative line artists, she admits that evolving a personal colour idiom was a painstaking process: 'I didn't use colour with any kind of confidence for a whole number of years.' There is frequently an underdrawing in pencil or sepia, which may then be overworked in chalks and watercolour, with the final detail of the drawing restated and pointed up by brush. This technical procedure is frequently varied, always individualistic, and inevitably it has become much more accomplished over the years. The singularity is that sepia acts as a kind of interface between drawing and colour rendering, sometimes an intended autumnal atmosphere pervades; more generally it provides depth of field and a reassuring ambience to everyday scenes at home or school, in playground or park.

The criticism is often voiced that there is a sameness about Shirley Hughes's drawings of children, but it is not difficult to show that in a number of ways nothing could be further from the truth. The adult eye can tend to scan artwork for children's books at a rather superficial level of concentration – sufficient to allow certain exciting qualities in drawing, colour handling or viewpoint to register, but rarely relating drawing and text in the way that a child does. I confess myself to a long-standing habit of enjoying drawings with scant reference to the text until it becomes necessary to pay proper attention for critical purposes. Shirley Hughes's work suffers badly when subjected to this malpractice, but it is possible to make amends as soon as one sees that she really understands the way the age-levels for whom she is writing and drawing respond to the page, and that in this work she is constantly making technical innovations of a very sophisticated kind.

In her early stories, as well of course as in her interpretative illustration of other writers' texts, she is precisely aware of how the young eye and imagination can be drawn right into a scene and travel about within it, and that this can be opened up into quite an immense experience. But only under the right conditions; for if an illustrator's communicative intention is flawed, or his technique inadequate or inappropriate, then the child will unerringly sense this and little or no communication can take place. The illustrating grown-up has to keep on form, stay fresh and be stimulating, if he or she is not to become the kind of person who churns out the same book all the time.

Shirley Hughes has illustrated some 200 titles since 1950, of which roughly one in six are to her own texts. It is on these that future critical interest in her work will centre, and it has already been noted that in recent years she has increasingly devoted the greater part of her working time to her own picture books. Comparatively few of the large number of titles illustrated for other writers are likely to stay in print indefinitely – many were routine productions squeezed in between family and publisher's deadlines – yet there are nevertheless lasting successes and hidden gems to be found. Space allows only a small handful to be mentioned here: Noel Streatfeild's *Bell Family* books; *The Faber Book of Nursery Stories; Dorothy Edwards's *My Naughty Little Sister* books; *Peter Pan and Wendy;* and Sara and Stephen Corrin's story-anthologies for various age groups.

'I have a loyalty to the characters I have created – Lucy and Tom have gone on and on, and I've by no means exhausted my interest in Alfie.' The first book Shirley Hughes illustrated to her own storyline was *Lucy and Tom's Day* (1960), but Alfie did not make his début until 1981 with *Alfie Gets in First;* a book remarkable for using facing pages to show what is going on inside and outside a house – inside is Alfie who has inadvertently locked his mother and sister outside – a technique which will be familiar to children of all ages from the use of the split-screen in vintage Hollywood comedies. But in contrast to those characters who retain a life of their own for her, Shirley Hughes will not be induced to try to repeat a signal success such as *Dogger* (which won the Kate Greenaway Medal in 1977) when there are new ideas waiting to be tackled.

In the gradual process of becoming an assured writer, the whole act came under her direct design control, and there was no longer any danger of disparity of aim or achievement between the words and pictures. She has always been fascinated by adventurous page layout, and saw the scope for a new picture book genre at roughly the same time as several of her contemporaries. It was to involve the rehabilitation of cartoon strip conventions, and their integration with certain features of the traditional picture book format in order to provide a fresh range of storytelling techniques. One of the best-known exponents of this must be Raymond Briggs, who has found a distinctive emotional key for each of his major books in the new idiom, though other artists were content merely to revive the surreptitious pleasures of their childhood in non-

77 *Trouble with Dragons, 1978*

78 'A Farmhouse in Tuscany', from an unpublished *Umbrian Journal,* 1981

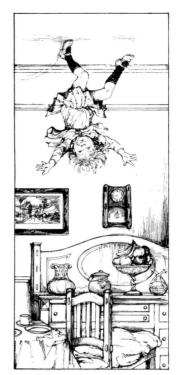

79 *Up and Up,* 1979

confiscatable form. Shirley Hughes had long been fascinated by what the picture book might be able to do for those who can't yet read, and one idea – for a wordless book that would encourage them to deduce and elaborate a story to tell from the pictures alone – resulted in *Up and Up* (1979). This first full-scale venture into strip cartoon[5] almost created its own rules, and in mastering them her style and subject matter were channelled away from naturalism and into fantasy and humour. The book was a resounding success.

With *Chips and Jessie* in 1985, Shirley Hughes found an entirely fresh synthesis of words and pictures and strip cartoon techniques:

> This book took a colossal time to work out, but represented a great breakthrough for me. The text was first written down conventionally and was originally much longer. I then extracted all the dialogue which would normally appear in quotes, and put this into speech balloons. For example, Chips' conversation with his mother – where he is saying that he wants to bring the school hamster home, and she says: 'You can't, the cat will eat it!' – actually becomes a row across the spread. It is incredible what starts to happen to design and speech structure when you use cartoon strip; but on the other hand I am using chunks of proper text as well, interspersed with the sequences of pure clowning which appear as strip cartoon. And then there are

pages where there are no words at all. There are also animals who make comments, a questionable procedure to attempt in written narrative, but simplicity itself when they can be placed in thought balloons!

The real *tour de force* comes later in the same story, where Chips and Jessie are in the kitchen in the gathering gloom and she's telling him a spooky story about a film which she has seen on television. So – for the person who can't read at all – we have a picture narrative of her telling him this story. The text of the story which she's telling appears above. Chips's interjections as he gets more and more gripped by the story are given in speech balloons. A written text at the foot amplifies the situation even further. As a sub-plot, the missing hamster turns up at the crucial moment. All the wiles of the skilled picture book page designer are in action here, with the object of signposting a rich and multi-layered narrative to read and return to. Parallel paths are laid out which avoid the alternative dangers of ambiguity or tautology.

80 *Another Helping of Chips,* 1986

81 *Lucy and Tom's ABC*, 'M is for moon', 1984

Few illustrators can have done more than Shirley Hughes to enable children to come to grips with the complex processes involved in learning to read, and to comprehend pictorial and typographic notations and modes of presentation. [6] Rather than work from the theoretical remoteness of the artistic ego, she has sought to provide an abundance of the most nourishing fare for non-readers and beginners onwards, based on a lifetime's caring observation of growing children in their real environments.

NOTES

1. Other commentaries on her work include 'Shirley Hughes', Authorgraph No. 26, *Books for Keeps,* (May 1984), 14–15; and Kate Moody, 'A is for artists', *Contact* (Spring 1984), 24–5. See also Elaine Moss, *Part of the Pattern* (Bodley Head, 1986), 107–12.
2. Extracts unless otherwise attributed are from a conversation recorded at Holland Park, London, on 30 April 1987.
3. She married John Vulliamy, architect and etcher, in 1952. They have three grown-up children.
4. A conversational transcript, not drawn from the Journals. Some of Shirley Hughes's recent views on illustration are expressed in 'Word and Image', the 1983 Woodfield Lecture at Loughborough University, reprinted in Margaret Fearn [ed.], *Only the Best is Good Enough: The Woodfield Lectures 1978–85* (Rossendale, 1985).
5. A successful experiment in transferring direct speech to balloons – but within the setting of an otherwise conventionally illustrated story for six-year-olds and upwards – had been made two years earlier, with *It's Too Frightening For Me!*
6. In 1984 she received the Eleanor Farjeon Award for distinguished services to children and books.

BIBLIOGRAPHY

1950
THE HILL WAR   Olivia Fitz Roy   Collins

1951
FOURWINDS ISLAND   Vega Stewart   Collins
GREAT-UNCLE TOBY   John Hale   Faber
MONSTER CREEK   Kathleen Mackenzie   Collins

1952
LUCY CUCKOO   Mary Coventry   Faber
MAGIC IN THE AIR   Dorothy Lovell   Faber
THE MARVELLOUS MERLAD   Judith Masefield   Collins
WORLD'S END WAS HOME   Nan Chauncy   OUP

1953
FOLLOW THE FOOTPRINTS   William Mayne   OUP
LARKING AT CHRISTMAS   Judith Masefield   Collins
SECRET IN THE SAND   Mary Edmonston   Hammond
A WEEK OF STORIES   Doris Rust   Faber

1954
ALL THROUGH THE NIGHT   Rachel Field   Collins
APRIL FOOLS   Judith Masefield   Collins
THE BELL FAMILY   Noel Streatfeild   Collins/Random House [as FAMILY SHOES]
THE JOURNEY OF JOHNNY REW   Anne Barrett   Collins/Bobbs-Merrill
THE SECRET MOTOR CAR   Norman Dale   John Lane
A STORY A DAY   Doris Rust   Faber/Transatlantic
THE WORLD UPSIDE DOWN   William Mayne   OUP

82 *Peter Pan and Wendy,* 1976

1955

ALL SORTS OF DAYS   Doris Rust   Faber/
Transatlantic

1956

THE ANIMALS AT NUMBER ELEVEN
Doris Rust   Faber/Transatlantic
THE CURIOUS ADVENTURES OF TABBY
E. H. Lang   Faber
GUNS IN THE WILD   Ian Serraillier
Heinemann
HOLIDAY   Judith Masefield   Collins
LOST LORRENDEN   Mabel Esther Allan
Blackie/Ryerson
THE MAN OF THE HOUSE   Allan Campbell
McLean   Collins
MR PUNCH'S CAP   Kathleen Fidler
Lutterworth
WILLIAM AND THE LORRY   Diana Ross
Faber

1957

ADVENTURE ON RAINBOW ISLAND
Dorothy Clewes   Collins
THE ANIMALS AT ROSE COTTAGE
Doris Rust   Faber/Transatlantic
KATY AT HOME   Ian Serraillier   Heinemann

1958

THE BOY AND THE DONKEY   Diana Pullein-
Thompson   Collins
THE JADE GREEN CADILLAC
Dorothy Clewes   Collins
MIXED-MUDDLY ISLAND   Doris Rust   Faber/
Transatlantic

1959

KATY AT SCHOOL   Ian Serraillier
Heinemann

1960

FELL FARM CAMPERS   Marjorie Lloyd
Penguin
FLOWERING SPRING   Elfrida Vipont   OUP
LITTLE WOMEN   Louisa M. Alcott
Blackie/W. R. Scott
THE LOST TOWER TREASURE   Dorothy
Clewes   Collins
LUCY AND TOM'S DAY   Shirley Hughes
Gollancz

NEW TOWN   Noel Streatfeild   Collins
ROLLING ON   Mary Cockett
Methuen/Ryerson
TROUBLE AT KITTIWAKE ROCK
Anne Westwood   Blackie

1961

THE BRONZE CHRYSANTHEMUM   Sheena
Porter   OUP/Van Nostrand
FAIRY TALES   Hans Andersen [ed. Jean
Roberton]   Blackie
MARY ANN GOES TO HOSPITAL
Mary Cockett   Methuen/Ryerson
THE PAINTED GARDEN   Noel Streatfeild
Penguin
PLAIN JANE   Barbara Softly   Macmillan/St
Martin's
THE RAILWAY CHILDREN   E. Nesbit
Heinemann
THE SINGING STRINGS   Dorothy Clewes
Collins

1962

THE COTTAGE BY THE LOCK   Mary Cockett
Methuen
LITTLE WARRIOR   Ailsa Wills   Hutchinson/
Nelson, Foster & Scott
NUMBER ONE VICTORIA TERRACE
Kathleen O'Farrell   Blackie/Ryerson
PLACE MILL   Barbara Softly   Macmillan
A TREASURE IN TIME OF TROUBLE
Valerie Hughes   Faber

1963

MEET MARY KATE   Helen Morgan
Faber/Transatlantic
THE MERRY-GO-ROUND   Diana Ross
Lutterworth
THE SHINTY BOYS   Margaret MacPherson
Collins
THE SIGN OF THE UNICORN   Mabel Esther
Allan   Dent/Criterion
SUMMER SILVER   Eric Houghton   Oliver &
Boyd/McGraw-Hill [as MYSTERIES OF THE
OLD FIELD]
TALES OF TIGG'S FARM   Helen Morgan
Faber/Transatlantic
WILLY IS MY BROTHER   Peggy Parish
Gollancz/W. R. Scott

1964

BEAUTY AND THE BEAST [unattributed text] Nelson

THE CAT AND MRS CARY Doris Gates Methuen

FIONA ON THE FOURTEENTH FLOOR Mabel Esther Allan Dent

JACKO, AND OTHER STORIES Jean Sutcliffe Bodley Head

OPERATION SMUGGLE Dorothy Clewes Collins

ROLLER SKATES Ruth Sawyer Bodley Head

A STONE IN A POOL Barbara Softly Macmillan/St Martin's

STORIES FOR 7 YEAR OLDS Sara and Stephen Corrin [eds.] Faber/Watts

STORIES FROM GRIMM [unattributed text] Blackie

TIM RABBIT'S DOZEN Alison Uttley Faber

1965

A DREAM OF DRAGONS Helen Morgan Faber

KATE AND THE FAMILY TREE Margaret Storey Bodley Head

LUCINDA'S YEAR OF JUBILO Ruth Sawyer Bodley Head

TALES THE MUSES TOLD Roger Lancelyn Green Bodley Head

THE TWELVE DANCING PRINCESSES Mark Twain Nelson

UP WITH THE JONESES Penelope Balogh Gollancz/Doubleday

1966

THE FABER BOOK OF NURSERY STORIES Barbara Ireson [ed.] Faber

LITTLE BEAR'S PONY Donald Bisset Benn

SATCHKIN PATCHKIN Helen Morgan Faber/M. Smith

THE SMALLEST BRIDESMAID Margaret Storey Faber

THE SMALLEST DOLL Margaret Storey Faber

SOMETHING TO DO 'Septima' Penguin

WAYLAND'S KEEP Angela Bull Collins

WISH ON PIG Barbara Ward Collins

THE WITCH'S DAUGHTER Nina Bawden Gollancz

1967

A DAY ON BIG O Helen Cresswell Benn

HOME AND AWAY Ann Thwaite Brockhampton/Follett [as THE HOLIDAY MAP]

MARY KATE AND THE JUMBLE BEAR Helen Morgan Faber

PORTERHOUSE MAJOR Margaret Baker Methuen/Prentice-Hall

STORIES FOR 6 YEAR OLDS Sara and Stephen Corrin [eds.] Faber/Watts

THE WOODEN SWALLOW Dana Faralla Hamish Hamilton

1968

A CROWN FOR THE QUEEN Ursula Moray Williams Hamish Hamilton/Meredith

FLUTES AND CYMBALS Leonard Clark [ed.] Bodley Head/Crowell

GRANDPA'S BALLOON John Randle Benn

MRS PINNY AND THE BLOWING DAY Helen Morgan Faber

THE NEW TENANTS Margaret MacPherson Collins/Harcourt Brace

STORM OVER SKYE Allan McLean Collins

THE TOFFEE JOIN William Mayne Hamish Hamilton

THE TOYMAKER'S DAUGHTER Ursula Moray Williams Hamish Hamilton/Meredith

A VICARAGE FAMILY Noel Streatfeild Penguin

VOICES IN THE FOG Elizabeth Walton Abelard-Schuman

WHEN MY NAUGHTY LITTLE SISTER WAS GOOD Dorothy Edwards Methuen

THE WOOD STREET SECRET Mabel Esther Allan Methuen/Abelard-Schuman

1969

ALL ABOUT MY NAUGHTY LITTLE SISTER [anthology] Dorothy Edwards Methuen

THE BICYCLE WHEEL Ruth Ainsworth Hamish Hamilton

GOLDIE Irma Chilton Hamish Hamilton

MOSHIE CAT Helen Griffiths Hutchinson/Holiday House

MRS PINNY AND THE SUDDEN SNOW Helen Morgan Faber

1970
CINDERELLA   Charles Perrault
   [ed. R. Samber]   Bodley Head/Walck
EIGHT DAYS TO CHRISTMAS
   Geraldine Kaye   Macmillan
MARY KATE AND THE SCHOOL BUS
   Helen Morgan   Faber
MORE MY NAUGHTY LITTLE SISTER
   STORIES   Dorothy Edwards   Methuen
RAINBOW PAVEMENT   Helen Cresswell   Benn
THE RUTH AINSWORTH BOOK
   Ruth Ainsworth   Heinemann/Watts
THE THREE TOYMAKERS   Ursula Moray
   Williams   Hamish Hamilton/Nelson
THE TROUBLE WITH JACK   Shirley Hughes
   Bodley Head
THE WOOD STREET GROUP   Mabel Esther
   Allan   Methuen

1971
BURNISH ME BRIGHT   Julia Cunningham
   Heinemann
DANCING DAY   Robina Beckles Wilson   Benn
FEDERICO   Helen Griffiths   Hutchinson
THE LITTLE BROOMSTICK   Mary Stewart
   Brockhampton/Morrow
THE LITTLE CAT THAT COULD NOT SLEEP
   Frances M. Fox   Faber
THE LOST ANGEL   Elizabeth Goudge
   Hodder & Stoughton
MALKIN'S MOUNTAIN   Ursula Moray
   Williams   Hamish Hamilton/Nelson
MOTHER FARTHING'S LUCK   Helen Morgan
   Faber
ROBBIE'S MOB   Jo Rice   World's Work
THE SMELL OF PRIVET   Barbara Sleigh
   Hutchinson
SQUIB   Nina Bawden   Gollancz
STORIES FOR 8 YEAR OLDS   Sara and
   Stephen Corrin [eds.]   Faber/Prentice-Hall
THE WOOD STREET RIVALS   Mabel Esther
   Allan   Methuen

1972
THE FIRST MARGARET MAHY STORY BOOK
   Margaret Mahy   Dent
GINGER   Geraldine Kaye   Macmillan
HOSPITAL DAY   Leila Berg   Macmillan
THE HOUSE IN THE SQUARE   Joan Robinson
   Collins

MOTHER'S HELP   Susan Dickinson [ed.]
   Collins
MRS PINNY AND THE SALTY SEA DAY
   Helen Morgan   Faber
THE THIRTEEN DAYS OF CHRISTMAS
   Jenny Overton   Faber/Nelson
WHERE DO WE GO FROM HERE?
   Josephine Kamm   Brockhampton

1973
THE HOLLYWELL FAMILY   Margaret Kornitzer
   Bodley Head
LUCY AND TOM GO TO SCHOOL
   Shirley Hughes   Gollancz
SALLY'S SECRET   Shirley Hughes
   Bodley Head
THE SECOND MARGARET MAHY STORY
   BOOK   Margaret Mahy   Dent
STORIES FOR 5 YEAR OLDS   Sara and
   Stephen Corrin [eds.]   Faber
THE WOOD STREET HELPERS   Mabel Esther
   Allan   Methuen

1974
CLOTHES   Shirley Hughes   Bodley Head
THE GAUNTLET FAIR   Alison Farthing
   Chatto & Windus
MISS HENDY'S HOUSE   Joan Drake
   Brockhampton
MY NAUGHTY LITTLE SISTER AND BAD
   HARRY   Dorothy Edwards   Methuen
THE PHANTOM FISHERBOY   Ruth Ainsworth
   Deutsch
STORIES FOR UNDER FIVES   Sara and
   Stephen Corrin [eds.]   Faber

1975
AWAY FROM WOOD STREET   Mabel Esther
   Allan   Methuen
HAZY MOUNTAIN   Donald Bisset   Puffin
HELPERS   Shirley Hughes   Bodley Head/
   Prentice-Hall [as GEORGE, THE
   BABYSITTER]
THE THIRD MARGARET MAHY STORY BOOK
   Margaret Mahy   Dent

83 *The Secret Garden,* 1988

1976

LUCY AND TOM AT THE SEASIDE
Shirley Hughes   Gollancz

PETER PAN AND WENDY   J. M. Barrie [ed.
May Byron]   Hodder & Stoughton

THE SNAKE CROOK   Ruth Tomalin   Faber

TATTERCOATS AND OTHER FOLK TALES
Winifred Finlay   Kaye & Ward/Harvey
House

1977

DOGGER   Shirley Hughes   Bodley Head/
Prentice-Hall [as DAVID AND DOG]

DONKEY DAYS   Helen Cresswell   Benn

IT'S TOO FRIGHTENING FOR ME!
Shirley Hughes   Hodder &
Stoughton/Prentice-Hall [as
HAUNTED HOUSE]

MAKE HAY WHILE THE SUN SHINES
Alison Abel [ed.]   Faber

THE PHANTOM ROUNDABOUT
Ruth Ainsworth   Deutsch/Follett [as
THE PHANTOM CAROUSEL]

A THRONE FOR SESAME   Helen Young
Deutsch

1978

BOGWOPPIT   Ursula Moray Williams
Hamish Hamilton

FROM SPRING TO SPRING   Alison Uttley
[ed. K. Lines]   Faber

MORE STORIES FOR 7 YEAR OLDS
Sara and Stephen Corrin [eds.]   Faber

MOVING MOLLY   Shirley Hughes
Bodley Head/Prentice-Hall

POTTLE PIG   Nancy Northcote   Kaye & Ward

THE SNAILMAN   Brenda Sivers
Little, Brown [USA]/Abelard-Schuman [as
TIMOTHY AND THE SNAILMAN]

TROUBLE WITH DRAGONS   Oliver G. Selfridge
Addison-Wesley [USA]

1979
STORIES FOR 9 YEAR OLDS   Sara and
   Stephen Corrin [eds.]   Faber
UP AND UP   Shirley Hughes   Bodley Head/
   Prentice-Hall

1980
BABIES NEED BOOKS   Dorothy Butler
   Bodley Head
HERE COMES CHARLIE MOON   Shirley
   Hughes   Bodley Head/Lothrop
OVER THE MOON: A BOOK OF SAYINGS
   Shirley Hughes   Faber
THE PIRATE SHIP AND OTHER STORIES
   Ruth Ainsworth   Heinemann
WITCHDUST   Mary Welfare   John Murray

1981
ALFIE GETS IN FIRST   Shirley Hughes
   Bodley Head/Lothrop
LUCY AND TOM'S CHRISTMAS   Shirley
   Hughes   Gollancz

1982
ALFIE'S FEET   Shirley Hughes   Bodley
   Head/Lothrop
A CAT'S TALE   Rikki Cate   Harcourt Brace
   [USA]/Methuen
CHARLIE MOON AND THE BIG BONANZA
   BUST-UP   Shirley Hughes   Bodley Head

1983
ALFIE GIVES A HAND   Shirley Hughes
   Bodley Head/Lothrop
SALLY'S SECRET   Shirley Hughes
   Bodley Head

1984
COUSIN PONS   Honoré de Balzac   Folio
AN EVENING AT ALFIE'S   Shirley Hughes
   Bodley Head/Lothrop
LUCY AND TOM'S ABC   Shirley Hughes
   Gollancz

1985
BATHWATER'S HOT   Shirley Hughes   Walker
CHIPS AND JESSIE   Shirley Hughes
   Bodley Head/Lothrop
MAHY MAGIC   Margaret Mahy   Dent
NOISY   Shirley Hughes   Walker/Lothrop
WHEN WE WENT TO THE PARK
   Shirley Hughes   Walker/Lothrop

1986
ALL SHAPES AND SIZES
   Shirley Hughes   Walker/Lothrop
ANOTHER HELPING OF CHIPS
   Shirley Hughes   Bodley Head
COLOURS   Shirley Hughes   Walker/Lothrop
TWO SHOES, NEW SHOES   Shirley Hughes
   Walker/Lothrop

1987
THE HORRIBLE STORY, AND OTHERS
   Margaret Mahy   Dent
LUCY AND TOM'S 123   Shirley Hughes
   Gollancz

1988
OUT AND ABOUT   Shirley Hughes   Walker
THE SECRET GARDEN   Frances Hodgson
   Burnett   Gollancz

8 · JOHN LAWRENCE

JOHN LAWRENCE was born in Hastings in 1933. His visual outlook was attuned to sea and landscape from the start and he was ever happiest with pen and paper in hand, and still recalls the first and enduring magic of making marks on paper. But he admits that during his boarding school years from the age of seven to seventeen[1] this talent drifted towards caricature, more influenced by comic papers than direct observation, and that he left with a career either as journalist or cartoonist in mind.

In fact he enrolled at Hastings Art School, which he remembers as a quiet backwater in which he was able to produce masses of drawings and watercolours, since the then Principal, Vincent Lines (1909–1968), was an able watercolourist and introduced him to the work of A. S. Hartrick (1864–1950) and Thomas Hennell (1903–1945), which he found very exciting. After two years at Hastings, two years of compulsory National Service intervened, most of which was spent with the army in West Africa – though he concedes that his duties left plenty of time to produce the many drawings which are still kept hidden away somewhere.

He then studied book illustration at the Central School of Arts and Crafts from 1955–57, and was initiated into engraving in the weekly evening classes given by Gertrude Hermes (1901–1983). He remembers her kindness at the time when he left the Central in inviting him to make use of her press when needed, and the help he derived through keeping in touch with her. By all accounts she was an inspiring teacher and at the epicentre of progressive wood engraving for several decades; certainly she exhibits an astonishing technical range and her finest prints – the later ones in particular – carry a great dramatic and intellectual charge.

Other influences dating from his college days include Palmer and Bewick, and the contemporary work of Keith Vaughan; ' . . . Vaughan certainly helped me, I learned a lot about the tonal possibilities of black and white from him, and he was also a great advocate of John Minton's work.'

Although he confesses that 'sometimes I feel that I've been influenced by too many people . . . ', the truth is that everything is transmuted in his work. It is difficult to think of any other illustrator who shares in quite the same way such a detailed knowledge of the highways and by-ways of British history, of popular and primitive crafts as well as the high culture of art and design, and can let it be reflected in their output at so many levels.

The nature of this dialogue is touched on in the following remarks:

> If you are working in different periods, re-doing a classic for instance, then I think that it should have something of your own, but it should also have something of its own time surely? . . . Cross my heart, I've never been conscious of pastiche, but if at the other extreme you transplant the thing totally – as Steadman does with *Treasure Island* – then, (and of course Steadman has done some remarkable things) in my view you are simply making a book for your own sake. [2]

Another characteristic of John Lawrence's art is its very Englishness, which is not at all the same thing as insularity, since he also loves to draw in the French and Italian landscape. Notwithstanding his affection for the countryside, he was ready to make a home in London provided he could be close to water and to riverside walks. This and much more he found in Chiswick where his young family grew up, and where he continued to live until 1986 when he moved with his wife to a smaller property in Stamford Hill, this time close to the River Lea.

84 'Chiswick House', wood engraving, 1965

Chiswick is a recurrent theme, from an early uncommissioned engraving of Chiswick House, the exterior of which also appears as the setting for Cinderella's ball in the *Blue Fairy Book,* to recent titles such as *Mabel's Story,* where he'll exclaim: 'There's a lot of Chiswick in that!' The house and studio are described by Lesley Macdonald:

His home, the top floor of an Edwardian villa in Chiswick, close to the Thames, is altogether in character with this unassuming but nevertheless very gifted artist. The huge garden surrounding the house has an unkempt, almost mysterious atmosphere. Two massive chestnut trees, coming up to three hundred years old, dominate the scene. A maple rises to almost twice the height of the house. At the bottom of the garden, the studio stands beneath one of these sweet chestnuts; a flat, glass-faced shed around which squirrels scuttle collecting chestnuts for their winter stores.

A fine-looking handpress stands in this workshop, a Hopkinson Albion, the printmaker's indispensable piece of equipment. The walls are covered with shelves and compartments, filled with woodblocks, printing-rollers, cans of ink and tools. A work-table for the draughtsman/engraver takes up the remaining space; truly an ideal setting for concentrated work, in which Lawrence strives to perfect his craft. [3]

The subject-matter of John Lawrence's mature bibliography attests to this affinity with English literature and the British countryside over the ages, with *Watership Down, The Shepherd's Calendar, Our Exploits at West Poley* and *The Magic Apple Tree* as just one stream of a tradition, another being the chapbook-inspired picture books, his own and those done in collaboration with Brian Alderson or Allan Ahlberg.

At the Central and in the years immediately following, John Lawrence attained a mastery of wood engraving and emerged as a leading exponent at an exciting time for the technical and aesthetic expansion of that medium. It calls for a fellow-engraver to evaluate this achievement:

Lawrence's engravings are very busy and his wit and humour are essentially English. In some respects he is the Rowlandson of the twentieth-century engraving school. His engravings are tightly packed, highly charged and with the exact number of burin [or engraving tool] thrusts to make a salient form. It is in the burin thrusts where, when he so chooses, he splits the form through from the black to white poles.

In draughtsmanship Lawrence is confident enough to enable him to sublimate it to the point of implying a form where it is most telling . . . He cuts shapes with his tools and each one is clearly defined but only the form is implied, yet the reviewer receives just enough visual information to cause him or her to complete the form mentally. [4]

Worthwhile commissions were slow to come his way, however, although some delightful bookplates and letterhead devices were produced for friends, and occasional ephemeral work for advertisers and others. He had married while still at the Central and had to undertake whatever illustrative work was on offer, and to begin to consolidate a position within book publishing. This turned out to be a slow route, paved with all sorts of inappropriate projects which he now prefers to forget.

Part-time lecturing has played a basic role from the outset to the present, but early on he decided that it should never occupy more than one or two days a week at most.[5] In this way he can give his best as a teacher and still cope with the most demanding of briefs.

The books illustrated by John Lawrence fall into two groups: those in which the original image was engraved either in wood or vinyl,[6] or linocut; and those where autographic media – pen, line and watercolour, or gouache – have been used singly or in a diversity of combinations. The artist once wrote: 'I don't like to be tied down stylistically, and ideally I believe that each new book, if one is inspired by it, should produce a new response so that all the time one is adding to one's repertory and keeping a fresh eye.'[7] For practical purposes it is simpler to look at some of the major engraved books as they enable changes in approach and intent to be discerned, and then to return and trace the development of his direct draughtsmanship and colour work.

> Almost every year some of the work has been engraved, and the rest drawn, and so whether it was actually a book or a more ephemeral sort of job, I've engraved all the time. Publishers who saw my engraved work early on took to it but didn't actually seem prepared to use it, whereas companies such as Shell BP and others were happy to place commissions in the early 'sixties. And so it was nine whole years after leaving art school – and I'd been engraving all the time – before the first commission came along. This was through Peter Guy at the Folio Society, who has ever since remained a helpful and sustaining influence, and it was for *Colonel Jack* . . .

This significant commission resulted in twelve two-colour wood engravings, and a case-binding design which was carried out as a woodcut and printed in black on yellow linen. It is a triumph, a young man's book, exuberant, animated, capable of taking risks, but exhibiting a fully developed style and technique.[8] The binding design is handled in broader terms than the engravings to the text, and has the effect of a theatre drop-curtain, an evocation of low-life as if viewed through a street-ballad woodcut of the period. The frequently reproduced frontispiece still goes off like a firework.

Engraving is essentially a black and white process; the need to introduce colour rarely arises, and is notoriously difficult to bring off when attempted. The illustrations to *Colonel Jack* form a series of variations on the basic theme of relegating simple, flat areas from within each of the completed black engravings to appear in a second colour (sepia) in reproduction. Interest is held since the scale, placement, and inventive use of these sepia passages is deliberately varied in an off-beat manner. Sepia is frequently made to stand in for wood; there may be hidden punning intent as the engraver's wood is textured by a multiple graver, and then inked in a colour to match wood and printed

85 *Colonel Jack*, 1967

to represent floorboards, wainscoting, and timber shop-fronts. When land is sighted (facing p.282), what the watchman sees through his spy-glass appears in sepia. In the Rowlandsonian quay-side scene (facing p.313), an impossibly congested block is focused through the expedient of consigning sky and water – along with a few small craft – into the second colour.

It seems fair to conclude that at this early juncture there already existed a wealth of good humour on, or just below, the surface; and a boundless confidence that most illustrative problems may be tackled by means of wood engraving with every bit as much vitality and versatility as through autographic line. *Tristram Shandy,* the next engraved book for Folio Society, although crammed with delightful period detail, is, however, a rather conservative performance to have followed *Colonel Jack:* possibly the result of the brief requiring the 41 engravings to be treated as rectangles within the text area, as well as imposing a rush date for completion.

With *Rabbit and Pork, Rhyming Talk,* a mid-career masterpiece falls under consideration. At long last a children's book publisher – Hamish Hamilton – had given the go-ahead for a wood-engraved picture book: 'I was able to get into that book so many of the 'isms and things that had interested me over a long period of time, and I worked on this, an important book for me, for about a year – ''in the background''.' The resultant plates are self-sufficient in black and white, but the artist devised an effective means of adding colour wash, to which the printer (Lund Humphries) did full justice. The caption text is integrated within each engraving with skill and verve, and there is a clever interplay between the effects of two- and three-dimensionality. Stare for a few moments at the flat cut-out elephants, and they seem to revolve in a lumbering dance! This is a children's book of lasting quality, which won't long let itself remain out of print as is sadly the case at the time of writing.

For a long time it has been known that the *Nuremberg Chronicle* (1493), makes use of only 645 woodcuts to supply 1,809 illustrations (the same crowned heads, effigies and city-views stand in time after time for quite different personalities and places). But then that printer did not have the services of John Lawrence, who derived 56 illustrations from just two engraved blocks for *The Road to Canterbury* (1979). These two massive composite subjects stand as frontispiece and conclusion in the design of the book, highly effective compositions in their own right after the manner of medieval tapestries or bronze cathedral doors. The original woodblocks measured 12 inches x 9 inches, and had to be reduced by over one third to fit the page. Each subject had been pre-designed to yield the artwork for twenty-five or more self-contained illustrations or decorative motifs, to the scale of the original engraving for the most part.

This solution made possible a fine piece of book production within the framework of trade publishing (and in addition a built-in rainy afternoon game was there for those children who caught on to what was afoot). Although *Canterbury* is arguably its finest application, John Lawrence apparently first hit upon the idea of 'taking things out of the print and using them elsewhere' whilst working on the linocuts for *Rogues,*

86 *The Road to Canterbury,* 1979

Vagabonds and Sturdy Beggars for the Imprint Society. Further variations on this composite formula were evolved for *English Folk Tales, John Clare's Autobiographical Writings,* and other projects.

It is sad to think that the cost of the wood alone must have accounted for the lion's share of the fees which incunabula printers and post-war British publishers alike were in a position to offer, and so the economy in materials and labour which John Lawrence devised here was not inconsequential. Further, the artist's ability to keep a project in progress under constant revision within the confines of a minimum number of working surfaces must also have contributed to the unity of the finished product.

In describing some of his engraving procedures,[9] Lawrence explains the difficulty of 'tying the work together' on such large-scale blocks; since for the first day or two — although guided by an accurate plan — he has to set out literally from the top left-hand corner of the block on what is likely to prove three weeks of intensive work during which everything gradually takes shape. Lemonwood is his favourite choice for really large blocks where jointed boxwood would be impractical; but he has worked with most woods, as supplied to all leading engravers by the old-established business run for many years by his unrelated namesake, T. N. Lawrence & Son, blockmaker extraordinary and importer of specialist papers, of Bleeding Heart Yard, Greville Street.

Naturally nothing suits an engraving better than to be printed directly from the wood by the letterpress process. This practice has been restricted to fine editions for most of the present century even whilst the letterpress process itself remained commercially viable, and now it plays an even more significant role in making out a case for keeping that process alive within art schools and a handful of specialist firms (not to mention the work of amateur enthusiasts of the kind capable of reactivating the age of steam locomotion). *The Shepherd's Calendar* and *Good Babies, Bad Babies* were designed to be printed by the Whittington Press in this way, and the Camberwell Press has printed *A Selection of Wood Engravings* by John Lawrence from the original blocks.

These are splendid books, to be sought out for themselves, and only incidentally because they reveal how much detail and nuance is lost through routine commercial printing. It is accepted that fine art reproduction and colour printing in general is at best an approximation to the original, but less widely known how severely all forms of black and white drawing and engraving suffer for much of the time. A case in point is *A Pair of Sinners,* where an immense commitment was marred through changes in the publisher's staff and the printer's lack of co-operation at the proofing stage. John Lawrence hoped, reasonably enough, that the success of *Rabbit and Pork* could be repeated, but in fresh terms by virtue of Allan Ahlberg's involvement. The engraver invested in individual woodblocks for each subject and five months' labour in the engraving. Despite going to extreme lengths to get things right and with every expectation of success, 'it somehow slipped through the floorboards': to an experienced eye the printed result when compared with the artwork supplied can only be described as a travesty – the choice of paper and the printer's failure to get the balance right affected the freshness of colour; yet there is such a wealth of imagination and craftsmanship present that it is to be hoped that one day this interesting book will be re-designed and originated afresh from the surviving material.

In each of the books illustrated by engraving techniques, there is a fresh approach that will reward careful examination. Behind the visual effect each picture plane makes at first glance, hidden levels of humour and observation await. At times the experience resembles entering one of the celebrated Central European rococo churches; the visitor comprehends a basic pattern underlying the riot of virtuosity and is made to smile, or feel serene.

John Lawrence's artistic and professional commitment usually goes far beyond the briefing contract in order to contribute something of value to each individual book. He can move effortlessly between narrative and decorative illustration – or into pattern-making for endpapers or binding design – in response to the possibilities presented by text and commission. In this briefest of surveys of the engraved work, it is only possible to mention the existence of a large corpus of so-called ephemeral work; labels and bookplates, publisher's devices (such as the one for Julia MacRae that appears in the margin), wrapping papers and so much else, as part and parcel of the expressive range of his genial talent.

Five of John Lawrence's picture books were published by Hamish Hamilton between 1968 and 1976, and he illustrated a range of other titles for them over a slightly longer period. 'In those days it was very nice at Hamilton. Julia MacRae and Michael Brown had just started off there; in a way they created a stable of artists, they did a lot of entertaining, one was in and out all the time, meeting authors and colleagues. As they built up their children's list, although you were only a freelance artist, you were made to feel part of it.'

The first two picture books, *The Giant of Grabbist* and *Pope Leo's Elephant*, were illustrated in gouache. As he himself admits, 'some early colour books were crucified'; and this was in the heyday of the full colour, international co-edition boom to which most contemporary picture book illustrators and publishers were avidly committed. At the time he may have felt some lack of the colour confidence he has more recently acquired, and he does appear once again to have been poorly served by his printers. But the real explanation is surely to be sought in what he was trying to say – to which colour was largely incidental in any case – and in this light these books should not be regarded as failures.

There was a bland common denominator current in the content of picture books during the first wave of the co-edition market, and those who fared best had a painterly approach to colour allied to a graphic designer's approach to line. Those illustrators whose art was rooted in specific draughtsmanship and a love of local detail, or deployed quirky or untranslatable humour and allusion, were to be on a bad wicket for a time, and it is probable that John Lawrence realised this. In consequence he continued along his own picture book path, independently of the colourists, and of his fellow wood-engravers.[10] This path was to lead several years later to the classic *Rabbit and Pork,* and more recently to *George, His Elephant and Castle* and to exciting projects currently in progress.

When John Lawrence exchanges the graver for the pen or watercolour brush, the faster working tempo leads to another type of exhilaration in his work, to all kinds of experiment in a range of media so that at times it is not always easy to identify the artist from the style he has generated. 'With every job I do, I'm never entirely sure how it's going to turn out . . . one doesn't know how its going to jump.'

There is what might be thought of as his 'Bank Holiday' style, a sketchbook line that is in complete contrast to the discipline of engraving and as though in relaxation from it, opening up fresh ways of illustrating and designing books that would be beyond the scope of engraving techniques. This line is racy and sparkling, and can be seen as a strong keyline in combination with gouache for the early picture books, including *The Mule of Avignon.* Since *Watership Down,* it is more common to find it used with watercolour wash in landscape settings, where the natural world is limpidly but convincingly conjured onto the page with an absolute economy of means.

The Diary of a Nobody provides an interesting example of the subtle modulation of this line in a historical direction. It is probable that he sensed that this *faux-naif* text wouldn't bear the weight of full page illustrative treatment but called instead for some form of inspired doodling. The only formal illustration appears on the binding case, serving to set the scene; for the rest there are spot drawings, single character observations, brilliantly evoking the period with apparent spontaneity. Peter Guy reveals the background research and effort that went into achieving this effect: ' . . . [he] absorbed the earlier editions and then retired behind piles of ancient copies of the *Illustrated London News* making occasional forays to Islington to capture the surroundings of nineteenth-century genteel suburbia. He produced the illustrations as if [Weedon] Grossmith had been reborn with a gift for draughtsmanship.'[11]

87 *The Diary of a Nobody,* spot drawings, 1969

88 *Rabbit and Pork,* 1975

To refer to John Lawrence's mastery as a designer of books here, as in so many instances, is not intended to belittle the contribution of his book typographers and other collaborators, but to highlight an attribute rare among even the best illustrators, namely the ability to think creatively about all sorts of approaches to the various parts of different kinds of books and to come up with fresh answers most of the time. Pre-eminently it is knowing in advance just how a book will look and feel as a result of the angle adopted by the illustrator, so that the publisher's design and production team follow the lead given rather than having to contrive a framework for drawings which, however fine in themselves, have not been visualised for a given format and its consequent typography. This design versatility becomes apparent in comparing a group of such different books as *The Diary of a Nobody, The Blue Fairy Book, Watership Down* and *Entertaining with Cranks.*

For *The Blue Fairy Book* historical research again provided a point of departure, and this is best understood as a process of familiarisation with the climate and conventions of the period rather than accepting direct influence from stylistic elements contained within the work of individual artists. Then the process, which has already been noted,

of relating this historical ethos to his own current thinking could take place, and an unusually elaborate style was evolved for these illustrations, some of which incorporate decorative borders. There were to be 100 subjects, and this effectively ruled out wood engraving, but there appears to have been a conscious decision to build white line and other features of engraving technique into the penmanship so that a kind of hybrid resulted, enabling the artist to veer towards a drawn or an engraved look from passage to passage as he felt inclined.

An illustrated *Watership Down* was bound to be widely noticed at the time it appeared, and proved instrumental in securing a further series of attractive commissions for the artist, and in enhancing his reputation in the field of landscape and natural history, although he says disarmingly; 'I've never been terribly knowledgeable about the countryside in any scientific sense, but I've always had a great feeling for it.' He tackled these drawings in pen and watercolour, making use of many small marginal studies as well, to produce a gently observed book, not lacking in power where appropriate, and sharing the author's avoidance of sentimentality in depicting wildlife.

Entertaining with Cranks marks a further development in his non-engraved illustrative idiom, and one which he considers it will be possible to build on in the future. Line and wash, incorporating a little white-line technique through the use of a resist, come into a fresh balance that has potential for extension into full-colour work as well. To over-simplify, line and tone and colour are now fully integrated, and there is no tension or dichotomy between line drawing and the introduction of colour.

The emergence of this more recent and assured style merits more attention than can be given here, since it is reasonable to predict that it could overtake wood engraving as his primary resource in the years ahead, with particularly fascinating implications for the children's picture book world. Despite the high artistic quality of John Lawrence's earlier picture books, elements of his style and the use of wood engraving at times may have acted to inhibit their wider recognition and popular success. Working from within these media bounds it was natural for him to have been drawn towards the early history of children's picture books, although in his own books he always succeeds in creating a modern counterpart to the chapbook tradition rather than merely alluding to it.

George, His Elephant and Castle, which when it was published in 1983 was the first book both written and illustrated by John Lawrence to have appeared for several years, is an altogether delightful performance. The textures of the brown line fuse with the texture and handling of the full-colour wash in a light and atmospheric way, characterisation is splendid, and the fantastic and everyday elements in this picture-book world work convincingly from start to finish. Drawings for Jenny Koralek's *Mabel's Story,* Richard Adams's *A Nature Diary* and Philippa Pearce's *Emily's Own Elephant* among other titles, refine and develop characteristics of this later style.

What is so special about these more recent pen and wash illustrations is that they

89 *The Blue Fairy Book,* 1975

90 *Watership Down,* 'Hazel', 1976

pick up the threads of a different tradition, and one which has largely remained dormant since the death of Edward Ardizzone. This is not to imply any conscious indebtedness or stylistic resemblance to the work of the older master; but to suggest that there exists a latent magic, whose sole concern is with true and direct visual converse with children at certain levels, and which determines its own line of succession, its own means of survival.

91 *Christmas in Exeter Street*, 1989

NOTES

1. At the Sussex village of Burwash, and later at the Salesian College, Cowley, Oxford.
2. Except where otherwise stated, quotations are based on interviews recorded at Stamford Hill, North London, on 30 September 1986, and 31 March 1987.
3. Lesley Macdonald, 'Der Illustrator John Lawrence', *Illustration 63,* 18/3 (November 1981), 83−8. This extract is re-translated from the German. An earlier review of the artist's work had appeared in 9/3 (1972).
4. Albert Garrett, *A History of British Wood Engraving* (Midas Books, 1978), 296. The emergence of a British school of wood engraving is superbly chronicled and illustrated in this book; each artist's style and achievement is evaluated in relation to influences and developments both past and present. John Lawrence's work is set in a precise and carefully balanced context.
5. As part-time lecturer at Maidstone College of Art (1958−60), at Brighton College of Art (1960−68), and at Camberwell School of Art and Crafts (since 1960).
6. Many engravers disdain working on vinyl, but Lawrence is rather attracted to its 'rumbustious, chapbook-like quality'. Much closer to linoleum than to wood, yet offering a clean consistent cut and no resistance worth mentioning, it is easily corrected, inexpensive and incredibly fast to work with. Thus it enables him to take on appropriate commissions to budgets and deadlines that would rule out wood engraving.
7. From a brief note about his life and work written for L. Kingman, G. A. Hogarth and H. Quimby (compilers), *Illustrators of Children's Books 1967−1976* (Boston, Mass.: The Horn Book, 1978), 138.
8. *Colonel Jack* shared second prize in the 1972 Francis Williams Book Illustration Award with Peter Reddick's *The Return of the Native;* in 1977 *Rabbit and Pork* shared the first prize with titles by Raymond Briggs and Michael Foreman.
9. These brief practical notes are only contextual to Lawrence's own view of his artistic development within the medium. He converts a freehand drawing to a precise compositional *line* drawing on tracing paper, which is turned over and traced-down onto the wood or vinyl through carbon paper. This line is established in waterproof ink so that it stays there when the surface of the wood is next darkened in order to make the progressive removal of wood visible as light though dark. Lawrence also rubs in precipitated chalk from time to time to highlight the lines he is making.

   He is a great admirer of the Victorian engravers who reproduced the detailed drawing on the block with fidelity and technical virtuosity, and in his own early work found that he was going along this same path to a degree. Now he regards the line drawing as a general guide to interpretation and feels that all the texturing and tonality should come from the tools. He speaks of 'cutting the drawing', and 'working out things from the wood'; and uses his favourite tools in a more experimental way – rocking multiple tools from side to side to produce fresh textures rather than using them for routine hatchings, for example – and engraving lines and textures through or over each other in ways that cause them to interact and enliven the print. 'What I'm looking for is the excitement of metal going through wood and coming up with interesting marks – I hope it isn't just fireworks – but a way of drawing.'
10. That is to say, he could encounter such superlative engravers as Peter Reddick, and Garrick Palmer on equal terms in their respective titles for the Folio Society, but no other contemporary British engraver has ventured such a sustained contribution within the children's book field.
11. Peter Guy, 'The wood-engravings of John Lawrence', *Matrix 3* (Winter 1983), 21−41. Peter Guy also contributed a brief introduction to *A Selection of Wood Engravings* (Camberwell Press, 1986).

BIBLIOGRAPHY

Note: it can be taken that books are illustrated by drawings unless ascribed to one of the following categories: [1] lino cuts; [2] lino engravings (i.e. where the material has been worked mainly with engraving tools); [3] wood engravings; [4] vinyl engravings.

1959

A BOOK OF MODERN STORIES Hester Burton [ed.] OUP

1960 –

1961

BLACK'S CHILDREN'S ENCYCLOPAEDIA [2 vols.] W. Worthy and R. J. Unstead [eds.] [drawings as contributor] A & C Black

1962

THE LITTLE STORE ON THE CORNER Alice McCarthy [lino cuts] Abelard-Schuman

1963 –

1964

JAGGER'S SECRET CHALLENGE Richard Bickers Macdonald
REDCOAT SPY John Redmayne Macdonald
TOMPKINS AND TALUKDARS Christine King Chatto & Windus

1965

THE LIFEBOAT HAUL Frederick Grice [with] ELIZABETH WOODCOCK Dora Saint OUP
A SAXON SETTLER Rosemary Sutcliff OUP
SUBSTITUTE GENERAL John Redmayne Macdonald
WINGS FOR PINKY Arthur Waterhouse Univ. London Press

1966 ·

KIT BAXTER'S WAR Frank Knight Macdonald
SOUTH OF THE ZAMBESI: POEMS FROM SOUTH AFRICA Guy Butler [lino cuts] Abelard-Schuman
THE STUMPFS John Onslow Cape

1967

A CHILD OF THE CHAPEL ROYAL Elfrida Vipont OUP
COLONEL JACK Daniel Defoe [wood engravings] Folio
ENJOY READING! BOOK 2 R. E. Rogerson and C. M. Smith [eds.] Chambers
PRINCE OF CAVALIERS: LIFE AND CAMPAIGNS OF RUPERT OF THE RHINE Frank Knight Macdonald

1968

THE GIANT OF GRABBIST John Lawrence Hamish Hamilton/White
GUNPOWDER TREASON Margaret J. Miller Macdonald
HISTOIRES COMME CI, COMME ÇA Daniel Roberts [ed.] John Murray
REBEL ADMIRAL: LIFE AND EXPLOITS OF ADMIRAL LORD COCHRANE Frank Knight Macdonald
TARTARIN OF TARASCON Alphonse Daudet [binding design only] Folio

1969

THE DIARY OF A NOBODY George and Weedon Grossmith Folio
DRAGONS COME HOME Janet McNeill Hamish Hamilton
ENJOY READING! BOOK 3 R. E. Rogerson and C. M. Smith [eds.] Chambers
THE HERO: VICE-ADMIRAL HORATIO VISCOUNT NELSON Frank Knight Macdonald
POPE LEO'S ELEPHANT John Lawrence Hamish Hamilton/World
THE SPUR AND THE LILY Howard Jones Macdonald
STUMPF AND THE CORNISH WITCHES John Onslow Cape

92 Patrick Hardy Books, letterhead engraving

93 *Mabel's Story,* 1984

94 *Good Babies, Bad Babies*, 1986

1972

COOK BOOK   Nicolas Freeling   Hamish Hamilton

JEMIMA AND THE WELSH RABBIT   Gillian Avery   Hamish Hamilton

THE MULE OF AVIGNON   Alphonse Daudet   Hamish Hamilton/Crowell

NO MAGIC EDEN   Shirley Guiton   Hamish Hamilton

ROBINSON CRUSOE   Daniel Defoe   [lino cuts]   Folio

1973

A FAIRY CALLED ANDY PERKS   Janet McNeill   Hamish Hamilton

THE LOST SEA   Jan de Hartog   Hamish Hamilton

THE MOUTH OF THE NIGHT   Iris Macfarlane [ed.]   Chatto & Windus/Macmillan

ROGUES, VAGABONDS AND STURDY BEGGARS   Arthur F. Kinney [ed.]   [lino engravings]   Imprint Society, Barre, Mass. [USA]

1974

THE SOUND OF COACHES   Leon Garfield [lino engravings]   Kestrel

1975

THE BLUE FAIRY BOOK   Andrew Lang [ed. Brian Alderson]   Kestrel/Viking

RABBIT AND PORK, RHYMING TALK   John Lawrence [wood engravings]   Hamish Hamilton/Crowell

SHERSTON'S PROGRESS   Siegfried Sassoon   Folio

1976

DRAGONS AND MORE   Mildred Davidson [vinyl engravings]   Chatto & Windus

FANNY'S SISTER   Penelope Lively   Heinemann

TONGUE TWISTERS   John Lawrence   Hamish Hamilton

WATERSHIP DOWN [illustrated edn]   Richard Adams   Kestrel

1977

FOOD BY APPOINTMENT: ROYAL RECIPES SINCE 1066   Michèle Brown   Elm Tree

THE HAPPY CAPTIVE   Francisco Núñez de Pineda y Bascuñán   [vinyl engravings]   Folio

A WORLD BY ITSELF   Shirley Guiton   Hamish Hamilton

1978

A CHRISTMAS CARD   Paul Theroux   Hamish Hamilton/Houghton Mifflin

OUR EXPLOITS AT WEST POLEY   Thomas Hardy   [vinyl engravings]   OUP

THE SHEPHERD'S CALENDAR   John Clare [wood engravings]   Whittington Press and David Paradine

TOO MANY HUSBANDS   Sheila Lavelle   Hamish Hamilton

95 *Good Babies, Bad Babies*, 1986

1979

FANNY AND THE MONSTERS   Penelope Lively
   Heinemann
LONDON SNOW   Paul Theroux   [wood
   engravings]   Michael Russell (limited edn);
   Houghton Mifflin [USA]/Hamish Hamilton
   1980
THE ROAD TO CANTERBURY   Ian Serraillier
   [wood engravings]   Kestrel

1980

FANNY AND THE BATTLE OF POTTER'S
   PIECE   Penelope Lively   Heinemann
A PAIR OF SINNERS   Allan Ahlberg and
   John Lawrence   [wood engravings]   Granada
THE UNLUCKY FAMILY   Mrs Henry de la
   Pasture   Folio

1981

EVERYMAN'S BOOK OF ENGLISH FOLK
   TALES   Sybil Marshall [ed.]   [wood
   engravings]   Dent

1982

THE CRANKS RECIPE BOOK   David and Kay
   Canter and Daphne Swann   Dent
THE MAGIC APPLE TREE:
   A COUNTRY YEAR   Susan Hill   [wood
   engravings]   Hamish Hamilton/Holt,
   Rinehart
PRECISELY PIG   Michael Berthoud   Collins

1983

GEORGE, HIS ELEPHANT AND CASTLE
   John Lawrence   Patrick Hardy
JOHN CLARE'S AUTOBIOGRAPHICAL
   WRITINGS   Eric Robinson [ed.]   [wood
   engravings]   OUP

1984

CHRISTMAS POEMS   George Mackay Brown
   [wood engravings]   Perpetua
MABEL'S STORY   Jenny Koralek   Patrick
   Hardy
NOTHINGMAS DAY   Adrian Mitchell and
   John Lawrence   [wood engravings]
   Allison & Busby/Schocken
UNINVITED GHOSTS AND OTHER STORIES
   Penelope Lively   Heinemann/Dutton

1985

CHRISTMAS STORIES   George Mackay Brown
   [wood engravings]   Perpetua

ENTERTAINING WITH CRANKS   Kay Canter
   and Daphne Swann   Dent
A NATURE DIARY   Richard Adams   Viking

1986

AWFUL ANNIE AND PERFECT PERCY
   J. B. Simpson   Julia MacRae
THE CANTERBURY TALES   Geoffrey Chaucer
   [2 wood engravings as contributor]   Folio
GOOD BABIES, BAD BABIES   John Lawrence
   [wood engravings]   Whittington Press and
   Lorson's Prints and Books (limited edn); Julia
   MacRae 1987
THE KNIGHTS OF HAWTHORN CRESCENT
   Jenny Koralek   Methuen
A SELECTION OF WOOD ENGRAVINGS
   John Lawrence   Camberwell Press
THE WORD PARTY   Richard Edwards
   Lutterworth

1987

AWFUL ANNIE AND NIPPY NUMBERS
   J. B. Simpson   Julia MacRae
EMILY'S OWN ELEPHANT   Philippa Pearce
   and John Lawrence   Julia MacRae/
   Greenwillow
JANCIS ROBINSON'S FOOD AND WINE
   ADVENTURES   Jancis Robinson   [vinyl
   engravings]   Headline
WHISPERS FROM A WARDROBE   Richard
   Edwards   Lutterworth

1988

THE FOLIO SHAKESPEARE   [2 wood
   engravings as contributor]   Folio
GOING OUT WITH HATTY   Jenny Koralek
   Methuen
JOHN LAWRENCE'S PICTURE BOOK   John
   Lawrence   [wood engravings]   J. L. Carr
OENONE IN JANUARY   Kevin Crossley-Holland
   [wood engravings]   Old Stile Press
SONGS FOR ST MAGNUS DAY
   George Mackay Brown   [wood engravings]
   Perpetua
THE STORY OF CHAMPAGNE   Nicholas Faith
   [vinyl engravings]   Hamish Hamilton

1989

CHRISTMAS IN EXETER STREET
   Diana Hendry and John Lawrence
   Julia MacRae/Knopf

9 · JAN PIEŃKOWSKI

JAN MICHAL PIEŃKOWSKI was born into a family of artists and architects in Warsaw in 1936, although due to the war his upbringing was largely rural – in Poland until he was eight, in Bavaria whilst nine, and in Italy when ten years old. He retains very vivid memories of those early years:

> Where we lived, in Poland, the folk-art tradition was still alive, surviving despite mass production and austerity, and sustained in part by the Church: with paper flowers and Christmas decorations, which we would start to make about a month beforehand from paper, straw and egg-shells – although it was war-time and we didn't have very much coloured paper, we continued the tradition as far as we could.

> One strong memory is of an old woman who came to make paper curtains for the the kitchen windows: they'd be cut out of thin white paper. She'd fold the paper and make her cuts – it was like a music-hall act – and then she'd open it up and there would be a wonderful piece of paper lace with swans and roses and things. I thought it was magic and was completely overwhelmed by her skill . . .
> I remember going to the woods to collect mushrooms. The woods were very much part of our lives. I also remember being given a fretsaw and doing fretwork with my father – we made a sleigh and horses . . .

> Again, during the Rising in Warsaw, I remember sitting in a cellar with my mother. I didn't like it at all, but a man came in from the fighting and entertained the children by cutting animals out of paper – just extempore – that made a big impression on me. So there was a general climate of these paper cut-outs and wood cut-outs, everybody knew how to do it, it was a living tradition.[1]

The silhouette is the strongest element underlying Pieńkowski's draughtsmanship. He returns to it in a pure form at intervals, with a mastery that is possibly only to be matched in the cartoon films made in the 1930s by Lotte Reiniger; but it is also a way of seeing which pervades his work in the most diverse media:

> Perhaps this awareness of silhouette, of the profile rather than the detail of things, is connected with a heavily wooded environment, where people are used to looking out of forest gloom into bright clearings, seeing contours against a lighter background. And it does seem to be from the dark woods that this art comes; from Switzerland, south Germany, Poland and all that great swathe of forest that still covers much of Europe.

When Jan Pieńkowski arrived in England in 1946, he was already familiar with the classic English children's books from Polish editions. He had yet to pick up the language, but the various boarding schools he attended saw to that fairly quickly. He discovered in the comics, *Hotspur* and *Eagle* in particular, an excitement which made him one of the first to use the strip cartoon form successfully in children's books. (Illustrators, it seems, may conveniently be divided into those who truly enjoyed the comics and those who missed out on the forbidden fruit.)

He went on to read Classics and English Literature at King's College, Cambridge; and it was at this time that he encountered and started to collect the work of Aubrey Beardsley, an illustrator still not highly regarded at that time outside specialist circles: 'I admired his amazing use of empty space, never my strongest suit. I think that the Japanese have a word for it, for space as a positive element in any design.'

After Cambridge he did a spell of advertising art direction, long enough to make plain that it was not for him, but nevertheless not time he considers wasted: 'The discipline of the seven-second commercial; organising the information, presenting it with economy, holding interest and ensuring that the information gets across, remains fundamental to planning children's books.'

Towards the end of the 1950s it became possible for him to revisit Poland, and it was then that Pieńkowski became very aware of his heritage and of the exciting things that were being done there in the contemporary arts. In England the distinct but related worlds of theatre and television, advertising and publishing, each exercised a fascination for him; but it must have been apparent that no irrevocable choice between them had to be taken. He is a person who works on the principle that once you feel you have mastered something to the extent that you could repeat the success, it's time to move on.

Whereas Sendak, Hockney and Scarfe came to theatre design after their careers were established, Pieńkowski in a sense began his with a series of university productions which included *Samson Agonistes, The Jew of Malta,* and Machiavelli's *Mandragola.* Later he designed *Aladdin* for Watford Palace, and the Unicorn Theatre's production of David Wood's *The Meg and Mog Show* for Christmas 1981. He was invited to design *Beauty and the Beast* by the Royal Opera House in 1986, and welcomed this challenge as a sabbatical from book illustration. *Anything for a Quiet Life* for the Théâtre

96 *The Kingdom Under the Sea,* 1971

97 *Past Eight O'Clock,* cut paper, 1986

de Complicité followed in 1988, in which year an exhibition of his designs for the stage was shown at the Lyric Theatre, Hammersmith. Despite these successes in the theatre, he is content that they should remain well spaced out.

In 1961, with Angela Holder he founded *Gallery Five,* the continuingly successful producer of greetings cards, posters, children's friezes and decorative papers. For the first five years or so he drew most of the cards himself, and then progressively began to commission the work of other artists and to introduce engravings and existing material. He phased himself out from the running of the company as involvement in the practice of book illustration grew; until finally he became an arbiter: 'someone who just comes in and says what he thinks, although I have never stopped designing for the company. I find it a challenging discipline and an exhilarating one.'

During the years 1960–61, he began to receive commissions for book jackets from Tom Maschler at Jonathan Cape; later in the 1960s Maschler, who liked the set of drawings already prepared for a collection of rhymes, *Annie, Bridget and Charlie,* published this as Pieńkowski's first illustrated book. Those years also saw Pieńkowski's first involvement with television: graphics and cartoons for the BBC children's educational series *Watch!*

His own first picture book, *Meg and Mog* (created with Helen Nicoll), took much longer to find a publisher. It was shown around and shelved for three to four years until it came to the notice of Judith Elliott, then at Heinemann. She immediately saw in it a prototype for a new style of popular small-format book that she wanted to launch for the youngest audience. The success story of *Meg and Mog* continues, and the most recent title is considered later in this chapter.

The distinctiveness of Pieńkowski's colour work in a range of styles can be linked to individual technical methods which he evolved in direct reponse to his dislike of the standard process for four-colour reproduction.[2] This he sees as a sausage-machine through which most illustrators' coloured drawings are passed; some colour palettes may be enhanced, others enfeebled. It is a levelling process nonetheless, permitting colour results within set parameters, and ruling out other quite printable colour effects.

In all his work, then, he seeks to by-pass this standard method of colour reproduction from flat painted artwork: 'I have embedded in my mind that *artwork is not art.* It is a signal showing the way to the printed page.' His aim may be very different from title to title, ranging from flat areas of brilliant colour to delicate and complex colour appearances that rival the multi-colour printing of earlier generations. The common denominator is that his black is always line – silhouette – the recalled paper cut or stencil. Black as an admixture is never allowed to sully the purity of the colour spectrum, which must be derived from the three primaries alone. Some of the means through which this is achieved make a fascinating and non-technical story, although it takes a master craftsman to put them into practice.

Imagine a stained glass window, in which the leads form an intense black pattern, and the colours resonate like jewels the more the light streams through, by virtue of being set within a black surround. And there you have the *Meg and Mog* principle. The artwork consists of his black line, and each 'pane' of colour is laid by the printer in the form of a flat tint from a palette which Pieńkowski has evolved. A preliminary colour rough is drawn up to evaluate the effect, but every colour area is specified by a pencilled percentage strength for each constituent ink – an operation which parallels the earlier experiment of Laszlo Moholy-Nagy, who in 1922 made history by ordering a painting from an enamel factory by telephone, giving colour specifications from shade cards and dimensions using co-ordinated grids, thus anticipating much later steps in design and information technology.[3] A rudimentary form of colour specification by mechanical tint strength has of course long been in use to supply routine flat

98 *Tale of a One-way Street,* 1978

99 *Zoo*, 1985

100 *Weather*, 1979

101 *Food*, 1986

102 'Nursery Books' series, 1983

103 *Mog's Box*, 1987

background colour to comics and cheap colour publications – but Pieńkowski's refinement of the technique enables him to communicate an individual colour vision designed for younger readers, and to achieve the standards of print quality he constantly demands.

A chance breakthrough came in the late 1960s, when Gallery Five bought some commercial marbled papers. Immediately Jan Pieńkowski wanted to experiment, for here was one of the earliest processes of all for fixing fluent coloured patterns and images on paper,[4] pre-dating any but the most rudimentary forms of colour printing – and if it could be brought into aesthetic harmony with the even older silhouette technique something very special might result. He is far too intelligent an artist not to have realised at the time that it would be impossible to use this discovery repeatedly, and yet difficult ever to make such a strikingly original synthesis again. Pieńkowski's comments on this experiment reveal much about his aims in general:

> We followed a Dryad handbook on marbling with little success, but evolved our own way of doing it. Anybody who came into the house – the milkman or window-cleaner even – was encouraged to produce a sheet, and their results were strikingly different. That is something else my Polish background has given me: this idea of everyone joining in. When we were making the Christmas decorations everyone had a go, and I think that in a way this is why I enjoy working with children; not to show them how to do it necessarily, but just to do it with them so that we all learn from each other. I think it a great pity that people are labelled artists or whatever whereas in fact everyone can do these things – it's just that some are very much more experienced.

However, this egalitarian and experimental approach becomes channelled, somewhere along the line, into the most rigorous professionalism and perfectionism in his own work and in what he expects of others. The published findings of the adventure with marbling techniques appeared as illustrations for *The Golden Bird* and *The Kingdom under the Sea,* in which areas of marbled paper are reproduced facsimile, matched in colour, mood and movement to a frequently storm-tossed line. These are illustrations destined to be measured on the scale of the classic children's artists of the past, and particularly in relation to Kay Nielsen and others among his personal favourites. It may be reasonable to detect here as well, not a debt but homage to *Fantasia,* his favourite film (almost to the point of obsession). With the acclaim these titles received Pieńkowski's course as a children's book illustrator was set, although he would always reserve time for other ventures.

In the years that followed, it does seem that his acceptance of this special role, and the acknowledgment that children had now become his primary audience, impelled him into participatory efforts to identify their current interests and to discover those things that truly engaged and entertained them:

Possibly because I have no children of my own, I work with children quite
a lot; I tell children stories, I draw with them and I find that world in some
ways very attractive. On the other hand, I don't have the grind of putting
up with them all day long, so they're sort of luxuries to me. We have fun
together.[5]

The time which elapsed between the two Kate Greenaway Medals awarded to Jan
Pieńkowski (for *The Kingdom under the Sea* in 1972 and *Haunted House* in 1980),
measures a shift in emphasis from children's book illustration as a studio activity
towards making books based on this involvement with children, through which he
could observe what was truly mega-fun or hyper-scary for them; and thereby enabling
him to break new ground in children's book publishing.

Haunted House, Robot and later titles are pop-up books which pull out all the stops
of that medium in its recent Colombian flowering. The skill of the world's top paper
engineers, and the bizarre alliance of advanced print technology and intensive hand
labour established at this specific South American location, provide the illustrator with
an opportunity to push towards the creative limits, whilst staying within the
remarkably high safety margins set for fair wear and tear. Pieńkowski's meticulous
attention to detail and his patient insistence that print production should come up to his
exacting standards, meant that he was an ideal artist to devise such intricate three-
dimensional moving objects. It must, by contrast, have been sheer relaxation to take
time off with children to deck out and transform a railway train, as he did some years
ago for a children's book week.

The *Meg and Mog* books achieved their fifteen-year anniversary with the
publication of *Mog's Box* in 1987. Staying power of that order is obviously something
which publishers look for, but it is especially intriguing where the latest product in
such a series proves to be the authors' favourite and to break new ground at the same
time: 'The books follow a proper cartoon technique; there are bubbles, balloons and
sound-effects and you can tell which is which.' But the sheer vibrancy of colour
demanded is now understood and reciprocated by the printer, and the traditional
resources are augmented by novel graphic fusions of word and form.

Shortly after 1980, Pieńkowski was at a peak in his career and aware also that he had
become caught up in the children's book world to the exclusion of most of his other
personal artistic plans and aspirations. He began to feel some discomfort in this
situation; the achievement was real enough, but critics are bound to look to the next
stage in development. Pieńkowski is equally driven to change the focus of his concerns.
He has always realised that book illustration should not consist only in offering
entertainment, although few have done it with more colour and verve in recent years
through the media of cartoon and pop-up book, and their exceptional level of sheer
delight has led to the wide use of his books in education.

Pieńkowski decided that the great Christian themes of *Christmas* and *Easter* lay before him as the next challenge, and – although a Catholic – he chose the King James version of the Bible as his text. These were to represent a summation of his work to date as an illustrator.

It is very rare for anyone working in publishing to concede that a book has been superbly produced in every detail, but this has to be said of *Christmas* in both its cased and paperback versions. So often the paperback issue of an illustrated children's book is a compromise, but Pieńkowski quietly insists on paper and print quality; and the way his books look set a standard of achievement. The technical production planning for this title was formidable, but the Tien Wah Press of Singapore was well able to cope. A description of the form which the artwork eventually needed to take illustrates his own view that it is as unnecessary for the illustrator to leave behind a trail of finished and signed drawings to authenticate his presence as it is for the theatre designer to turn scene-painter.

Pieńkowski was eager to use the bronze-powder technique for gold printing,[6] the line artwork for which he drew twice-size in black. For the colour interstices – initials and decoration – he pencilled in percentaged values for flat tri-colour tints. The black silhouette artwork he drew separately for a massive reduction. When it came to colour, then the hated three-colour separation process had to be subverted at all costs; and this involved hundreds of hours of skilled craftsmanship in generating a range of textures and subtle colour variations through techniques of resist, splatter, stipple, chalking and controlled precipitation of pigment from washes onto the texture of hand-made paper. The large initials were drawn by the artist Jane Walmsley, and the entire text was 'Letraset' by hand to yield a more precise result than could be specified from any of the 'state-of-the-art' phototypesetting systems. The credits state, in a form customary to Jan Pieńkowski, that 'the illustrator would like to thank the following for their help . . .' – an acknowledgment that might well have been given from the beginning of the record of printed book illustration, for, with very few exceptions, artists in earlier times also involved the work of intermediate or interpretative craftsmen in translating their vision into print.

These two volumes, in particular, were such vast projects that some assistance was vital: it took five months' uninterrupted effort to collate the words of the four Evangelists into a working text for *Easter*. This is a book with deep personal significance into which he wanted to put all the experience and best qualities he has gained as an illustrator. He likens it to the time of life when an artist wishes to make a large-scale gesture of affirmation – as when, for example, a composer feels ready and impelled to write a Requiem Mass.

When I last met Jan Pieńkowski, he admitted that his interest in work outside the field of children's book illustration has grown in recent years. Other artistic challenges beckon, and he has increasingly made time alongside his commitments to publishing and the theatre for free artistic work, as was to be seen in his first one-man exhibition,

105 *Easter,* 'Jesus washing Peter's feet', 1989

'Works in Cut Paper, Wood and Metal' at the Oxford Gallery in 1988 – a direction which nevertheless reflects the innovatory cut and torn paper vignettes for *Past Eight O'Clock.* For an artist with a declared intention to move onwards, nothing may be predicted, beyond a constant willingness on the part of his younger audience to follow new initiatives – which will inevitably come.

NOTES

1. Quotations, unless otherwise stated, are from a conversation recorded in Barnes, West London, on 17 August 1987.
2. The almost universal method of reproducing full-colour photographs or drawings, by analysing each colour modulation in terms of the presence of constituent strengths of the standard yellow, magenta, cyan and black inks from which the resultant plates will be printed, formerly by using filters and angled screens to produce an overlapping pattern of dots of different sizes, nowadays by digital scanning. See also *Glaister's Glossary of the Book,* 2nd edn (Allen & Unwin, 1979), colour plates between pp. 432–3.
3. Laszlo Moholy-Nagy, *Malerei, Fotografie, Film,* facsimile reprint of 1927 edn (Mainz: Kupferberg, 1967).
4. 'A slimy fluid is produced from a watery solution of gum tragacanth and carrageen moss, then filtered into a dish which should be slightly bigger than the sheet to be marbled. Certain vegetable dyes mixed with propellants are dripped or sprinkled on to this surface and then drawn with combs or sticks into the pattern desired. Then the sheet, which has been made absorbent with alum water, is laid in the dish and the floating colours transfer to it. It can then be carefully lifted and hung up to dry. Each single sheet requires the preparation to be made afresh on a new surface.' O. Hirsch, *Holzschnitt-Umschlage und Buntpapiere* (Köln: Wallraf-Richartz-Museum, 1959), trans. Douglas Martin.

   'To succeed in this craft one needs to be diligent, have a dexterous hand and the ability to transfer sudden bright ideas straight into patterns on liquid.' Daniel Schwenter (1585–1636).

5. 'An interview with Jan Pieńkowski', *Puffin Post,* Summer 1984.

6. The line image is first printed 'blind' in gum or size and then dusted with bronze-powder. Before industrial health legislation clamped down on this technique in Europe it was always a poor relation to other processes, for characteristically there would be a sprinkling or dispersal of loose particles from the finished work, and it was therefore restricted to cheap greetings cards and so forth. Pieńkowski had identified its current use to an exemplary quality standard in the Far East in connection with religious festivals and for decorative wrapping papers. It has an aesthetic far removed from the effect of gold-blocking, and its integration into a finely produced picture book proved a signal success.

BIBLIOGRAPHY

1967

ANNIE, BRIDGET AND CHARLIE   Jessie Gertrude Townsend   Cape/Pantheon

1968

A NECKLACE OF RAINDROPS   Joan Aiken Cape/Doubleday

1969 –

1970

THE GOLDEN BIRD   Edith Brill   Dent/Watts
JIM ALONG JOSIE   John and Nancy Langstaff OUP

1971

THE KINGDOM UNDER THE SEA   Joan Aiken Cape

1972

MEG AND MOG   Helen Nicoll and Jan Pieńkowski   Heinemann/Atheneum
MEG'S EGGS   Helen Nicoll and Jan Pieńkowski Heinemann/Atheneum

1973

CONCEPT BOOKS   [*Colours, Shapes, Sizes, Numbers*]   Jan Pieńkowski   Heinemann/ Harvey House
MEG ON THE MOON   Helen Nicoll and Jan Pieńkowski   Heinemann/Harvey House
MEG AT SEA   Helen Nicoll and Jan Pieńkowski Heinemann/Harvey House

1974 –

1975

MEG'S CAR   Helen Nicoll and Jan Pieńkowski Heinemann/David & Charles
MEG'S CASTLE   Helen Nicoll and Jan Pieńkowski   Heinemann/David & Charles
QUEST FOR THE GLOOP   Helen Nicoll and Jan Pieńkowski   Heinemann

1976

THE AMBER MOUNTAIN   Agnes Szudek Hutchinson
MEG'S VEG   Helen Nicoll and Jan Pieńkowski Heinemann/David & Charles
MOG'S MUMPS   Helen Nicoll and Jan Pieńkowski   Heinemann/David & Charles

find our way sure enough." And when the full moon had risen he took his sister by the hand and followed the pebbles, which shone like newly minted pieces of silver, and showed them the path.

106 *Hansel and Gretel,* 1977

107 *Past Eight O'Clock*, cut paper, 1986

108 'Figure Three', work in cut paper, undated

1977
FAIRY TALE LIBRARY   [*Cinderella, Hansel and Gretel, Jack and the Beanstalk, Puss in Boots, Sleeping Beauty, Snow White*]   Jan Pieńkowski
Heinemann with Gallery Five/Crowell

1978
GHOSTS AND BOGLES   Dinah Starkey
Good Reading
TALE OF A ONE-WAY STREET   Joan Aiken
Cape

1979
CONCEPT BOOKS   [*Homes, Weather*]
Jan Pieńkowski   Heinemann/Harvey House
HAUNTED HOUSE   Jan Pieńkowski   [paper engineering, Tor Lokvig]   Heinemann/Dutton
MEG AND MOG BIRTHDAY BOOK   Helen Nicoll and Jan Pieńkowski   Heinemann/David & Charles

1980
CONCEPT BOOKS   [*ABC, Time*]   Jan Pieńkowski
Heinemann/Harvey House

1981

DINNER TIME   Jan Pieńkowski   [paper
    engineering, Marcin Stajewski, James Roger
    Diaz]   Gallery Five/Price Stern
ROBOT   Jan Pieńkowski   [paper engineering,
    James Roger Diaz, Tor Lokvig, Marcin
    Stajewski]   Heinemann/Delacorte

1982

MOG AT THE ZOO   Helen Nicoll and Jan
    Pieńkowski   Heinemann/David & Charles

1983

GOSSIP   Jan Pieńkowski   [paper engineering,
    Marcin Stajewski, James Roger Diaz]
    Gallery Five   [reissued with new text and
    cover as SMALL TALK,   Orchard/Price Stern
    1987]

1984

CHRISTMAS   Extracts from the Authorized
    King James Version of the Bible
    Heinemann/Knopf
MOG IN THE FOG   Helen Nicoll and Jan
    Pieńkowski   Heinemann/David & Charles
OWL AT SCHOOL   Helen Nicoll and Jan
    Pieńkowski   Heinemann/David & Charles

1985

NURSERY BOOKS   [*Farm, Zoo*]   Jan
    Pieńkowski   Heinemann/David & Charles
LOOK AT ME   [*I'm Cat, I'm Frog, I'm Mouse,
    I'm Panda*]   Jan Pieńkowski   Walker/Little
    Simon

1986

NURSERY BOOKS   [*Faces, Food*]   Jan
    Pieńkowski   Heinemann/David & Charles
LITTLE MONSTERS   Jan Pieńkowski   [paper
    engineering, Marcin Stajewski, James Roger
    Diaz, David A. Carter]   Orchard/Price Stern
PAST EIGHT O'CLOCK   Joan Aiken   Cape

1987

MOG'S BOX   Helen Nicoll and Jan Pieńkowski
    Heinemann/David & Charles

1988 –

1989

EASTER   Extracts from the Authorized King
    James Version of the Bible
    Heinemann/Knopf

109   *The Children's Book*, cover design, 1985

110   *I'm Panda*, cut and torn paper, 1985

10 · HELEN OXENBURY

KOKOSCHKA'S international school of art met under the banner of 'the school of seeing',[1] and I propose to borrow his title as the theme for this look at ways in which different modes of seeing come into play within the illustrative process generally, and particularly in the specific artistic achievement of Helen Oxenbury.

A natural dichotomy exists between habits of perception in everyday life and the individual artist's highly selective and structured vision, and, in this situation, the illustration of books for children can frequently afford one of the best possible bridging-points. Helen Oxenbury – besides drawing fluently and splendidly – has an innate way of observing and presenting her material which, however sophisticated the hidden artistic means deployed, succeeds in making her results a direct and uncomplicated delight for the viewer; and it is this rare ability which has helped in her personal quest for fresh ways in which to communicate with the very youngest of children.

Clearly she has an unerring eye for the overall *contour* made by a single figure or group together with the rhythms and movements which animate it, and for ensuring that this key aspect of the drawing is read as one take, free from distraction or ambiguity. Other figure artists have their own skills for ordering and reducing complex visual fields into universally intelligible imagery, but Helen is particularly able to adapt her everyday domestic surroundings at a variety of levels without conventionalising her viewpoint or compromising the sensitivity of her drawing.

Format and functional considerations dictate to a degree the burden of content of books from the pre-reading age onward, but Helen has been content to extend and exploit these limitations to the full during that phase of her career spent in this chosen field of practice, which will be found to correlate with the years of her youngest daughter, Emily's, progression to primary school. The essence of her success here as elsewhere still resides in her insistence on drawing characters and situations directly from life, and in finding the best places to incorporate domestic props and treasures, whether mundane or exotic.

III *Meal One*, 1971

Helen Oxenbury was born in Ipswich, Suffolk, in 1938, the daughter of an architect. After leaving school she attended Ipswich School of Art, and it was at that time that she discovered her tremendous enthusiasm for the theatre, not through art school but as a result of vacation work, at first with a repertory company at Felixstowe (so tiny that it could not afford actors, with the result that small parts immediately came her way alongside the scene-painting for which she had been engaged), and later with another company in Ipswich. The progression from fine art to theatre design was a logical one and the Central School of Art and Design in London the natural place to study, and it was there in the years 1957–9 that she was to meet John Burningham for the first time. However, her practical experience of the stage, slight though it was, sufficed to awaken reservations about the relevance of academic studies in isolation from real-life conditions; and so she was happy to be able to join Colchester Repertory Theatre as

assistant to the designer, where opportunities arose to design complete productions towards the end of her stay. For the most part, however, work consisted of painting, striking, and reassembling sets, along with all the endless chores and long hours that went with provincial rep at seven pounds a week.

In contrast, there followed three creative years as set painter and designer for the Habimah Theatre in Tel Aviv,[2] and it would have seemed that Helen Oxenbury was poised for success at the top in her chosen field when she returned to London in 1962. She was out of touch after three years in Israel, but did some designing for ABC Television and at Shepperton Film Studios. Her personal reasons for abandoning work for the stage simply reflect the age-old incompatibility of theatrical and family life – for she was about to marry John Burningham and must have sensed the extreme contrast in working lifestyle between the bustle of the theatre and the solitude of the illustrator's studio at home.[3] She had watched John illustrating books and knew what it was all about, and must have been attracted to making her own individual and totally different books for children as well.

But her initial step in a freelance direction was to consider the greetings card idiom and to attune her style to the newly fashionable, up-market image that Jan Pieńkowski had established at Gallery Five, and for whom she was shortly to design. Helen affirms that 'Jan's art direction is brilliant',[4] and that he was quick to point her towards children's books; he has remained a staunch personal friend and artistic mentor. Her very first book, *Numbers of Things,* still in fact shows the influence of modes of design thinking and compositional treatment growing out of the greetings card market, whilst at the same time coming to terms with the conventions of the book page. She found it an advantage in starting out not to have studied illustration formally at college: 'that's where you get influenced'; and abiding favourites aside – E. H. Shepard and of course Edward Ardizzone ('it is that wonderful seaside atmosphere I like about his work') – 'it was marvellous not to have to carry about the impedimenta of stylistic influences, and to be able to analyse and respond freshly to new design problems'. *Numbers of Things*

112 *The Great Big Enormous Turnip,* 1968

has charm and has retained its popularity; a cumulative counting scheme gives the book its structure, and this renders immaterial the slight lack of continuity in artistic handling from plate to plate that is to be expected of a first venture.

The books of the decade 1968–78 show Helen's increased preoccupation with textural surface treatment involving mixed media, and in particular with the range of effects to be drawn from coloured crayon pencils in relation to pen or soft pencil line. The drawing is firmly realised but never overworked, the elaboration of incidental pattern and detail builds up a rich and credible pictorial surface. The influence of set design can still be detected in the way domestic backdrops are handled, notably in the stylishly modified perspective of the interiors for Ivor Cutler's *Meal One*. There is no assertive staginess about the way characters inhabit these sets, yet her earlier theatrical experience seems in a quiet way to inform and coordinate many of the effects

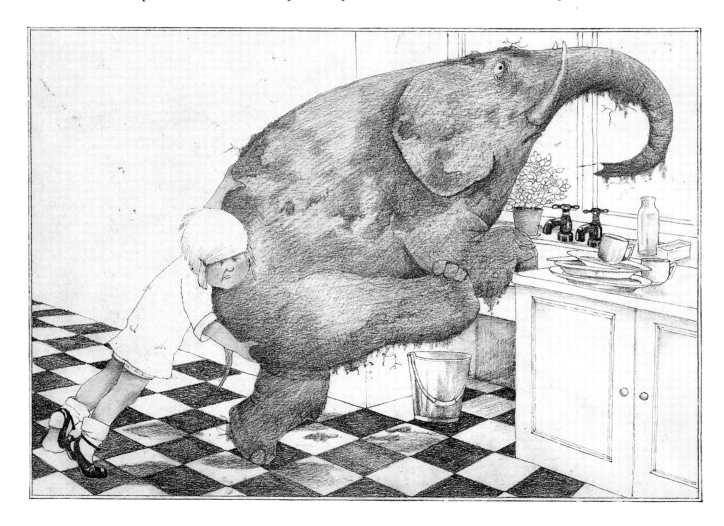

113 *Balooky Klujypoop,* 1975

114 *Cakes and Custard,* 1974

115 *The Dancing Class*, 1983

produced. The years which led up to *Cakes and Custard* in 1974 must have been creatively satisfying ones for the artist, bringing the Kate Greenaway Medal for *The Hunting of the Snark* and *The Quangle Wangle's Hat*, as well as her own splendid *ABC* among other projects. *Cakes and Custard* itself contains much fine drawing but is unfortunately flawed as a piece of book design and production.

One of her greatest strengths as an illustrator is that Helen Oxenbury has always seemed to allow issues of scale and content to flow naturally from her current design preoccupations, and as these have changed the adaptations involved have been considerable; she doesn't work concurrently on different types of project but finds that a shift of focus occurs every so often – from the theatre to greeting cards and thence to the group of chidren's books to which those mentioned above belong. The next transition was towards the board book idiom with which her name has become closely identified, and which in turn must have called for something of a stylistic re-appraisal. She started to work on these in about 1980, partly, as already indicated, as a result of having a younger daughter at a time when her first two children were already teenagers, and because this new mother–daughter relationship and the unhurried exploration of the domestic scenarios which arose, provided a fresh fund of ideas for such books; but there was also another reason:

> Walker Books was being established at the time, and so I did these books with no other thought than that it would be quite fun to work with somebody who was starting a publishing house, and to watch it get off the ground. Naturally I didn't want to do the sorts of book I'd been doing for Heinemann, my regular

116 *The Check-up*, 1983

publisher, and so I developed these titles for very young children which took off in an extraordinary and unexpected way because somehow they filled a gap in the market.

The shifts in style and technique which have accompanied these developments are simple to see and to describe: line and wash has become her preferred medium; an earlier interest in juxtaposed surface pattern (for instance, of dress against carpet or wallpaper) has been subordinated to compositional clarity; and shading and texture are indicated more economically now to that same end. I am sure that she would not wish it to be made to sound any more complicated than that, since she feels that rapport with children in her work has to remain instinctive, that books are there for entertainment and to foster the love of reading, and not for any overtly educational end. She has no wish ever to teach, and is distrustful of theory: 'It is hard enough without added market research or the need to worry about age or level.' Nevertheless, her outstanding success in this field stimulates a few supplementary reflections, and the desire to go into a little more detail.

Her books for the very young may be seen in contrast to other recent approaches by virtue of the instinctive freshness of her drawing, and demonstrate that in the common task of establishing basic conventions for pictorial storytelling at these levels there is greater scope for individuality, and a variety of starting points,[5] than some may have thought. When a study of earlier ventures along the road to graphic simplification for pre-school and primary users of books is eventually made, it may well be found that instinctive − even primitive − approaches from around the world and from the past emerge as more productive than post-war examples based on received educational theory. The modernist reduction to a design idiom where features are represented by conventional signs, drawing by rigid black outline, and colour by primary infill, may come to be viewed as the social equivalent of the 1960s tower block or the misused sans serif typeface. Some illustrators have gone a long way in attempting to reform that tradition from within, but the return to a more instinctive and humanistic approach exemplified by Helen Oxenbury and others should hold more for the future.

'Line and wash' is a cataloguer's bald description for what is surely a very personal synthesis, which in her hands becomes a means of fixing the intended image with precision. The soft pencil line remains virtually continuous to define the contour, inflected to make it come alive spatially but without violating the essential two-dimensional convention. Degas said that 'figures are activated by pressure points within the contour itself', and this helps to convey rhythm and momentum. Colour wash runs up to the defining line and softens it as required − slight variations in the strength and reticulation of the wash say all that is necessary about form and establish the natural presence of the characters.

The overall shape on the page has much to do with the way in which very young children take in Helen Oxenbury's drawings for them: the first, instantaneous impression is likely to be of a single memorable image which subsumes content and context, explaining it in a way that subsequent scanning of detail only confirms and reinforces. This ability to reduce a story into a dominant shape or contour is quite rare among illustrators, although its value in the early learning process can be readily appreciated. Historical examples of a similar technique in action can be found in both the Western European and Japanese woodcut, where shapes and outlines can give rise to imagery which is comparable in effect to the equally instinctive work of modern illustrators such as Helen Oxenbury who possess such a mastery of contour.

It has been seen that Helen Oxenbury's work has progressed through a number of successive and distinct phases, and she now acknowledges an eagerness to move on towards fresh subject-matter at different levels of age and complexity. It is always a challenge for any artist to relinquish a successful formula, all the more so where this has been dedicated to the solution of specialised problems in an innovatory way. Whilst relishing a return to the fuller use of illustrative resources on a broader canvas, she finds it slightly unnerving not to be able to pinpoint the precise direction which this is likely to take in the immediate future, but knows that it is sure to involve work for older children, moving gradually towards the illustration of books for adults: 'I haven't yet done a book that requires research into place or period or a section of people or an animal that I don't know.' In view of her distinguished achievement at each stage in her career, and proven ability to adapt from one to the next, it is only possible to look forward in eager anticipation when such an artist confidently asserts: 'the best is still to come'.

NOTES

1. Oscar Kokoschka (1886-1980) was the guiding spirit of the 'Schule des Sehens': International Summer Academy for the Study of the Creative Arts, founded at Salzburg in 1953.
2. Habimah 'The Stage' was founded in 1918 in Moscow and after years of displacement in Europe and a rift that took part of the company to the United States, it found a home in Tel Aviv in 1932 where it was well funded once it became a national theatre. The 1960s were vintage years since here was an ensemble of tremendous energy, able to draw on the talents of the great Russian performers who were still active, and yet extending its lively and enterprising international repertoire to include such contemporary English works as Arnold Wesker's *Billy Liar* and Willis Hall's *The Long and the Short and the Tall*, with sets designed by Helen Oxenbury.
3. The place of the family in her books and the problems of working under the same roof as another children's book illustrator are well conveyed in an interview with Hilary Macaskill, 'The art of keeping chaos in the family' (*The Guardian*, 26 May 1983), 10.
4. Quotations are from a conversation recorded in Hampstead on 13 March 1987.
5. In establishing the requisite near two-dimensional picture plane and the balance between bounding outline and contained colour, the background influence of the illustrators for the Evans workshop and of the Japanese woodcut can surely be sensed.

117 *We're Going on a Bear Hunt:* pencil studies

BIBLIOGRAPHY

1967
NUMBERS OF THINGS Helen Oxenbury
   Heinemann/Watts

1968
THE GREAT BIG ENORMOUS TURNIP
   Alexei Tolstoy Heinemann/Watts
THE QUANGLE WANGLE'S HAT Edward Lear
   Heinemann/Watts

1969
THE DRAGON OF AN ORDINARY FAMILY
   Margaret Mahy Heinemann/Watts

LETTERS OF THANKS Manghanita Kempadoo
   Collins/Simon & Schuster

1970
THE HUNTING OF THE SNARK
   Lewis Carroll Heinemann/Watts

1971
HELEN OXENBURY'S ABC OF THINGS
   Helen Oxenbury Heinemann/Watts
MEAL ONE Ivor Cutler Heinemann/Watts

1972 –

120 *Trubloff, the mouse that wanted to play the balalaika,* 1964

I've never been one for the technicalities of printing, and I know that my early work has a naive quality which it is impossible to recapture. I wasn't then conscious even of the need to leave areas for the type to appear; this had simply to overprint the drawing or a background be contrived – one was just 'doing a picture' – and it didn't matter in the long run, in the way that superb reproduction doesn't really matter: reproduction entails a certain loss, and ultimately it's a question of have you done a good drawing and have you written a good story? I mean 'Tea for Two' is as good on a penny whistle as with a symphony orchestra, and nowadays there is a lot of superbly reproduced work which is completely arid and meaningless in content.

Before *Borka,* John Burningham had spent a time in New York, where he had worked on a lot of educational material. Although it has not proved possible to trace his own contribution to specific projects, it is well known how advanced American publishing was at this time in presenting basic concepts of science and number with exemplary directness, and it is likely that this interest in deploying illustration freshly and simply in objective learning situations resurfaced much later in his own number scheme. But however satisfying and well paid this work may have been at a certain level, what continued to elude Burningham on both sides of the Atlantic was illustrative work of the kind he really wanted and which he knew he could do best: 'It was the same old story as one took a portfolio around: − ''If somebody else will use you, we will too''. ' And so *Borka* was born of this frustration: 'I thought to hell with it, I'll just do the whole lot on spec!'

Tom Maschler at Jonathan Cape accepted this first book virtually as it stood, and it sailed into a Kate Greenaway Medal just as Brian Wildsmith's first picture book, for Oxford University Press, had done in the previous year. The stage was set for a new full-colour approach to the picture story book, and for Burningham's long creative association with that format and with Cape: in his own mock rueful words −

I was a prisoner of the success of *Borka,* it became a question of 'Let's have another one', and I had another idea, and it has been going on like that for 20-odd years and every time I've consciously wanted to stop doing them I've had an idea that I couldn't resist working out.

Everyone will have their favourites from among the sequence of Burningham picture books, but it is interesting to note what has remained constant as his art as illustrator

and storyteller has refined and developed. The story-line has tended to become less discursive, and is pared down to a classic telling shared out between text and pictures in order that many of the same motifs – notably his grasp of the near inevitability of mutual incomprehension between adult and growing child – can be developed with greater subtlety and economy. The graphic means of expression are similarly subdued to the point that they are adequate for the task in hand, whilst opening the door to a greater range of contrasts than was possible with the full-blown chromaticism of *Borka* or *Trubloff* (and which proved at its most effective in the *Wall Friezes,* which had to operate over optical distances ranging from right across a room to close up). The *Wall Friezes* were an exciting landmark at the time, and opened up the world of his 'books' to thousands of children before they could read – a great introduction!

A striking stylistic transformation is fully evident by the time he came to do the drawings for *Mr Gumpy's Outing* (1970); it is as though a major line artist has emerged from the chrysalis of a painterly and frequently bravura handling of gouache. That is not to say anything as absurd as that Burningham's drawing has suddenly improved –

121 *Chitty-Chitty-Bang-Bang,* 1964

122 *Mr Gumpy's Outing*, 1970

123 *Come Away from the Water, Shirley,* 1977

he has always been a superb draughtsman, however much his line may have had to be broadened and simplified to support the textural slabs of resonant colour in some of the early plates – but rather that now, where he wishes, a drawing can be made to appear effortlessly self-sufficient in that most difficult of all media: colour line. Linear cross-hatchings (with each distinct colour ink adopting a horizontal, vertical or diagonal axis) can build up into a landscape shimmering with light, atmosphere and movement. This hatched line is ideally suited to the pastoral progress of Mr Gumpy's punt, whether on the sepia pages or in the full-colour encounters, and the line angles can be freed up or scribbled-in almost wildly to contrast a scudding night sky with noonday calm. Here he has evolved so magical a means of bringing the countryside on to the page that it must be linked to his own rural upbringing in its freedom from artifice or sentimentality. It is not always easy to see how an award jury comes to prefer one achievement rather than another in the work of the same artist, but seldom can the choice of title on which to confer a second Kate Greenaway Medal have been more right and inevitable than it was for *Mr Gumpy's Outing.*

In considering the mixture of media and the range of techniques used within any single book, it does seem that Burningham works from the principle that visual awareness is stimulated by contrast and surprise: frequently he will hit upon a brilliant technical solution which many artists would be content to consolidate and sustain throughout in a series of unified drawings, but he prefers to create an imaginative garden with scope for wilderness and decay, tended plot and formal vista, life and growth generally.

The sequence of John Burningham's own full-scale picture books began to be interspersed after about ten years with the first of several series of smaller, squarish format books for much younger readers (the *Little Books* of 1974–5) in which the sketchy sepia line with its scratchy crayon pencil infill borrows from the universally restricted technical resources of the child as a method of address. Needless to say, the sophistication in observation and draughtsmanship far transcends anything a child actually does, but is unerringly right in projecting what he or she would *like* to achieve, and thus a valid channel of communication is established without any talking-down on the artist's part. [5]

Once this line and wash demotic had been evolved it was found that it could be used as a springboard in the full-scale picture books. The archetypal Burningham theme for slightly older readers is the ever-present dichotomy between the prosaic routine of adult life and the boundless inner world of the imagination; and it is the refinement of his technical means for conveying this which makes the sequential study of his published books so rewarding. *Come Away from the Water, Shirley* (1977) provides a clear-cut exposition of one of the basic mechanisms: Mum and Dad park themselves in deckchairs on the left-hand pages in drab line and wash – Shirley's colourful adventures with the pirates fill the facing pages – and the day passes without any real connection.

Without underestimating the difficulties of making it work in practice, there is the danger that this static repetition of the contrast formula will in itself be read as agitprop by the child, and so more subtle means of organising the transitions and the page sequence are sought in *Where's Julius?* (1986), in which the everyday routine of preparing and carting meals about, and of the family sometimes eating together and sometimes not, goes on regardless of Julius's imaginary travels to exotic and far-away places which are realised through a more varied gamut of graphic techniques and with a greater element of ambiguity. Burningham's overriding concern is with the story to be told and with the resonances it stimulates, provided that these are either unambiguous or thought-provoking, according to his intent. This may be further exemplified and possibly clarified through *John Patrick Norman McHennessy – the boy who was always late,* a recent title of which the author has observed: 'I consider this one of the very best things that I have ever done, and yet it has been totally ignored by the critics.' On the surface, both textual and illustrative story lines appear to be quite straightforward, but the reader is left to choose whether or not to identify the crocodile who 'came out of a drain and got hold of his satchel' with the dreadful schoolmaster himself, or to take in the message (that sometimes it is only possible to 'set off along the road to learn' after the effects of bad schooling have been shaken off) only if it is pertinent; the book works equally well without this interpretation. And so an enterprising point may have been reached in the development of the structure and mechanism of these picture books where the tracks have nearly been covered up: sub-text and illustration nowhere underline each other; nothing is explicitly stated; the contrast principle is no longer the mainspring of the mechanism but just an incidental; but *if* there should be a message or a moral to be inferred then no child need fail to perceive it. In all John Burningham's picture books there is an undertow of humanism or consolation for the underdog and of visual poetry to be found for those ready to take it aboard; and for the rest there is wit, colour and observation in plenty.

An average output of two titles per year should hardly be considered as slender,[6] but it also reflects John Burningham's concern for the quality and integrity of ideas. He gives an impression of restlessness when work's afoot, and evidently needs a fixed point or a counterfoil against which his thinking can be keyed up to a suitable pitch between bursts of studio activity. Evidently this is provided by his energetic work in creating the remarkable garden at the house close to Hampstead Heath to which he, his wife Helen Oxenbury and their son and two daughters moved over ten years ago. This family villa had been broken into a number of flats, but the opportunity was there to rescue and restore the whole stage by stage and to provide a setting for the beautiful objects from all periods which these artists joy in finding. John seems to bear a certain wistful awareness of the impermanence of things, which calls for mention since to it must be attributed the poetic insight so frequently to be glimpsed in his work; its counterpart in everyday life possibly finding expression through his custom of haunting demolition sites, which in turn accounts for the presence in his garden of items as various as a bell tower from a demolished church on the Finchley Road and a re-assembled Victorian greenhouse – an operation reminiscent of the way in which Mr Gumpy collects up his boatload of characters, eventually dispersing them to make a new pattern.

One option open to the children's book artist is the interpretative illustration of the writings of others; for some this is part of the excitement of the game and for others simply a corollary of building up a practice in the early stages. John Burningham's views on this topic hold a particular fascination since, apart from a couple of early ventures,[7] he has produced only a single book of this kind – but a masterly one.

> What I've never wanted to do is to illustrate endless and rather indifferent children's books. When asked to do *The Wind in the Willows,* I accepted because I hadn't read it and didn't know it . . .

This being so, it is remarkable that he should earlier have approached so close to the landscape of the book in *Mr Gumpy's Outing* – rivers, beasts, a watery sense of

125 *John Patrick Norman McHennessy – the boy who was always late,* 1987

timelessness – that a certain continuity is evident; the unusual outcome is a book in which the illustrations are pure Burningham and yet at the same time marry perfectly with Kenneth Grahame's text. When the public have taken the original illustrator of a classic to their hearts, as with Tenniel and Shepard, it is heresy and folly to dissent, but whilst admiring Shepard's original achievement it has to be said that I prefer Burningham's version, which deserves to be regarded as a classic in its own right.

124 *The Wind in the Willows,* 1983

NOTES

1. cf. A. S. Neill, *That Dreadful School* (Herbert Jenkins, 1937), for an account of the philosophy behind this celebrated liberal progressive school.
2. Extracts are taken from a conversation recorded in Hampstead on 9 December 1987.
3. Burningham acknowledges that he learned quite a lot from Keith Vaughan (1912–77) in particular, and the influence of the senior artist's freedom and sureness of touch in handling gouache at this period may be detected at certain points in *Borka.*
4. It must be hard for a younger generation of art students to imagine the prestige and excitement generated by graphic poster art until it was largely eclipsed by other genres in the late 1960s. cf. Harold F. Hutchinson, *London Transport Posters* (London Transport Board, 1963) and Michael F. Levey, *London Transport Posters* (Phaidon, 1976).
5. One of the few pedagogical parallels which spring to mind is that of Carl Orff's *Schulwerk,* where real music is cast within the span of classroom instruments and children's choral resources.
6. Friezes and individual titles in small-format series have been included to arrive at an estimated total of 51 titles produced over 26 years.
7. *Chitty-Chitty-Bang-Bang,* although an unqualified success, came from a commission given in only his second year of practice as an illustrator, when it would seem fair to assume that both artist and publisher were keen to cement a professional accord and to explore the range and volume of work which might be entailed.

BIBLIOGRAPHY

1963

BORKA, THE ADVENTURES OF A GOOSE WITH NO FEATHERS   John Burningham   Cape/Random House

1964

CHITTY-CHITTY-BANG-BANG   Ian Fleming [ed. Sheila Lane and Marion Kemp, 3 vols., 1964–65]   Cape/Random House
JOHN BURNINGHAM'S ABC   [lettering drawn by Leigh Taylor]   Cape/Bobbs-Merrill
TRUBLOFF: THE MOUSE THAT WANTED TO PLAY THE BALALAIKA   John Burningham   Cape/Random House

1965

HUMBERT, MISTER FIRKIN & THE LORD MAYOR OF LONDON   John Burningham   Cape/Bobbs-Merrill

1966

CANNONBALL SIMP   John Burningham   Cape/Bobbs-Merrill
WALL FRIEZES   [*Birdland, Lionland, Storyland*]   John Burningham   Cape/Braziller

1967

HARQUIN: THE FOX WHO WENT DOWN TO THE VALLEY   John Burningham   Cape/Bobbs-Merrill

1968

THE EXTRAORDINARY TUG-OF-WAR   Letta Shatz   Bodley Head/Follett
WALL FRIEZES   [*Jungleland, Wonderland*]   Cape/Braziller

1969

SEASONS   John Burningham   Cape/Bobbs-Merrill

1970

MR GUMPY'S OUTING   John Burningham   Cape/Holt, Rinehart

1971 –

1972

AROUND THE WORLD IN EIGHTY DAYS   John Burningham   Cape/Braziller
WALL FRIEZE   [*Around the World*]   Cape/Braziller

1973

MR GUMPY'S MOTOR CAR   John Burningham
   Cape/Crowell

1974

The Baby, The Rabbit, The School, The Snow
   John Burningham   Cape/Crowell

1975

The Blanket, The Cupboard, The Dog, The Friend
   John Burningham   Cape/Crowell

1976 –

1977

COME AWAY FROM THE WATER, SHIRLEY
   John Burningham   Cape/Crowell

1978

TIME TO GET OUT OF THE BATH, SHIRLEY
   John Burningham   Cape/Crowell
WOULD YOU RATHER . . .   John Burningham
   Cape/Crowell

1979 –

1980

THE SHOPPING BASKET   John Burningham
   Cape/Crowell

1981 –

1982

AVOCADO BABY   John Burningham
   Cape/Crowell

1983

JOHN BURNINGHAM'S NUMBER PLAY
   SERIES [*Pigs Plus: Learning Addition, Ride
   Off: Learning Subtraction, Read One: Numbers
   as Words, Five Down: Numbers as Signs, Count
   Up: Learning Sets, Just Cats: Learning Groups*]
   Walker/Viking
THE WIND IN THE WILLOWS
   Kenneth Grahame   Kestrel/Viking

1984

FIRST WORDS [*Cluck baa, Jangle twang, Skip
   trip, Slam bang, Sniff shout, Wobble pop*]
   John Burningham   Walker/Viking
GRANPA   John Burningham   Cape/Crown

1985 –

1986

WHERE'S JULIUS?   John Burningham
   Cape/Crown

1987

JOHN BURNINGHAM'S [*Alphabet Book,
   Numbers Book, Colours Book, Opposites Book*]
   Walker/Crown
JOHN PATRICK NORMAN MCHENNESSY –
   THE BOY WHO WAS ALWAYS LATE
   John Burningham   Cape/Crown

1988

RHYMETIME [*A Good Job, The Car
   Ride*] Walker

1989

RHYMETIME [*Animal Chatter, A Grand
   Band*] Walker

126 *The Wind in the Willows,* 1983

12 · RAYMOND BRIGGS

ON A DARK November day at the end of 1987, a car drew up outside Haywards Heath Station on the dot and in heavy rain. For an instant a copy of *When the Wind Blows* fluttered behind the windscreen, and then the passenger door was opened. On the dashboard a neat, *Fungus*-like list set out the car's future from first service to MOT-time. These opening frames were so characteristically Briggsian that their author had effectively introduced himself.

My interest in his work as an illustrator dates from long before *Father Christmas* and the fame which ensued, and therefore I was concerned to follow a chronological thread from the outset towards the future. It is hoped that this approach will complement that of Richard Kilborn, who takes a cross-sectional view over a shorter time-span in his seminal study of the media adaptation of *WTWB* (Briggs's own abbreviation).[1]

Raymond Briggs was born at Wimbledon Park, South London, on 18 January 1934, the son of a Co-operative Dairies milkman. His parents never moved from this address, and he stayed with them until he left London after the Slade. Large pencil drawings of his father Ernest and his mother Ethel hang in his sitting-room; unsurprisingly, they do not in the least resemble Jim and Hilda. His working-class, 'like most of us', values are the absolute bed-rock of his personality, and, I'm convinced, provide the most serviceable key towards an understanding of his skill as a communicator. In the process of learning to become middle class, he neither rejected nor complained about his heritage, as was fashionable at the time.

His earliest ambition was to be a newspaper reporter, but this changed to becoming a cartoonist when he first began to draw seriously at about the age of thirteen. He was much influenced by the cartoonists of the day, notably those whose work appeared in *Punch.* The continuity of this lifelong absorption is shown in his recent foreword to 'Trog's book',[2] and – for one reluctant to name names – an admiration for the work of Steve Bell: 'Wonderful! I wish they'd give him more space.'[3]

127 *Fungus the Bogeyman,* cover drawing, 1977

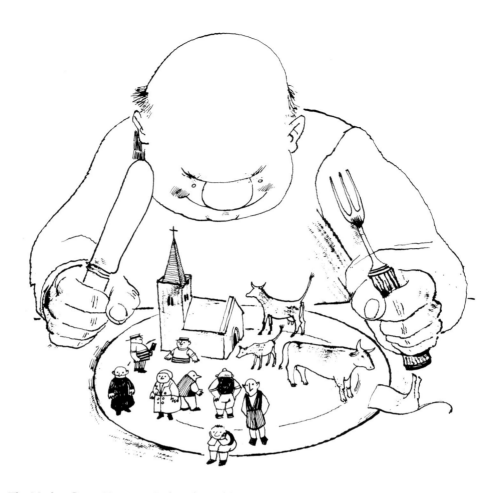

128 *The Mother Goose Treasury*, 'Robin the Bobbin', 1966

Briggs attended Wimbledon School of Art from 1949 to 1953, completing the NDD course in painting:

> We kept hearing rumours that the school was regarded almost as a joke outside because no-one did anything remotely modern. We were told that painting had stopped in about 1880 and that art had gone downhill from then on, culminating in the horrors of modern art. We were encouraged in the main to base ourselves on the Renaissance – Michelangelo, Piero della Francesca and people like that – a very old-fashioned, traditional training. It was actually jolly good for an illustrator. [4]

The years 1953–55 were spent in National Service, and although he was offered a choice between postings in Egypt or Germany, or Catterick, he derives amused satisfaction from having spent the whole time at Catterick: 'I'm a bit against travelling about – although I did go to Sark this year (1987) – that's abroad enough for me!'

He did some painting in the army; and when his *3am on the 'Catterick Flyer'* was shown at the Young Contemporaries, it attracted an enthusiastic and lengthy piece from John Berger within his review of the exhibition as a whole.[5]

> This gave me the idea that I was going to be a famous painter. I felt that if I can get that far on the strength of a painting done in the army, I'll go to the Slade and get two years experience there among all their sophisticated tutors and sophisticated students, and then I'll be alright. But I didn't achieve anything at the Slade at all.

He left the Slade School of Fine Art at twenty-three, convinced that he wasn't very good at painting and lacked a feeling for its media and procedures. But he did see that he had an ability to draw and paint from imagination and memory: '. . . which I hadn't thought about because at Wimbledon we considered that that was what *painting* was all about, but of course it wasn't. It is, however, what *illustration* is all about, and I realized that I had the knack for being able to do it, and should be doing it . . .'

In his first year as an illustrator he made contact with Hamish Hamilton, his publishers to this day.[6] The beginnings were unexceptional; illustrations to a half-dozen routine children's books in the 'Antelope' and 'Look Books' series. Briggs felt that he could do as well, and offered to write the stories. *Midnight Adventure* and *The Strange House* appeared in this way, and show him as a natural writer, well able to strike the reading tempo and interest of a specific age-group. This is fascinating, since – as his subject-matter has become deeper and more individual – he has often chosen to eliminate age and other categories from his thinking. These become matters for his publishers and critics to deliberate upon, whilst a large and motley audience discover the books for themselves.

In 1961 he became a part-time lecturer at Brighton College of Art, now a constituent college of Brighton Polytechnic, where he still teaches for one day each week. Property

129 *The Elephant and the Bad Baby*, 1969

130 *Jim and the Beanstalk,* 1970

in either London or Brighton fell beyond his combined income as illustrator, author and teacher at the time; and so he went for a while to 'somewhere in Burgess Hill, a not very thrilling town a little way away', before finding his present home which is isolated but seemingly sheltered behind the sweep of the South Downs. He married, in 1963, the painter Jean Taprell Clark, who died ten years later.

His next novel for young readers, *Sledges to the Rescue* – in which Tim and Mary help milkman Ernie on a snowy morning – is one in which he acknowledges a sentimentality which he has since striven to eliminate from his work. It also contains some fine drawing, including (in 1963) a figure who recurs at the close of *The Tin-Pot Foreign General* (1984), and who in the meantime has also put in appearances as *Gentleman Jim* and as the definitive Jim of *WTWB*. This is a figure of 'Everyman' which is based to some extent on his own father, just as there may well be an autobiographical element in his depiction of the quite different characters of *Fungus* and *Wally*.

Three short picture books of nursery rhymes date from the working years 1961 to 1963, of which the last, *Fee Fi Fo Fum,* may be regarded as a dry-run for the 897 illustrations to *The Mother Goose Treasury.* At a crucial point in his career as a children's book illustrator, Briggs must have viewed this material from the Peter and Iona Opie

132 *Gentleman Jim*, 1980

131 *Sledges to the Rescue*, 1963

133 *When the Wind Blows*, 1982

134 *The Tin-Pot Foreign General and the Old Iron Woman*, 1984

collections, upon which he had been encouraged to draw, as a plateau between illustrating other people's titles and defining some of the possible directions that his own future books might take.

The lasting success of *Mother Goose* is that it works for both children and parents as the finest modern illustrated compilation from traditional sources. As well as being a delight, it causes all parties to think. Briggs (who finds *Ring-a-Ring O'Roses*, his first essay in the genre, to be soft-centred), here deploys alienation-effects in a manner totally consonant with the origins and structure of his subject-matter:

> They [nursery rhymes] contain quite rude, quite tough, quite gutsy material
> about money and marriage and work and laziness and theft – not sweet
> innocent pink and blue baby stuff. [7]

Raymond Briggs has consistently refused to accept that young children lack the requisite open-mindedness and stamina to take in the realism of folk material and his own unsentimental gloss on it. He believes that they will take it in their stride and relish it, and that educational treason consists in adulterating or suppressing the message. If individuals of any age are not quite ready for the nuclear debate or other aspects of his subject matter, then no damage will be inflicted since they will simply avert their concentration for a time; it is, however, becoming apparent that many can identify with these issues much earlier than was previously supposed.

He was awarded his first Kate Greenaway Medal for *The Mother Goose Treasury* (1966), after which he did not attract much critical attention until *Father Christmas* appeared in 1973 to elicit a comparable response from the Greenaway judges, and unpredicted and unprecedented acclaim from the public at large.

However, he was far from inactive during these years; distinguished illustrative work continued to appear, and he became committed for a time to the 'Briggs Books' concept which Richard Hough (then his editor at Hamilton) had devised, and which featured the pioneers of navigation, aviation and motor racing.

It does appear that he was in greatest demand as an illustrator at just the point that he was beginning to call into question his own future role as an accompanist. Asked recently whether any circumstances might induce him to illustrate another person's words, he replied that he had in fact been invited by Kestrel to select any classic text that appealed to him for illustration and that the choice had momentarily fallen upon *Robinson Crusoe.* On reflection, he concluded that this would involve enormous labour on a book which already existed in hundreds of editions, and so the project was dropped.

Looking back to this time which fell between successes, one is acutely conscious of a man of immense talent approaching his fortieth year, and about to find a voice which was to reach out to address the nation and humanity – a remark which should be construed in the context of an earlier, unsententious tradition: one which Hogarth, Rowlandson, or Gillray – leaving aside artists of the nineteenth-century – would have seen as the aim and object of a suite of engravings, a caricature, or a cartoon strip for that matter.

Father Christmas and the seven books that have followed to date have to be marvelled at for their sheer diversity in terms of graphic and communicational technique, as well as for a thematic gamut that ranges from the innocence of *Snowman* to the black spread with which *WTWB* concludes. This makes it almost impossible to survey these eight titles collectively for most useful purposes; accordingly the author has become something of an enigma, presenting Fleet Street with a running challenge to get things wrong, frequently with Briggs's own passive encouragement.

But the present concern is with Briggs's artistic personality and intentions – about which he is himself very straightforward – as the following extracts in which he discusses the reception of various titles may make clear:

> I think that the people who hated *Wally* got the wrong idea, they couldn't see beyond the surface. I think that does happen with people – it happened with *Fungus* a bit, a lot of bad reviews – and they couldn't see that all the so-called nastiness is very much on the surface; and they couldn't see in *Father Christmas* that his grumpiness and so on was also on the surface and underneath all that he was fundamentally very warm, kindly, and all the things that Father Christmas is meant to be. The fact that when he looks at a tie he's been given, and says 'Blooming awful tie from Aunty Elsie!', then superficial people regarded that as curmudgeonly – Father Christmas must not be like that and so on – but his treatment of his cat and his dog, and his self-sufficiency and everything, show he has quite admirable qualities as well. It's the same with *Fungus* – there's all this repulsive slime and stuff – but that's not really the point. It's all to do with middle age, and struggling-on and all those Philip Larkin-ish kinds of preoccupation . . . a similar sort of subject-matter, I suppose.

The foregoing clues may point to an apprehension common to those in middle age, of being in the front line, and to the suggestion that *Fungus* and *Wally* are in part the autobiographical offspring of the same *malaise.* The book in prospect mentioned at the end of the following extract would strengthen this notion:

> I don't think it [*Unlucky Wally*] is particularly wonderful. It's just a bit ordinary really; nothing particularly original. I think *Fungus* and *Father Christmas* are slightly original. *WTWB* did something for strip cartoon, and the use of it in book design – having a blank spread for the explosion and so forth – this showed that strip cartoon could deal with a serious subject.
>
> I don't think that *Wally* is just a book full of fairly trivial things and faintly offensive details, I don't believe that it's that bad, but that there *is* a human figure beginning to emerge from it which I'm doing in a new book – which is

135 *Father Christmas*, 1973

136 *The Snowman*, 1978

what happens to him 20 years on, when he's over 50 – and that has something more serious to say . . .

Each of the strip cartoon titles have involved the artist in for up to twenty-four months' gestation and the sheer slog of producing the artwork to a detailed plan and holding the consistency of characterisation (in fact the artwork for *Father Christmas* occupied eighteen months, and that for *Fungus* a full two years). Allowing for the blank pages in *WTWB* (which have an immensely greater function than those in *Tristram Shandy* – their sole precursor in the history of book illustration), there are scarcely fewer than 600 frames. An examination of the publication pattern that emerges from Briggs's bibliography reveals the time taken up by drawing, media adaptation and promotion, in the non-publication years 1967, 1971, 1974, 1976, 1979, 1981, 1983, 1985 and 1988. Certainly the over-productivity of some illustrators may be self-defeating in marketing terms, and Briggs is very conscious of this danger. Although he might appear to be in the enviable position of devoting to each project the single-minded time and attention that it demands, I'm sure that in practice it doesn't work out quite like that:

137 *Unlucky Wally,* 1987

I couldn't in any case produce a book a year. I don't believe in churning out that number anyway, and the market probably wouldn't stand for it. And one does other things – I wrote *Gentleman Jim* for the Nottingham Playhouse, and I designed *Toad of Toad Hall* for the Northcott Theatre, Exeter. These call for quite a lot of work, which very few people inside or outside book publishing ever come to hear of.

It has to be remembered that the radio adaptation of *WTWB* was submitted to the BBC by Briggs as an unsolicited MS;[8] and that several other scripts of his have since arrived at Broadcasting House. Radio attracts him as a medium to write for, and he is undaunted by the failure so far of his serious work in this field to win acceptance. Media adaptation is a constant challenge; he is currently working on a 90-minute live action film version of *Fungus,* cheerfully accepting the fact that the book has no real story-line to provide a basic structure and that he'll need to rectify this deficiency.

The avoidance of compromise is an instinctive accomplishment; it is somehow accepted that Briggs's intention will prevail in the natural order of things, without hassle and without undue assertion on his part. It is as though an innate professionalism catches the media moguls – whether in film, radio or the theatre – completely off-guard; so that there can be no question of subverting or diluting Briggs' message. Facing the title-page of *WTWB* are eighteen statements from parliamentarians and the press. These represent the unorthodox residue of the celebrated publicity campaign to lobby each MP, each trade union leader and press commentator of significance – some 1,500 in all – with a free copy of the finished book.

A few years ago I saw Europe's first university professor of children's literature staggering under a pile of essays all on the theme of 'Depth psychology and *Where the Wild Things Are',* a sight that has stayed with me for some absurd reason; and no other book until *WTWB* can have generated such a secondary literature. Kilborn devotes an entire chapter to its use in the classroom,[9] newspaper indexes bulge with references; but its imagery has in any case already become part of the mass iconography of nuclear war, alongside the shadow sprayed on the sidewalk and the nightmare recall of Hiroshima:

> When I did the book I was not remotely a CND supporter. I simply thought it was a good subject. It is highly depressing and fairly political, and I could not even think who was going to buy it. But I never think of the potential audience when I embark on a book; this was not even done specifically for children.[10]
> . . . I expect accusations of exposing children to anti-nuclear propaganda to follow.[11]

It appears that Briggs was contemplating work on a further picture book along pacifist lines: *How Many Days has My Baby to Play?,*[12] but this would have been precisely at the time that the Falklands Adventure was being enacted, and this must have switched his attentions to *The Tin-Pot Foreign General and the Old Iron Woman*. There is a current of non-political humanism which the Thatcherite political establishment in Britain evidently can't brook, and Briggs won't easily be forgiven his clear-sightedness into what was actually taking place; for giving permanent visual form to the obscene but fleeting newsreel image: 'Later on, a boat came back to the Old Iron Woman's kingdom with a big iron box full of dead bodies'; for his invocation of Samuel Johnson's masterly dictum: 'Patriotism is the last refuge of a scoundrel'; and for his candour and compassion generally.

And yet this is the same man who gave all children *The Snowman*, whilst retreating grumpily to his greenhouse as it receives its annual Christmas airing on the box.[13] He also possesses a comic genius which I believe may eventually surface to greater effect in the sequel to *Unlucky Wally* than at any time since the two *Father Christmas* books. 'What sort of a person is he?' – A private man, whose communications with the outside world are universal and life-enhancing.

NOTES

1. Richard Kilborn, *The Multi-Media Melting Pot: Marketing 'When The Wind Blows'* (Comedia, 1986).
2. 'The greatest cartoonist of our time', from RB's preface to Frank Whitford, *Trog: Forty Graphic Years: The Work of Wally Fawkes* (Fourth Estate, 1987).
3. Kilborn, *Multi-Media Melting Pot*, 31.
4. Quotations, unless otherwise stated, are from author's interview with Raymond Briggs, Westmeston, Sussex, 25 November 1987.
5. John Berger, 'The reaction of the young contemporaries', *New Statesman* (29 January 1955), 156.
6. Hamish Hamilton published the paperback editions of *Fungus, Gentleman Jim* and *The Tin-Pot Foreign General*; but sold the rights of the *Father Christmas* titles, *The Snowman*, and *WTWB* to Penguin in the interests of the mass-marketing potential of the latter titles. (Hamilton was taken over by Penguin in 1985.)
7. Elaine Moss, 'Raymond Briggs: on British attitudes to the strip cartoon and children's book illustration', *Signal* (January 1979).
8. 'The script didn't need a lot of work on it ... it was extraordinary ... So together we worked on the reduction of the script [to an optimum 75-minute length] ... There was very little in the way of re-writing. Raymond's stage directions and sound directions were fine ... he'd auralized the thing perfectly.' John Tydeman (director), quoted in Kilborn, *Multi-Media Melting Pot*, 57. The radio play won the Broadcasting Press Guild's award for the most outstanding radio programme of 1983.
9. Kilborn, 'Learning from *WTWB*', in *Multi-Media Melting Pot*, 91–107.
10. *The Times*, 13 May 1982, 12a.
11. *The Times*, 23 November 1985, 22h (interviewed in connection with the animated film version).
12. *The Sunday Times*, 14 March 1982, 15.
13. 'Snowman's an island', *The Observer*, 13 December 1987, 16.

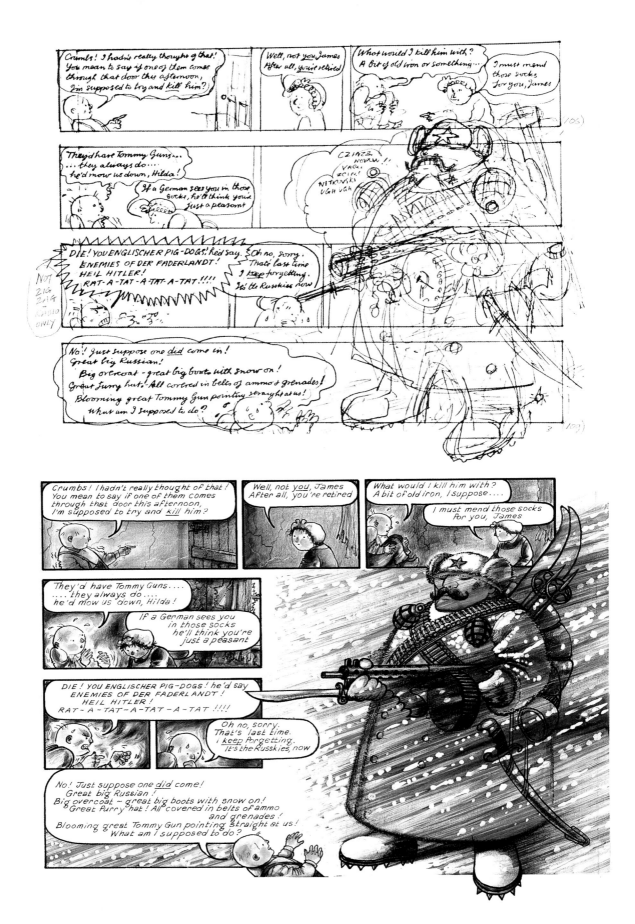

BIBLIOGRAPHY

1958

PETER AND THE PISKIES: CORNISH
    FOLK AND FAIRY TALES   Ruth Manning-
Sanders   OUP/Roy 1966
THE WONDERFUL CORNET   Barbara Ker
Wilson   Hamish Hamilton

1959

THE MISSING SCIENTIST   Sydney Frank
Stevens   OUP
THE ONION MAN   Alan Ross   Hamish
Hamilton
PETER'S BUSY DAY   Stephen Tring
Hamish Hamilton

1960

DANGER ON GLASS ISLAND   Alan Ross
Hamish Hamilton
LOOK AT CASTLES   Alfred Duggan
Hamish Hamilton

1961

LOOK AT CHURCHES   Alfred Duggan
Hamish Hamilton
MIDNIGHT ADVENTURE   Raymond Briggs
Hamish Hamilton
THE STRANGE HOUSE   Raymond Briggs
Hamish Hamilton

1962

THE FAIR TO MIDDLING   Arthur Calder-
Marshall   Penguin
RING-A-RING O'ROSES   Raymond Briggs
[ed.]   Hamish Hamilton/Coward

1963

SLEDGES TO THE RESCUE   Raymond Briggs
Hamish Hamilton
THE STUDY BOOK OF HOUSES
    Cliford Warburton   Bodley Head
THE WHITE LAND   Raymond Briggs [ed.]
Hamish Hamilton/Coward
WILLIAM'S WILD DAY OUT   Meriol Trevor
Hamish Hamilton

1964

FE FI FO FUM: A PICTURE BOOK OF
    NURSERY RHYMES   Raymond Briggs [ed.]
Hamish Hamilton/Coward
THE SWAN PRINCES   [unattributed text]
Nelson
WHISTLING RUFUS   William Mayne   Hamish
Hamilton/Dutton

1965

THE HAMISH HAMILTON BOOK OF
    MAGICAL BEASTS   Ruth Manning-Sanders
[ed.]   Hamish Hamilton/Nelson 1970 [as
    A BOOK OF MAGICAL BEASTS]
STEVIE   Elfrida Vipont   Hamish Hamilton
THE WRECK OF MONI   Alan Ross   Alan Ross

1966

THE FLYING 19   James Aldridge
Hamish Hamilton
THE MOTHER GOOSE TREASURY   Raymond
Briggs [ed.]   Hamish Hamilton/Coward
THE WAY OVER WINDLE   Mabel Esther
Allan   Methuen

1967 –

1968

THE CHRISTMAS BOOK   James Reeves [ed.]
Heinemann/Dutton
THE HAMISH HAMILTON BOOK OF GIANTS
    William Mayne [ed.]   Hamish
Hamilton/Dutton [as WILLIAM MAYNE'S
    BOOK OF GIANTS]
JIMMY MURPHY AND THE WHITE
    DUESENBERG   Bruce Carter   [a 'Briggs
Book']   Hamish Hamilton/Coward
LINDBERGH THE LONE FLIER   Nicholas Fisk
[a 'Briggs Book']   Hamish Hamilton/Coward
NUVOLARI AND THE ALFA ROMEO
    Bruce Carter   [a 'Briggs Book']   Hamish
Hamilton/Coward
POEMS FOR ME, BOOKS 4 & 5   Kit
Patrickson   Ginn
RICHTHOFEN THE RED BARON   Nicholas Fisk
[a 'Briggs Book']   Hamish Hamilton/Coward

138/139 *When the Wind Blows,* 1982: from pencilled rough to finished artwork

1969
THE ELEPHANT AND THE BAD BABY
Elfrida Vipont and Raymond Briggs
Hamish Hamilton/Coward
FIRST UP EVEREST   Showell Styles   [a 'Briggs
Book']   Hamish Hamilton/Coward
SHACKLETON'S EPIC VOYAGE   Michael
Brown   [a 'Briggs Book']
Hamish Hamilton/Coward
THIS LITTLE PUFFIN: FINGER PLAYS AND
NURSERY GAMES   Elizabeth Matterson [ed.]
[chapter head illustrations by Raymond
Briggs, decorations by David Woodroffe]
Penguin

1970
JIM AND THE BEANSTALK   Raymond Briggs
Hamish Hamilton/Coward
THE TALE OF THREE LANDLUBBERS
Ian Serraillier   Hamish Hamilton/Coward

1971 –

1972
THE FAIRY TALE TREASURY   Virginia
Haviland [ed.]   Hamish Hamilton/Coward
FESTIVALS   Ruth Manning-Sanders [ed.]
Heinemann/Dutton

1973
FATHER CHRISTMAS   Raymond Briggs
Hamish Hamilton/Coward
THE FORBIDDEN FOREST, AND OTHER
STORIES   James Reeves   Heinemann

1974 –

1975
FATHER CHRISTMAS GOES ON HOLIDAY
Raymond Briggs   Hamish Hamilton/Coward

1976 –

1977
FUNGUS THE BOGEYMAN   Raymond Briggs
Hamish Hamilton/Random House

1978
THE SNOWMAN   Raymond Briggs
Hamish Hamilton/Random House

1979 –

1980
GENTLEMAN JIM   Raymond Briggs
Hamish Hamilton

1981 –

1982
THE FUNGUS THE BOGEYMAN PLOP-UP
BOOK   Raymond Briggs
Hamish Hamilton
WHEN THE WIND BLOWS   Raymond Briggs
Hamish Hamilton/Schocken

1983
WHEN THE WIND BLOWS   [play, adapted by
Raymond Briggs, unillustrated]   French

1984
THE TIN-POT FOREIGN GENERAL AND THE
OLD IRON WOMAN   Raymond Briggs
Hamish Hamilton/Little, Brown

1985 –

1986
THE SNOWMAN POP-UP BOOK   [a pop-up
book with music]   Raymond Briggs with Ron
Van der Meer   Hamish Hamilton

1987
UNLUCKY WALLY   Raymond Briggs
Hamish Hamilton

1988 – *in preparation*
UNLUCKY WALLY TWENTY YEARS ON
Raymond Briggs   Hamish Hamilton

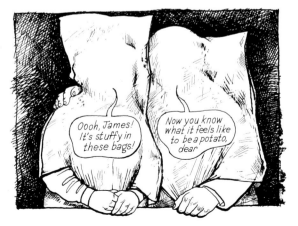

140   *When the Wind Blows*, radio play, 1983

13 · QUENTIN BLAKE

QUENTIN BLAKE'S is an apparently spontaneous art, but it springs from exacting working methods which few of his admirers will probably be aware of, though Mel Calman seized upon this particular paradox and analysed it brilliantly in his own case in *What Else Do You Do?* This art which conceals art has not prevented him from becoming a household name or from receiving the highest professional accolades,[1] but, in common with many book illustrators, surprisingly little critical attention has so far been paid to his work.[2]

Quentin Blake was born in 1932 at Sidcup in Kent and educated at Chislehurst & Sidcup Grammar School. There was nothing in his family background to predispose him towards drawing, but from about the age of nine or ten he became conscious that his natural instinct was developing strongly in that direction. An acquaintance who was a cartoonist explained how to go about submitting work to periodicals, and so from the age of fourteen he regularly sent things into *Punch* and after a couple of years the occasional small drawing met with acceptance. This continued throughout sixth form and National Service, but it was viewed as an avocation rather than a potential livelihood, although it may come as a surprise to learn that it was to take him some fifteen years from first being published as a cartoonist to effect the gradual transition into book illustration. He retains affinities and respect for the great band of British cartoonists and could easily have chosen to stay as one of their number: what appears to have happened instead is that he followed the path of English literature to a point where a possible synthesis between these two interests became apparent to him. The result is there to be seen in the mature work, which defies categorisation or comparison with the work of other illustrators, but exists as a deft, vital and original exploration of the interplay between words, ideas and images.

He acknowledges that he was taught well in literature and given an apposite pointer by a disciple of F. R. Leavis to Downing College, Cambridge, where he read English from 1953 to 1956. This laid a foundation which was to prove as pertinent to his subsequent achievement as his relatively brief formal artistic training. He trained as a

141   *The Boy Who Sprouted Antlers,* 1961

teacher at the London University Institute of Education (1956–57) and then held a post teaching English at the French Lycée in London for a short time: 'As soon as I saw that I could have become very involved in teaching as a career, then this was the time to decide not to pursue it further but to try my luck with illustration instead.'[3]

He sounded out Kenneth Bird[4] and others, and Chelsea School of Art commended itself to him because of the presence there of Brian Robb (1913–1979), the distinguished painter and illustrator. Quentin Blake enrolled for life classes for two days a week and found Robb's influence of tremendous importance both artistically and in his later career,[5] for after Robb became Head of Illustration at the Royal College of Art he offered his younger colleague, who was later to succeed him in that post, his first teaching appointment there.[6]

In these same years (1957–58) Quentin Blake struck up a working relationship as an illustrator with the *Spectator* which was to help him in his gradual drift away from cartooning in the direction of general illustration. He had already found through designing covers for *Punch* that he relished the visual challenge of producing more complex drawings that were not subject to the habitual constraints of the pocket cartoon.

> I experienced no pull between cartooning and illustrating because these developments took place in sequence. Initially it had proved possible to break into cartoons since up to a point your message can be conveyed with a minimum of drawing. Later I became bored with thinking of jokes and wanted my drawing to have greater depth and self-sufficiency. The cartoon approach simply faded out as part of a slow and natural process.

To transfer from one category of illustration to another, in this instance from journalism to book publishing, frequently involves a fresh beginning rather than the straightforward lateral move that might be anticipated. For this reason, Quentin Blake felt that he had to ask someone to write a book for him to illustrate since he simply didn't know how one made a start in this field, and that having an author solved the problem of how to find one – and in this way *A Drink of Water* came to appear as his first illustrated book and as the first of a long series of titles produced in collaboration with John Yeoman. *Come Here Till I Tell You* was a case of Patrick Campbell getting into print out of the pages of the *Spectator* with a collection in which the artist's original drawings were reproduced and for which he was asked to design a cover. Just as both these projects were about to be published, Brian Payne at Abelard-Schuman had the confidence and foresight to approach Blake with a commission for a children's book, Rosemary Weir's *Albert the Dragon*.

142 *My Son-in-Law the Hippopotamus*, 1962

From these beginnings publishing patterns can quickly be seen to emerge, notably that subsequent titles by these and future authors will find their way to Blake because he does such a splendid job and must clearly be a pleasure to work with, and also that: 'once the children's book bandwagon starts rolling, then nobody really believes you can do anything else.' And so there is evident a gentle acceptance of the reasons for which he has largely been typecast in the roles of humorist and children's book artist; and there is also, although he has been given much stimulating material to work with, an underlying disappointment that editors and art editors are not sometimes more adventurous. He would love to illustrate more classics and more books for adults generally.

> It might not work for the customers, but I don't think there is anything
> I wouldn't like to try. It is simply that one doesn't get asked, and I suppose
> that I regret not having suggested such things more often when the rare
> opportunities have presented themselves.

Many children's illustrators really prefer to evolve their own stories whenever possible, whereas Blake actually likes illustrating other people's texts, finding in them a potent stimulus to his way of working. He draws quickly but does not regard the total

143 *Listen and I'll Tell You*, 1962

144 *Uncle and the Treacle Trouble,* 1967

process as being quick. 'I like to work in a lot of rapid bursts, with much sitting about in between!' He likes to read and re-read, marking passages, and then to be able to leave the whole thing in a 'creative marinade' for a few days. Lots of rapid sequential drawings are generated at the rough stage, where instinct seeks out key situations and confrontations, most of which will survive in essence through to the finished drawing; at the same time problems of scale and sequence, breakdown into spreads and general layout are anticipated and largely resolved.[7]

When he is ready to execute the final drawing, a rough is placed beneath his drawing paper on a lightbox. This means that he doesn't have to worry about problems of content and compositional placing and can concentrate solely on the spontaneity of the line.

> Everything depends on the quality of the marks that are made – if these are not good the drawing will not work. I have to do it in a way that is in some respects similar to handwriting because this gives me the *accents* and it is not possible to put these in consciously. I've been told and recognise that there are resemblances to my actual handwriting, it skips about and makes the same sorts of mark.[8]

Quentin Blake believes that an artist learns through practice to cope with his own psychology, and to respect how the subconscious operates creatively whilst keeping a work discipline going: 'I can draw more cheerfully than I feel.'

In common with so many book artists, Blake draws analogies between the theatre and illustration as interpretative arts, but he places the emphasis not on direction or set design or ensemble as others have done, but on acting as being the more direct comparison. The text is the starting point to be studied closely in order to generate an individual performance; similarly his drawing aims to be dynamic and gestural in response to the unfolding action – in contrast to other, equally valid types of illustration which may be more passive or contemplative in intent. This view may serve to lead into a consideration of some of his best successes as well as to explain his yearning for some of the roles that have so far eluded him.

A glance at a list of the titles which Quentin Blake has illustrated reveals a further aspect of what Pevsner called 'the Englishness of English art'[9] (or literature for that matter); that is to say, the currents of observation which can be traced from the margins of illuminated manuscripts, and from Hogarth, as they flow into the mainstreams of later English satire, humour and eccentricity. The course of satirical caricature from Gillray to Gerald Scarfe and Ralph Steadman has frequently been plotted, but there is also a gentler stream which links Rowlandson to such present-day artists as Quentin Blake and John Lawrence and which is concerned with the observation of character without recourse to the cutting edge of the caricaturist school.

Blake's apolitical nature makes him a natural running mate for those whose patron saints are Lear and Carroll, the writers of humorous sense and nonsense at all levels, and the greatest number of the books which he has illustrated fall into this loosely defined category. There is an affinity between the drawings of Edward Lear and those of Quentin Blake which falls outside the accustomed pattern of stylistic similarities or influences; it is more that they share a sense of the absurd and an instinct for timing and, above all, that an equivalent mastery underlies the spontaneity and sparkle of their respective line techniques.

Quentin Blake has said that the selection of incidents and what he calls confrontations – the points at which illustrations should occur – is largely subjective and instinctive, and it can be shown that his procedures differ from those of most narrative illustrators by virtue of his stylistic individuality and creative intention. He has the quickest of minds and the readiest stylistic attack and so can go into action in situations which those with a more deliberate technique do well to avoid. It appears that he selects an instant in a developing situation and records it not as an arrested frame but in a way that engages the viewer in projecting the movement forwards in time; in a sense the focal point is frequently a little ahead of the drawing. All non-essentials are excised in the interests of making the situation plain and packing energy and movement into the figure drawing.

145 *The Birds*, 1971

Such footwork !

146 *Nonstop Nonsense,* 1977

His first commission from the Folio Society was for *The Hunting of the Snark* in 1976, and the volume which resulted is quintessential Blake. The Society's books frequently offer their illustrators a chance to stand aside a little from received commercial criteria, and this delightful book works because Blake's innately sophisticated approach to design is allowed to follow its course. 'It is the book as a whole which is the illustrator's canvas, and the placing on the page is as vital as timing is to verbal delivery.' The visual entrances and exits through printed binding cloth, preliminary and end pages, are superbly managed, as is the positioning of individual drawings in relation to text. The anticipatory reference to the Butcher and Beaver on the left page of the spread (pp.14−15) disguises the fact that text and illustration will terminate to great effect in the couplet which resolves 'Fit the First'. Blake believes that he has gained in insight through gradually changing his stance from one of initial willingness to leave the layout to the book designer to one of needing to control the detailed *mise-en-page* personally.

Four further books have followed for the Folio Society to date, widely separated in ambience and in the technical treatment they receive from the illustrator: Stella Gibbons's *Cold Comfort Farm*, Evelyn Waugh's *Black Mischief* and *Scoop*, and Orwell's *Animal Farm*. The tone of the first title elicits a virtuoso performance which is at the same time in line with the artist's accustomed wit and style, but it must have been difficult at the time to anticipate how he might tackle the others. The pigs in *Animal Farm* are recognisably his, but the expressions catch more than a dash of despondency − even pessimism − a quality not normally associated with his work but to be welcomed for the dimension it adds. Other titles that are of interest because they are slightly less humorous than usual include *The Adventures of Huckleberry Finn* and the French language edition of Patricia MacLachlan's *Sarah Plain and Tall*.

A more realistic, everyday style surfaces at times and may be seen as a response to the different problems posed in, say, Michael Rosen's off-beat books of poems for children; similar adjustments occur in the course of working for different publishers,

147 *The Twits*, 1980

each of whom regard him as a slightly different person. Earlier in his career, some editors had recourse to his talents for a handful of books on drab or serious topics that clearly cried out for the kind of light relief he could provide before he had fully emerged from his chrysalis as cartoonist turned illustrator.

The penalty for stylistic distinctiveness is sometimes to be thought guilty of sameness, but the assembled evidence does not point in that direction in Quentin Blake's case. Wit and invention are always sparklingly fresh, style of interpretation modulates from one author to the next, and his use of media is constantly varied to produce a range of line qualities and freely handled line and wash or watercolour effects. There are a number of repeated mannerisms or trademarks of a kind which follow from adopting such an autographic and quirky mode of address, and which will be noticed in any comparative review of the books, but these are not of a kind to obtrude in normal conditions of use.

As the number of volumes illustrated by Quentin Blake rapidly nears the 200 mark, it is surprising to reflect that this output has been achieved against a background of teaching, administrative and other outside commitments which frequently left only half the week free for drawing. With so many titles it helps to be able to trace a pattern of long-standing partnerships, where only the conjoint activity of author and artist allows characters and situations to enjoy a full existence. Everyone will have their favourites from among the *Agaton Sax, Arabel* and *Uncle* series, and the many titles produced in collaboration with such writers as Patrick Campbell, Roald Dahl, Michael Rosen and – over the longest time of all – with John Yeoman.

Joan Aiken's *Arabel* stories were written for children's television and Quentin Blake produced brilliantly successful caption drawings for the first nine of these, but he eventually tired of the sheer volume of work entailed and the ephemeral nature of television as contrasted with books and gave it up; however, the omnibus books based on this series are happily still in circulation many years later.

An illustrator frequently has to adapt to a pre-existing text and Blake finds it challenging to locate the optimum wavelengths for writers as individualistic as Dahl, Russell Hoban, and Rosen; and this he did nowhere more triumphantly for this particular trio than in Dahl's *The Giraffe and the Pelly and Me,* Hoban's *How Tom Beat Captain Najork and His Hired Sportsmen* (Whitbread Award 1974), and Rosen's *Mind Your Own Business.* In contrast the books produced with John Yeoman seem to be based on a closer affinity of style and intention. *Rumbelow's Dance* is a cumulative story delivered at Quentin Blake's pace and angled to his particular strengths and here, as in the felicitous *Mouse Trouble,* John Yeoman has provided splendidly crafted picture book texts. Another option open to the illustrator is to anthologise favourite material as he feels inclined – in contrast to his professional obligation to attend promptly to newly commissioned titles – and in this way Quentin Blake has made a selection from Ogden Nash (*Custard and Company*) and chosen apt verses from the vast Opie collection for his own *Nursery Rhyme Book.*

Quentin Blake is oddly diffident about the books for which he has supplied his own texts, although these clearly demanded a lot of careful work. Most began with an idea that generated a visual narrative to which he later added words. He was pleased that the pictorial structure of his first book, *Patrick,* proved so sound that when it came to making an animated film it was possible to leave out the words and use a violin accompaniment as soundtrack.

The Kate Greenaway Medal awarded to *Mister Magnolia* in 1980 recognised Blake's distinctive contribution through his own picture books, and the three titles he has since published show an augmentation of his inventiveness in developing stories in a way that is only possible given an integrated starting point – where words and images can play leapfrog in a fertile mind. The visual pace and energy in the earlier books lead the reader's attention forward from beginning to end, at times with such momentum that they carry the words along with them like a string of railway coaches. This provides a marvellous inducement to read or listen to the stories, as well as for the storyteller to make adventurous use of subject-matter and its presentation; but there is the attendant

148 *Quick, Let's get out of Here,* 1983

danger – which is fundamental to the case-bound picture book format – that everything may be over too quickly in terms of apparent length. There are a number of ways around this problem and the one which Blake chooses is the masterly control of pace. In *The Story of the Dancing Frog,* the central character can leap, almost literally, from page to page for sure-fire continuity, whereas the unnamed mother can recall episodes at a more leisurely tempo as flashbacks; pictures and words can be made to freeze-frame, leaving the development in time, back and forth from a set tableau, to the child's imaginings. This is storytelling and illustrative book designing at its most accomplished: the observer's eye follows as bidden, oblivious to the means deployed.

Mrs Armitage on Wheels uses the time-honoured device of cumulative additions to punctuate the progress of the scatty lady, her bike and her dog, which (after the fashion of 'This is the House that Jack Built'), lets the reader move back and forth between what is happening at each stage and what has gone before: the way the book ends by starting afresh (this time with roller skates) poises the reader on the edge of yet a further cycle of development, another movement, this time into the future.

The most recent of this group of picture books, *Our Village,* is one of the most interesting yet, since it lets us see the development of the structure beneath the surface. A bird's eye plan of the village and where its inhabitants live appears on the front endpapers, and again as the back endpapers – but this time at night. This simple device frames the story, which in pictures and John Yeoman's verses moves at a gentle pace, with occasional bursts of excitement, from dawn to dusk and from spring to winter.

Although all Quentin Blake's illustration is characterised by an abundance of humour and vitality, lightness of handling should not be equated with slightness in substance. His technical means are always adequate for what he has to say, and however much this may astonish us in terms of range, dexterity and unpredictability, it is invariably pertinent to the text. It must have taken initial courage to decide to draw in so direct a manner – where in a sense there is nothing to hide behind if inspiration flags – and to seek for applications in areas of publishing where on the face of it the chances of success looked the most precarious. As he stated in an earlier interview: 'If they like it, I'll do it. If they don't, I'll give up.'[10] Needless to say, they did. His inimitable style qualifies this widely gifted artist to illuminate fresh aspects of adult literature and the classics in the future as well as continuing to delight children of all ages with the witty and sparkling line which he has made his own.

149 *Mortimer Says Nothing*, 1985

NOTES

1. He was elected a Royal Designer for Industry in 1981, awarded an OBE, and in 1988 appointed a senior fellow of the Royal College of Art.
2. Quentin Blake's own book about his work is in preparation and will be published by Jonathan Cape. A further interesting text in preparation (by Chris Powling, for Ginn) takes Quentin Blake as its subject and covers some of the same ground, adapted for younger readers, in a thematic series *'What it is like to be an . . . illustrator'*.
3. Extracts have been adapted from a conversation recorded in London on 8 December 1988.
4. Cartoonist, working as 'Fougasse', art editor and for a time editor of *Punch*.
5. Quentin Blake makes a useful distinction between the influence of other artists on style and their influence by example; on the first count he finds that there are far too many influences not to result in an individual synthesis but acknowledges the considerable impression made by the achievement of André François at the time he set out on his own career. The exuberant and wicked pen line of that artist was only approached in the early 1950s by Searle and Steinberg, giving the trio an unprecedented following in art schools and universities. Brian Robb's influence of example was also to be a major one, and it is a pity that there is so little of this fine illustrator's work in circulation owing to the vagaries of publishing and the fate of most of the titles he was asked to illustrate. There are interesting parallels to Blake's line in the work of a number of European and American cartoonists and illustrators, though these are superficial resemblances in terms of brilliance of attack and the intentions can rarely be equated.
6. Quentin Blake has taught at the RCA from 1965 onwards, becoming Head of the Illustration Department in 1978. He relinquished the running of the department in 1986 but continues as a visiting tutor. On his influence as a teacher of illustration see Christopher Frayling, *The Royal College of Art: 150 Years of Art & Design* (Barrie & Jenkins, 1987), 191.
7. Quentin Blake discusses his own working approach in 'Research from an illustrator's point of view', *Research in Illustration: Conference Proceedings Part II* (Brighton Polytechnic, 1981), 25–61.
8. The kinship of draughtsmanship and handwriting is usefully explored in Dietrich Mahlow, *Schrift und Bild* (Frankfurt: Typos Verlag, 1963). Other research in the mid-1960s by Prof. Dr Hans A. Halbey was the subject of a lecture at the Klingspor Museum, Offenbach, at which slides of minute near-abstract background details from the work of Rembrandt, Van Gogh, and Carlfriedrich Claus among others were projected at colossal enlargement for identification and analysis – a technique which offers scope for further extension in the study of book illustration.
9. Nikolaus Pevsner, *The Englishness of English Art: an expanded and annotated version of the Reith Lectures broadcast in 1955* (Architectural Press, 1956), 20–7, 33–41 (plates) and *passim*.
10. With Elaine Moss for *Signal* in 1979.

BIBLIOGRAPHY

1960

COME HERE TILL I TELL YOU Patrick Campbell Hutchinson

A DRINK OF WATER, AND OTHER STORIES John Yeoman Faber

1961

ALBERT THE DRAGON Rosemary Weir Abelard-Schuman

THE BOYS' COUNTRY BOOK John Moore [ed.] Collins

THE BOY WHO SPROUTED ANTLERS John Yeoman Faber

GOOD MORNING, MISS DOVE Frances Gray Patton Penguin

THE WONDERFUL BUTTON Evan Hunter Abelard-Schuman

1962

CONSTANTLY IN PURSUIT Patrick Campbell Hutchinson

LISTEN AND I'LL TELL YOU Edward Korel Blackie/Ryerson

MY SON-IN-LAW THE HIPPOPOTAMUS 'Ezo' Abelard-Schuman

PUNKY, MOUSE FOR A DAY John Moreton Faber

1963

BREWING UP IN THE BASEMENT Patrick Campbell Hutchinson

HOW TO BECOME A SCRATCH GOLFER Patrick Campbell Blond/Norton

TALES OF A WICKED UNCLE Rupert Croft-Cooke Cape

1964

FURTHER ADVENTURES OF ALBERT THE DRAGON Rosemary Weir Abelard-Schuman

GARDENERS' QUESTION TIME F. Loads, A. Gemmell and B. Sowerbutts BBC Publications

THE GENTLE KNIGHT Richard Schickel Abelard-Schuman

LUCY Joan Tate Heinemann Educational

THE NEXT-DOORS Joan Tate Heinemann Educational

THE OXFORD BOOKS OF STORIES FOR JUNIORS (3 vols., 1964-66) James Britton [ed.] OUP

RIDDLES, RIDDLES EVERYWHERE Ennis Rees Abelard-Schuman

UNCLE J. P. Martin Cape/Coward

1965

AGATON SAX AND THE DIAMOND THIEVES Nils-Olof Franzén Deutsch

APHRODISIACS IN YOUR GARDEN Charles Connell Barker/Taplinger

MOTORING AND THE MOTORIST Bill Hartley with Roy McCarthy BBC Publications

THE P-P-PENGUIN PATRICK CAMPBELL Kaye Webb [ed.] Penguin

PUN FUN Ennis Rees Abelard-Schuman

ROUGH HUSBANDRY Patrick Campbell Hutchinson/Norton

UNCLE CLEANS UP J. P. Martin Cape/Coward

1966

ARISTIDE Robert Tibber Hutchinson/Dial

AROUND THE WORLD IN EIGHTY DAYS Jules Verne [ed. John Webber] Chatto & Windus

GARDENERS' QUESTION TIME, 2nd series F. Loads, A. Gemmell and B. Sowerbutts BBC Publications

HOME ECONOMICS Beryl Ruth Heinemann

UNCLE AND HIS DETECTIVE J. P. Martin Cape

1967

BITS AND PIECES Joan Tate Heinemann

GIVE A DOG A GOOD NAME Marjorie and Antony Bilbow Hutchinson

LIVING WITH TECHNOLOGY H. P. Rickman Hodder & Stoughton

LUKE'S GARDEN Joan Tate Heinemann

PUZZLES FOR PLEASURE AND LEISURE Thomas L. Hirsch Abelard-Schuman

TINY TALL TALES Ennis Rees Abelard-Schuman

UNCLE AND THE TREACLE TROUBLE J. P. Martin Cape

1968

ALBERT THE DRAGON AND THE CENTAUR
Rosemary Weir   Abelard-Schuman
THE ENERGY MEN   Miles Tomalin [chapter
openings by QB]   Hodder & Stoughton
PATRICK   Quentin Blake   Cape/Walck
PUT ON YOUR THINKING CAP   Helen Jill
Fletcher   Abelard-Schuman
SUCCESS WITH ENGLISH:
THE PENGUIN COURSE   [Stages 1-3:
Coursebooks, Teacher's Handbooks
1968-71]   Geoffrey Broughton [ed.]   Penguin
THOUGHTS AND APHORISMS FROM THE
FRUITS OF MEDITATION OF KOZMA
PRUTKOV   [16pp, chiefly illustration, date
uncertain]   Royal College of Art

1969

AGATON SAX AND THE SCOTLAND YARD
MYSTERY   Nils-Olof Franzén   Deutsch/
Delacorte
ALPHABET SOUP   John Yeoman   Faber/Follett
A BAND OF ANGELS   Drawings by Quentin
Blake   Gordon Fraser
THE BEAR'S WINTER HOUSE   John Yeoman
Blackie/World
THE FIRST ELEPHANT COMES TO IRELAND
Nathan Zimelman   Follett [USA]
GILLYGALOOS AND GOLLYWHOPPERS
Ennis Rees   Abelard-Schuman
GINGER MICK   Joan Tate   Almqvist & Wiksell
[Sweden]
JACK AND NANCY   Quentin Blake   Cape
MR HORROX AND THE GRATCH
James Reeves   Abelard-Schuman
UNCLE AND CLAUDIUS THE CAMEL
J. P. Martin   Cape
YOUR ANIMAL POEMS   Quentin Blake
Gordon Fraser

1970

AGATON SAX AND THE MAX BROTHERS
Nils-Olof Franzén   Deutsch/Delacorte
ANGELO   Quentin Blake   Cape
THE BEAR'S WATER PICNIC   John Yeoman
Blackie/Macmillan
THE BIRTHDAY PARTY   D. Mackay *et al.*
Longman for the Schools Council
DOCTORS AND NURSES   D. Mackay *et al.*
Longman for the Schools Council
THE GOOD TIGER   Elizabeth Bowen   Cape

HOGMANAY AND TIFFANY   Gillian Edwards
Bles
KIBBY'S BIG FEAT   Thomas I. Corddry
Follett [USA]
'QUOTE AND UNQUOTE'   Peter and Josie
Holton [eds.]   Arcadia Press

1971

AGATON SAX AND THE CRIMINAL DOUBLES
Nils-Olof Franzén   Deutsch
THE AGES OF MAN: FROM SAV-AGE
TO SEW-AGE   Marcus Cunliffe
American Heritage Press [USA]
THE BIRDS   Aristophanes [tr. Dudley Fitts]
Lion & Unicorn Press
MY FRIEND MR LEAKEY   J. B. S. Haldane
Penguin
PLAY SCHOOL PLAY IDEAS   Ruth Craft
BBC Publications
PUZZLES AND QUIZZLES   Helen Jill Fletcher
Abelard-Schuman
SIXES AND SEVENS   John Yeoman
Blackie/Macmillan
THE WITCH'S CAT   Harwood Thompson
Blackie/Addison-Wesley 1975

1972

AGATON SAX AND THE COLOSSUS OF
RHODES   Nils-Olof Franzén   Deutsch
HOME   Joan Tate   Almqvist & Wiksell [Sweden]
MCBROOM'S WONDERFUL ONE-ACRE FARM
Sid Fleischman   Chatto & Windus
MOUSE TROUBLE   John Yeoman
Hamilton/Collier 1976
PIGEON OF PARIS   Natalie Savage Carlson
Blackie
THE READER'S DIGEST TREASURY OF
AMERICAN HUMOR   American Heritage
Press [USA]

151 *The Witches*, 1983

1973

AGATON SAX AND THE LONDON
    COMPUTER PLOT   Nils-Olof Franzén
    Deutsch
EATING   Frances Knowles and Brian Thompson
    Longman for the Schools Council
MONSTER BOOKS   [*Monster on the Bus,
    Monster Cleans His House, Monster Comes to
    the City, Monster Goes to School, Monster Goes
    to the Museum, Monster Goes to the Zoo,
    Monster Has a Party, Monster Looks for
    a Friend, Monster Looks for a House, Monster
    and the Magic Umbrella, Monster Meets Lady
    Monster, Monster at School*]   Ellen Blance and
    Ann Cook   Longman/Bowmar
SNUFF   Quentin Blake   Cape/Lippincott
UNCLE AND THE BATTLE FOR
    BADGERTOWN   J. P. Martin   Cape
WIZARDS ARE A NUISANCE   Norman Hunter
    BBC Publications

1974

AGATON SAX AND THE LEAGUE OF SILENT
    EXPLODERS   Nils-Olof Franzén   Deutsch
THE ARMADA LION BOOK OF YOUNG
    VERSE   Julia Watson [ed.]   Armada
BEATRICE AND VANESSA   John Yeoman
    Hamish Hamilton/Macmillan
GREAT DAY FOR UP!   Dr Seuss
    Random House [USA]/Collins
GRIMBLE, and GRIMBLE AT CHRISTMAS
    Clement Freud   Puffin
HOW TOM BEAT CAPTAIN NAJORK AND
    HIS HIRED SPORTSMEN   Russell Hoban
    Cape/Atheneum
MIND YOUR OWN BUSINESS   Michael Rosen
    Deutsch/Phillips
THE PUFFIN JOKE BOOK   Bronnie
    Cunningham [ed.]   Puffin
TALES OF ARABEL'S RAVEN   [*Arabel's Raven,
    The Breadbin, The Escaped Black Mamba*]
    Joan Aiken   [these stories were first read on
    Jackanory and published individually as BBC
    paperbacks from 1972 onwards; they were
    brought together in this hardback volume and
    further similar collections are listed for 1980,
    1983 and 1985]   Cape and BBC
    Publications/Doubleday

1975

AGATON SAX AND THE HAUNTED HOUSE
    Nils-Olof Franzén   Deutsch
THE INCREDIBLE KIDNAPPING   Willis Hall
    Heinemann
KIDNAPPED AT CHRISTMAS   [a play]
    Willis Hall   French
LESTER AT THE SEASIDE   Quentin Blake
    Collins
LESTER AND THE UNUSUAL PET
    Quentin Blake   Collins
A NEAR THING FOR CAPTAIN NAJORK
    Russell Hoban   Cape/Atheneum
ONE HUNDRED AND ONE BLACK CATS
    Stephen Mooser   Scholastic [USA]
THE PUFFIN BOOK OF IMPROBABLE
    RECORDS   Quentin Blake and John Yeoman
    Puffin/Atheneum   [as THE IMPROBABLE
    BOOK OF RECORDS]

1976

AGATON SAX AND THE BIG RIG   Nils-Olof
    Franzén   Deutsch
THE BED BOOK   Sylvia Plath   Faber
HERE COMES MCBROOM!   Sid Fleischman
    Chatto & Windus
HORSESHOE HARRY AND THE WHALE
    Adèle de Leeuw
    Parents' Magazine Press [USA]/Dobson 1979
THE HUNTING OF THE SNARK
    Lewis Carroll   Folio
THE WORRIED GHOST   Seymour Reit
    Scholastic [USA]

152 *The Adventures of Huckleberry Finn*, 1983

153 *Our Village,* 'Mr Crumb the Baker', 1988

154 *The Story of the Dancing Frog,* 1984

1977

THE ADVENTURES OF LESTER
Quentin Blake   BBC Publications
COLD COMFORT FARM   Stella Gibbons   Folio
MONSTER BOOKS   [*Lady Monster and the Bike
Ride, Lady Monster Has a Plan, Lady Monster
Helps Out, Monster Buys a Pet, Monster Gets
a Job, Monster Goes Around the Town, Monster
Goes to the Beach, Monster Goes to the Circus,
Monster Goes to the Hospital, Monster and
the Mural, Monster and the Surprise Cookie,
Monster and the Toy Sale*]   Ellen Blance and
Ann Cook   Longman/Bowmar
NONSTOP NONSENSE   Margaret Mahy   Dent
OF QUARKS, QUASARS, AND OTHER
QUIRKS   Sara Brewton [ed.]   Crowell [USA]
PLAY SCHOOL IDEAS 2   Carole Ward [ed.]
BBC Publications
WILLIE THE SQUOWSE   Ted Allan
Cape/Hastings House
WOULDN'T YOU LIKE TO KNOW
Michael Rosen   Deutsch
THE YOUNG PERFORMING HORSE
John Yeoman   Hamish Hamilton/
Parents' Magazine Press

1978

AGATON SAX AND LISPINGTON'S
GRANDFATHER CLOCK   Nils-Olof Franzén
Deutsch
THE ENORMOUS CROCODILE   Roald Dahl
Cape/Knopf
FUNNY BUSINESS   Bronnie Cunningham
[ed.]   Puffin
THE GREAT PIRATICAL RUMBUSTIFICATION,
with THE LIBRARIAN AND THE ROBBERS
Margaret Mahy   Dent

1979

THE BAKERLOO FLEA   Michael Rosen
Longman
CUSTARD AND COMPANY   Ogden Nash
Kestrel/Little, Brown
A FEAST OF TRUE FANDANGLES   Patrick
Campbell   W. H. Allen
THE TRUE HISTORY OF SIR THOMAS
THUMB   anon.   Holp Shuppan, Tokyo
[published in Japanese only]
THE WILD WASHERWOMEN   John Yeoman
Hamish Hamilton/Greenwillow

1980

ACE DRAGON LTD   Russell Hoban   Cape
ARABEL AND MORTIMER   [*Mortimer and the
Sword Excalibur, Mortimer's Tie, The Spiral
Stair*]   Joan Aiken   Cape and BBC
Publications/Doubleday
BLACK MISCHIEF   Evelyn Waugh   Folio
MISTER MAGNOLIA   Quentin Blake   Cape
THE TWENTY-ELEPHANT RESTAURANT
Russell Hoban   Cape
THE TWITS   Roald Dahl   Cape/Knopf
WHAT DIFFERENCE DOES IT MAKE,
DANNY?   Helen Young   Deutsch

1981

CYRIL BONHAMY V MADAM BIG
Jonathan Gathorne-Hardy   Cape
GEORGE'S MARVELLOUS MEDICINE
Roald Dahl   Cape/Knopf
MCBROOM AND THE GREAT RACE
Sid Fleischman   Chatto & Windus
LES TRUCS DU DÉTECTIVE ET DE L'AGENT
SECRET   Georges Berton
Editions Brissonières, Gallimard [France]
UP WITH SKOOL!: CHILDREN'S OWN
CHOICE OF THE BEST SCHOOL JOKES
Tony Lacey [ed.]   Puffin
YOU CAN'T CATCH ME!   Michael Rosen
Deutsch

1982

THE BFG   Roald Dahl   Cape/Farrar, Straus
JOSEPH AND THE AMAZING TECHNICOLOR
DREAMCOAT   Tim Rice and Andrew Lloyd
Webber   Pavilion/Holt, Rinehart
ROALD DAHL'S REVOLTING RHYMES
Roald Dahl   Cape/Knopf
RUMBELOW'S DANCE   John Yeoman
Hamish Hamilton
SCOOP   Evelyn Waugh   Folio

1983

THE ADVENTURES OF HUCKLEBERRY FINN
Mark Twain   Puffin's Choice/Puffin
CYRIL BONHAMY AND THE GREAT DRAIN
ROBBERY   Jonathan Gathorne-Hardy   Cape
DIRTY BEASTS   Roald Dahl   Cape/Knopf
MORTIMER'S CROSS   [*Mortimer's Cross,
Mortimer's Portrait on Glass, The Mystery of
Mr Jones's Disappearing Taxi*]   Joan Aiken
Cape and BBC Publications/Harper & Row

QUENTIN BLAKE'S NURSERY RHYME BOOK
Quentin Blake   Cape/Harper & Row
QUICK, LET'S GET OUT OF HERE
Michael Rosen   Deutsch
THE WITCHES   Roald Dahl   Cape/Farrar,
Straus

1984

ANIMAL FARM   George Orwell   Folio
CRASH! THE WALDO AND WANDA BOOK
OF PRACTICAL HINTS   John Yeoman [ed.]
Magnet
CYRIL BONHAMY AND OPERATION PING
Jonathan Gathorne-Hardy   Cape
THE HERMIT AND THE BEAR   John Yeoman
Deutsch
HOW THE CAMEL GOT HIS HUMP
Rudyard Kipling   Macmillan/Bedrick
THE STORY OF THE DANCING FROG
Quentin Blake   Cape/Knopf

1985

DON'T PUT MUSTARD IN THE CUSTARD
Michael Rosen   Deutsch
THE GIRAFFE AND THE PELLY AND ME
Roald Dahl   Cape
A LAMP FOR THE LAMBCHOPS   Jeff Brown
Methuen
MORTIMER SAYS NOTHING   [*A Call at the
Joneses', Arabel's Birthday, Mr Jones's Rest
Cure, Mortimer Says Nothing*]   Joan Aiken
[illustrated for this collection only; no
drawings were made to accompany the
televised storytellings as hitherto]
Cape/Harper & Row

1986

ASK DR PETE   Peter Rowan   Cape/Messner
[as CAN YOU GET WARTS FROM
TOUCHING TOADS?: ASK DR PETE]
FRANKIE'S HAT   Jan Mark   [jacket and 3 half-
title drawings only]   Viking Kestrel
THE MARZIPAN PIG   Russell Hoban
Cape/Farrar, Straus
THE RAIN DOOR   Russell Hoban   Gollancz
SCRAPBOOKS   [*Smelly Jelly Smelly Fish, Under
the Bed*]   Michael Rosen and Quentin Blake
Walker/Prentice-Hall

1987

THE CAMPBELL COMPANION   Patrick
Campbell [ed. Ulick O'Connor]   Pavilion
CYRIL OF THE APES   Jonathan
Gathorne-Hardy   Cape
MRS ARMITAGE ON WHEELS   Quentin Blake
Cape/Knopf
SARAH LA PAS BELLE   Patricia MacLachlan
Folio Cadet, Gallimard [France]
SCRAPBOOKS   [*Hard-boiled Legs,
Spollyollydiddlytiddlyitis*]   Michael Rosen
and Quentin Blake   Walker/Prentice-Hall

1988

MATILDA   Roald Dahl   Cape/Viking
OUR VILLAGE   John Yeoman   Walker/
Atheneum

in preparation

MONSTERS   Russell Hoban   Gollancz
OLD MOTHER HUBBARD'S DOG   [*Needs a
Doctor, Learns to Play, Dresses Up, Takes Up
Sport*]   John Yeoman   Walker
QUENTIN BLAKE'S ABC   Cape
RHYME STEW   Roald Dahl   Cape

155   *The Hermit and the Bear*, 1984

14 · JANET & ALLAN AHLBERG

THIS IS THE STORY of the two-headed illustrator, although in reality one draws and the other doesn't. Although it might prove productive under certain circumstances to study just one half of a creative partnership, it is more customary to view it as a whole, and, since this book is about book illustrators, it may be best for this purpose to regard Allan Ahlberg as an honorary illustrator.

156 Drawing by Janet Ahlberg, aged about seven

157 *Burglar Bill,* 1977

The story concerns the genesis, design and illustration of picture books, but goes on to look at the question of how far it is possible for the originators themselves to monitor the detail of mass production to ensure the effective communication of their vision. It concludes by examining the extensions of this where Allan Ahlberg works with other illustrators for some of his picture books, novels and tales in verse.

Janet Hall was born in Huddersfield in 1944 but spent her childhood in Leicester. She attended Sunderland Teacher Training College from 1963 to 1966 – time spent discovering that she had no vocation for conjoining the talents of actress and policewoman as classroom teaching appeared to demand, but also time in which her sights could be gradually realigned towards art under the guidance of Charles Bray, a fine lecturer who encouraged her to paint and to draw, though with no thoughts as yet of illustration.

Allan Ahlberg was born in Croydon in 1938, grew up in the Black Country, and filled the years between the ages of eighteen and twenty-five variously as publishers' packager, conscripted army private, postman, gravedigger, plumber's mate and trainee time study engineer – in fact, all the occupations which are regarded as *de rigueur* for an author (although in common with Thurber he missed out on being a truck driver). He then determined to become a teacher, and loved and was obsessed by that career until the time came that 'as my teacher's train was slowing down, it was lucky for me that the writer's train came into the station and I was able to jump on it.' It was the chance outcome of several course applications that brought him to the Sunderland Teacher Training College in the same years as Janet.

He was to teach in primary schools on and off for the next ten years until he was able to launch his career as a writer, taking classes as young as five years old, which was still unusual for a man at that time – though in fact he never did become the headmaster his blurb-writers have seized upon: that episode has been enlarged from a term's temporary headship of a village school with all of thirty-eight pupils and one other teacher. He went to work in Leicestershire in the first place because of the prevailing conditions created by that county's progressive plan for schools – and also, of course, Janet was at college there; and, after spells in London and Oxfordshire, he returned to Leicestershire to teach.

On completing her course at Sunderland, Janet went back to Leicester since it was her home base and enrolled at the Polytechnic for a further three years, where she studied for Dip AD within the framework of a graphic design course which admitted a certain illustrative content whilst discouraging any form of specialisation. 'When producing specimen illustrations, then any texts issued as part of a project brief were there simply as a vehicle to hang nice pictures on. It was only much later that I realised that a book was quite a different thing, and that words and pictures both mattered profoundly in their interrelatedness.' [1]

André Amstutz was one of the visiting lecturers at Leicester at that time. His early style as an advertising and poster artist had considerable vigour and clarity; several of the students loved his work and were directly influenced by it for a time. He was to become a lasting friend of the Ahlbergs, and an artistic collaborator as his personal interests turned increasingly towards book illustration. Another influential tutor was David Howells, a calligrapher who imparted an abiding love of letter forms to any student sensible enough to listen. The fact that Janet habitually weighs up the possibility of a hand-lettered alternative to typeset titling, and has the confidence to use her own handwriting where appropriate (as in *The Jolly Postman*), can be traced back to his teaching.

On completing her studies, Janet Ahlberg (for by that time she and Allan were married) placed her portfolio with a London artist's agent as an initial step, being prepared to take on commissions from whatever source – whether advertising or publishing – they might arrive.

Both Ahlbergs regard their earlier involvement with teaching as a coincidence which is largely irrelevant to the fact that their joint work was to be with books for children, although such experience could hardly fail to be turned to good account. As Allan Ahlberg remarks: 'It just so happens that children read picture books. If, in our culture, old age pensioners read them – our work might have gone in another direction.'

Janet Ahlberg's very first book illustrations were for *Night,* in the 'Starter' series published by Macdonald, and they both found the arrival of finished copies of this special baby to be an unforgettable experience – never quite matched by the receipt of proofs or early copies of any of their later books. This was because, whatever its merits, it gave them (and Allan had not even been directly involved in this commission), the beginnings of thoughts about the book as a physical object, and of possible ways in which the picture book might evolve. If the first stage of the picture book revolution had consisted largely in revelling in the exuberance of colour which modern graphic processes could unleash, then future phases might explore the chamber music as contrasted to the symphonic aspect: a quieter interplay between words and pictures, a more intimate tone of voice?

The basis for Janet's professional practice when she began as an illustrator was located on the faultline that runs between educational and children's publishing; it would have been all too easy to note her earlier teacher training and the clarity and directness of her graphic exposition, and to see its application in the publishing of high quality visual aids material. This could have happened if commissions of the kind she initially received (for classroom arithmetic and crafts) had been admitted as more than a temporary foundation. She must have foreseen that danger and thought about ways

158 *The Vanishment of Thomas Tull,* 1977

159 *Each Peach Pear Plum,* 1978

of circumventing it, in the knowledge that at the same time Allan was undergoing a similar experience in attempting to exchange one creative activity for another. It was to take several years before they eventually found a way out of this impasse.

Allan Ahlberg had wanted to write more than anything else since the age of eleven or twelve, but apart from the usual school stuff, he felt that he couldn't make the necessary breakthrough.

> In my teens and 20s I would occasionally write a paragraph – which was about the most I ever managed – and so it went on until my mid-30s when one day Janet said: 'Could you write me a picture book? I'm getting all these books from publishers about how to make things out of yogurt pots, I'm sick of them!' And so I wrote a story, and it was as though someone had turned a key in my back. I was off, and have been writing children's stories ever since. I do have ideas for adult things, but usually they don't work. Whereas you could lock me in a room and I could give you a children's story a day with no trouble.

For a period of some eighteen months all their efforts went into one picture book proposal after another, but each submission to a publishing house was countered by a rejection slip – scores of them! They ran out of money and Allan Ahlberg had to return to teaching. Had they got things wildly wrong, or was the time-lag before they would be taken seriously just part of the common experience? They examined the current stock in bookshops and libraries in search of an answer: 'What sustained us was that there were usually plenty of poor books to be found; and we always had the idea that we could do better.'

The tide turned as soon as Collins accepted the concept for the *Brick Street Boys* series, and books for various publishers followed in rapid succession. *Jeremiah in the Dark Woods,* and *Each Peach Pear Plum* (awarded the Kate Greenaway Medal for 1978), represent high points achieved after relatively few years in professional practice. There is great fluency and distinction in Janet's work dating from these years, and this is unquestionably sustained through *Peepo!, The Baby's Catalogue,* and other more recent titles. In the best of the *Jeremiah* pictures, though, I think it not unreasonable to see a springboard from which to project the possible development of this illustrator's art along slightly different lines – towards a minority appeal, towards surrealism and closer affinities with international trends. This course (which might have brought the illustrator's name into greater prominence in art circles at an earlier date) was never adopted, since an independent path lay ahead.

By the early 1980s the Ahlbergs had found new ways of associating words and images which resulted from using numerous spot and marginal drawings in contrast to a sequence of full pages and spreads. These little drawings are ingeniously threaded through or clustered around a concisely tailored text, with the result that the 'mind's eye' is made to work hard without knowing it. The words in any case are calculated to trigger independent visual images. The reader's eye flits to Janet's tiny vignettes and

Daisychains

WHICH WITCH?

Janet & Allan Ahlberg

If you meet a witch,
    Don't scream and run;
Whatever she does
    It's only in fun.

If she turns you
    Into a frog – don't croak!
She's only teasing;
    It's only a joke.

If she sends you to sleep
    For a year or more,
Don't bat an eyelid,
    Just smile – and snore!

If she pops you
    Into a pot – keep calm.
Don't get in a stew,
    She means no harm.

But – if she pulls out a bib
    And cries, "Yum, yum!"
Then scream the place down
    And run home to mum.

160 *Which Witch?,* 1983

MR BIFF THE BOXER
Mr Biff trains for the big fight; his wife and children are trainer and sparring partners.
Meanwhile Mr Bop the other boxer is being trained by his family. The fight: Ding, ding! Round 1, 2 etc Mr Biff biffs Mr Bop. Mr Bop bops Mr Biff. They Biff and Bop each other out; a draw. Both families repair to Mr Wobble's cafe for friendly slap-up feed.
BIFF V BOP
Grand Charity Match
MR BIFF
V
MR BOP
In aid of the old boxers benevolent fund
Mrs Biff makes an embroidered silk dressing gown with Biff on the back.
Mr Biff has retired.
He comes back for a charity match
He needs toughening up.
shopping
full coal scuttle
They accustom him to blows to the head and body.
He runs paced by the children on a tandem bicycle. The dog runs too, snapping at his heels.
Mrs Biff
Mr Biff
Miss Biff
Master Biff
They put him on a diet and hide his beer, fags and slippers.
salt
mustard
vinegar
pepper
The champ
parrot
Ding ding
Seconds out!

161 *Mr Biff the Boxer,* the idea in words and pictures, 1980

and are teaming up with other specialists (such as paper engineers in the design of ingenious pop-up and other novelty books); but on the other hand there are a number of well-known illustrators who prefer to do their own book design or evolve it with the help of other freelance designer colleagues within production guidelines agreed with the publisher.

The Ahlbergs thrive on working in this way: the making of books is for them an integrated and indivisible activity, embracing writing, illustration, designing and using available technology creatively. However wide the circle of people involved from creative inception to production line, there must be a shared aim which leaves no place for conflicting views or compromise. They would doubtless regard the proliferation of the novelty book in some of its more baroque forms as a danger, but their own uses have been restrained and individual, ranging from *Peepo!* (1981) where each alternate illustration-free leaf has had a circle punched out so that it frames unexpected details of the larger illustrations on adjacent pages, to *The Jolly Postman* (1986) with its chain of letters that can be removed from their envelopes.

Once the line of a story or poem is established, then it is necessary to project it through to the point of reception, at the intended level of communication, and to visualise the way in which the book will feel and look as a manufactured physical object – but one with a certain personality and capacity to surprise or delight. The complex processes involved in this transfer of ideas into reality are such that extreme care has to be taken at all stages to ensure that nothing goes wrong *en route.* This might be as elementary as failing to get the cover titling exactly right – it could involve bad shrink-wrapping spoiling the look of the whole job at the last moment – any one of a thousand tiny factors might operate. Concern at all levels over the smallest particulars of design and production will reduce the risk of any such errors assuming significance for the general reader, and it is through this belief in co-operation rather than in any spirit of mistrust that the Ahlbergs have made it part of their working agreement with their publishers that nothing happens to their books without consultation. [5]

Both Janet and Allan Ahlberg agree on the need to be sure where the verbal/visual balance for a given title or series is heading at the earliest possible stage; this is where the first of Janet's miniature pencil dummies may come in to take over from Allan's schematic storyboard. At first glance her drawing may appear tentative and insubstantial, but in most cases it will prove a firm blueprint and be found to correspond to the finished page layout in most essentials. This is because the problems will have been ironed out in discussion, and the whole process of illustration anticipated with creative sensitivity and forethought. What lies ahead is the realisation of every detail in the drawing, the typesetting and paste-up stages, through to the final

162 *The Clothes Horse,* 1987

camera-ready artwork for each page — all constructed with the same meticulous attention.

In many cases, work of this kind is batted to and fro between the artist and a distant publisher's studio; communication is difficult and aims and levels of skill vary. For informational books in series the process can be streamlined and made to yield consistent results, but it simply can't be made to work for material as varied and personal as the Ahlbergs. The delight and charm of *The Jolly Postman* is that it looks to the child as though it came together on the kitchen table of two very clever artists who were enjoying themselves. The technical problems in manufacture were formidable but so well handled, by Robert Aspinall at Heinemann and by Wing King Tong (the printers in Hong Kong), that finished copies matched the authors' hopes and intentions.

Janet and Allan Ahlberg went on to design *The Clothes Horse* together, a book of short stories with full-colour illustration, which is both a fluent and brilliant performance within its 32-page compass and a pointer which, taken alongside the renewed interest which they have expressed in cartoon strip technique, may indicate that further innovatory developments are in the offing.

The idea for *Starting School* (1988) grew out of a duplicated booklet which they had drafted with a member of staff for use in the families of children about to start at the school which their own daughter, Jessica, already attended. This friendly induction to the routine of the school day was produced on the school's 'jumbo' typewriter and had exactly the right look for the job with its basic letterforms, extra wide spacing between letters and general unevenness. Clearly this typewriter was too primitive to be pressed into service again for the published version, and it is characteristic that absolutely every alternative should have been explored in order to recapture the intended effect. Janet made several trials at a style of handwriting that would be clear and unmannered enough for this now quite lengthy text, trials were run on other makes of typewriter, stencils were tried, specimen typesettings essayed, but in the end all of it was 'Letraset' by hand — a saga far removed from normal conceptions of the work of book illustrator or typographer.

Allan Ahlberg has a superb eye for what a collaboration with a chosen illustrator ought to yield, and knows those specific points in his own writing on which an experienced illustrator's eye will light. This first becomes apparent at the level of his series of readers entitled 'Happy Families'. Many early primers and readers had colourfulness, vigour and quirkiness despite the fact that these have always been utility productions, but a period of particularly bad neglect set in shortly after the Great War and lasted until comparatively recently when writers and artists of talent saw the potential scope offered by these poor relations of the expensive picture book. If restricted and structured vocabulary resulted in trite or dispirited stories and routine illustration the fault rested clearly with the makers; these books could and should be immense fun.

Not knowing how big the 'Happy Families' series might grow, it was Janet's idea that variety would be created by spreading the titles between different illustrators.

Janet Ahlberg, André Amstutz and Joe Wright each undertook two titles in the first series; André Amstutz, Faith Jaques and Colin McNaughton two titles each for the next; and André Amstutz, Faith Jaques, Colin McNaughton and Fritz Wegner a title apiece in the most recent series. Most of these artists have partnered Allan Ahlberg on other projects and he clearly values the unique character of each individual's style. The unity of the series is ensured by the way in which the author briefs through his initial text, listing objects and planting speech balloons in the knowledge of the kinds of response they are likely to receive from each individual illustrator. His plan for the 24-page books follows logically from the way the text has been made to fall, and so no artist could feel that he was being over-directed.

Each of Allan Ahlberg's later series of readers has been undertaken with a single illustrator. This change in approach allows a batch of titles to be tackled as a single project, with the advantages this brings in simplifying production and in allowing the series concept to be explored in greater depth by both participants.

Moving away from the problems which are unique to picture books into other categories, such as the novel or poetry collection for young readers, the author should rightly expect to exercise less influence on the way the illustrator goes about his or her own work, but of course it helps if illustrator and author have a mutual respect for each other's work and a willingness to co-operate (though where the author is visually unenlightened, it is undoubtedly for the best that an editor and/or art editor should provide a communication line).

Most authors would admit to writing first and foremost for themselves, but to feeling disconsolate if a hoped-for market or following fails to materialize. Allan Ahlberg wrote his story in verse, *A Pair of Sinners,* without giving any thought as to how it might be illustrated. As a poem it is lengthy but for book publication on its own it is really too short. He discussed it with John Lawrence, who devised and engraved illustrations and decorative borders on wood which succeed in augmenting the extent of the poem by at least 200 per cent without overpowering it. The result is a delightful collector's piece which, perhaps inevitably, failed to reach a children's audience in that form.

Some years later Allan Ahlberg had written four longer poems with diverse subject matter ready for publication as *The Mighty Slide,* and once again the problem of illustration had not been confronted in the course of literary composition.[6] This is perfectly understandable in that he had discovered his abilities in a new field of authorship, but fascinating in that it shows a reversal of his habitual approach to visual matters. He felt the only thing to be done was to approach an illustrator he had never worked with before and to offer an open brief and see what happened. Charlotte Voake agreed to illustrate *The Mighty Slide,* and the approach she adopted was to prepare a generous sheaf of pencil studies of characters, scenes, situations, suggestions for part-titles and for spreads. It was an approach based on alternatives made possible by her talent for looking at the problems posed by these contrasted stories from all sorts of angles and noting all her findings down at lightning speed. There was full agreement about which compositions to choose, the roughs were sized and pasted with a proof of the text into a dummy, and only at that stage was the author able to make a full assessment. Both author and artist were delighted to find that everything had fallen into place, and very few changes indeed were needed before the final artwork could go ahead.

During these exciting post-war decades, writers have perhaps been more fortunate in their contacts with children's book illustrators than some of them have appreciated. One could be forgiven for thinking that many authors have often had little idea of what was taking place, or to what extent the appeal of their books was actually being enhanced by the illustrator's contribution – a concept with which even Public Lending Right was initially slow to come to terms. But despite a much greater awareness of this contribution, true author/illustrator partnerships – of any conceivable configuration – are still comparatively rare: it is, perhaps, more usual for an illustrator to become his own author and write his or her own texts.[7] It is even more unusual for such a partnership to evolve and grow as Janet and Allan Ahlberg's has done, never repeating itself and with each partner stimulating the other to fresh discoveries and levels of achievement.

NOTES

1. Extracts, unless otherwise attributed, are from a discussion recorded in Oadby, Leicester, on 9 December 1987.
2. Ludwig Mies van der Rohe (1886–1969), German architect, emigrated to America in the 1930s.
3. After the sub-title of Hugh Williamson's classic, *Methods of Book Design: The Practice of an Industrial Craft* (3rd edn, Yale UP, 1983).
4. '. . . A general comment on publishing – I do the words, Janet does the pictures, together we design the book – but we only got involved in the *manufacture* of books, because we had to. The end product is a printed, bound object – we needed, gradually, to get control of the making of that object – not for the sake of having control – but in order simply to make our books. We needed good paper, good printing, good boards etc. – only because our publishers could not give us all that we asked for, did we get involved. Also note – it seems to me that there is an inevitable tension/tug of war between authors and publishers. We want

William Morris books at Penguin prices! It can't be done – disagreements are inevitable. But, really we regret all this – we would much rather sit at home, do the words and the pictures, and leave the making of the book to other people.' Letter from Allan Ahlberg, dated 26 March 1988.
5. 'A final thought about our relationship with publishers – by all means record that we do quarrel/conflict with our publishers – it's true and they know it – but would like to include also reference to the fact that they are our allies in making the books – after ourselves, they are the people who care most about making each book.' *ibid.*
6. *A Pair of Sinners* had gone out of print in the interim and so was added to this group of longer poems to which in a sense it belongs.
7. And here the hidden partner is frequently an unacknowledged editor talented enough to enable the illustrator – whose primary language is by nature a visual one – to achieve expression through the medium of words.

163 *The Jolly Postman,* postcard, 1986

BIBLIOGRAPHY

1972

LUCKY CHARMS   S. M. Lane, M. Kemp and Janet Ahlberg   Blackie

MY GROWING UP BOOK   Bernard Garfinkle and Janet Ahlberg   BMG Productions Inc.

NIGHT   ill. Janet Ahlberg   Macdonald

PROVIDENCE STREET   Ivy Eastwick and Janet Ahlberg   Blackie

1973

TOYSHOP MATHS   Leslie Foster [ed.] and Janet Ahlberg   Macdonald

1974

THINGS TO MAKE FROM CARD   Felicia Law and Janet Ahlberg   Collins

THINGS TO MAKE FROM JUNK   Felicia Law and Janet Ahlberg   Collins

1975

THE BRICK STREET BOYS   [*A Place to Play, Here are the Brick Street Boys, Sam the Referee*] Allan and Janet Ahlberg   Collins

1976

THE BRICK STREET BOYS   [*Fred's Dream, The Great Marathon Football Match*] Allan and Janet Ahlberg   Collins

THE OLD JOKE BOOK   Janet and Allan Ahlberg   Penguin/Viking

1977

BURGLAR BILL   Janet and Allan Ahlberg   Heinemann/Greenwillow

JEREMIAH IN THE DARK WOODS   Janet and Allan Ahlberg   Kestrel/Viking

THE VANISHMENT OF THOMAS TULL   Janet and Allan Ahlberg   A & C Black/Scribner

1978

COPS & ROBBERS   Janet and Allan Ahlberg   Heinemann/Greenwillow

EACH PEACH PEAR PLUM   Janet and Allan Ahlberg   Kestrel/Viking

1979

THE LITTLE WORM BOOK   Janet and Allan Ahlberg   Granada/Viking

SON OF A GUN   Janet and Allan Ahlberg   Heinemann

TWO HEADS   [*The One and Only Two Heads, Two Wheels, Two Heads*]   Janet and Allan Ahlberg   Collins

1980

FUNNYBONES Janet and Allan Ahlberg
Heinemann/Greenwillow

HAPPY FAMILIES [*Master Salt the Sailor's Son*
ill. André Amstutz; *Miss Jump the Jockey* ill.
André Amstutz; *Mr Biff the Boxer* ill. Janet
Ahlberg; *Mr Cosmo the Conjuror* ill. Joe
Wright; *Mrs Plug the Plumber* ill. Joe Wright;
Mrs Wobble the Waitress ill. Janet Ahlberg]
Allan Ahlberg Kestrel and Puffin/Golden
Press [as WACKY FAMILIES]

A PAIR OF SINNERS Allan Ahlberg and John
Lawrence Granada

1981

HAPPY FAMILIES [*Master Money the
Millionaire* ill. André Amstutz; *Miss Brick the
Builder's Baby* ill. Colin McNaughton; *Mr Buzz
the Beeman* ill. Faith Jaques; *Mr and Mrs Hay
the Horse* ill. Colin McNaughton; *Mrs Lather's
Laundry* ill. André Amstutz; *Mr Tick the
Teacher* ill. Faith Jaques] Allan Ahlberg
Kestrel and Puffin/Golden Press [as WACKY
FAMILIES]

PEEPO! Janet and Allan Ahlberg
Viking Kestrel [in USA as PEEK-A-BO!]

1982

THE BABY'S CATALOGUE Janet and Allan
Ahlberg Kestrel/Little, Brown

HELP YOUR CHILD TO READ [*Bad Bear,
Double Ducks, Fast Frog, Poorly Pig, Rubber
Rabbit, Silly Sheep*] Allan Ahlberg and
Eric Hill Granada

THE HA HA BONK BOOK Janet and Alan
Ahlberg Penguin

1983

DAISYCHAINS [*Ready, Teddy, Go!, Summer
Snowmen, That's My Baby, Which Witch?*]
Janet and Allan Ahlberg Heinemann

HELP YOUR CHILD TO READ [*Hip- Hippo-
Ray, King Kangaroo, Mister Wolf, Spider Spy,
Tell-Tale Tiger, Travelling Moose*]
Allan Ahlberg and André Amstutz Granada

PLEASE MRS BUTLER Allan Ahlberg and
Fritz Wegner Kestrel

TEN IN A BED Allan Ahlberg and André
Amstutz Granada

1984

DAISYCHAINS [*Clowning About, The Good Old
Dolls, Monster Munch, Rent-a-Robot*]
Janet and Allan Ahlberg and André Amstutz
Heinemann

FOLDAWAYS [*Circus, Families, Monsters, Zoo*]
Allan Ahlberg and Colin McNaughton
Granada

SLOT BOOKS [*Playmates, Yum, Yum*]
Janet and Allan Ahlberg Viking Kestrel

1985

DAISYCHAINS [*One True Santa*]
Janet and Allan Ahlberg Heinemann

RED NOSE READERS [*Bear's Birthday, Big Bad
Pig, Fee Fi Fo Fum, Happy Worm, Help!,
Jumping, Make a Face, So Can I,*]
Allan Ahlberg and Colin McNaughton
Walker/Random House

1986

THE CINDERELLA SHOW Janet and Allan
Ahlberg Viking Kestrel

THE JOLLY POSTMAN Janet and Allan Ahlberg
Heinemann/Little, Brown

RED NOSE READERS [*Blow Me Down, Crash!
Bang! Wallop!, Look Out for the Seals, One,
Two, Flea!, Me and My Friend, Push the Dog,
Shirley's Shops, Tell Us a Story*]
Allan Ahlberg and Colin McNaughton
Walker/Random House

WOOF! Allan Ahlberg and Fritz Wegner
Viking Kestrel

1987

THE CLOTHES HORSE AND OTHER STORIES
Janet and Allan Ahlberg Viking Kestrel

1988

THE MIGHTY SLIDE Allan Ahlberg and
Charlotte Voake Viking Kestrel

STARTING SCHOOL Janet and Allan Ahlberg
Viking Kestrel

HAPPY FAMILIES [*Master Bun the Baker's Boy*
ill. Fritz Wegner; *Miss Dose the Doctors'
Daughter* ill. Faith Jaques; *Mr Creep the Crook*
ill. André Amstutz; *Mrs Jolly's Joke Shop* ill.
Colin McNaughton] Allan Ahlberg
Viking Kestrel

15 · ANTHONY BROWNE

ANTHONY BROWNE is an extraordinary observer, a surrealist, a maker of images which ensnare the viewer. He is also a masterly constructor of picture books, who keeps a wealth of mood and detail under the control of a unifying plan.

Take *Hansel and Gretel,* an early book for him, but still one of his finest. He has seized upon the theme of encagement, emphasised by the device of prison bar verticals echoed through and through the design, indoors and out. These are at times explicitly stated, at others hidden away. A single landscape with rainbow escapes towards the end of the book in order to to modify the rules of the game. Each drawing – full-page or spot – exists within its own squarish box or frame. This funnels mind and eye to the interior of each drawing, where the illustrator's compositional skills detain both. The text, in consequence, tends to be rather up-staged for many readers on their first aquaintance with some of the early books where the visual storytelling is so compelling; but these are books to live with in any case, and so to return to them can only enlarge one's experience. 'One of the reasons I use surrealism is because I'm very bored with books which you read just once, and in which you're unable to find anything extra on subsequent readings.'[1]

Some 'hyper-realist' illustrators are prisoners of their own technical virtuosity, and children find much of their artwork bland and unstimulating. Certainly, this could never be said of Anthony Browne's work; and it is equally fascinating to study his developing approach to the balance between text and illustration, and the progress he has made in little more than a decade as a book illustrator. The brilliance and maturity of his first children's book is only to be explained in the light of experiences gained as an illustrator working in very contrasting fields over the several years leading up to his change of vocation.

Anthony Browne was born in Sheffield in 1946, but the family moved shortly afterward to the village of Hipperholme near Halifax. His father died suddenly in 1963, a traumatic experience which may have had a causative bearing on his later

development of an ability to face the realities of shape and form in human strength and
frailty, and a wish to create a balanced pictorial world for the young. This achievement
rests on a brilliant but hard-won synthesis: Browne never seeks to impose a dark view
of human experience, but on the contrary has mastered the optimistic surface quality
which characterises the seaside postcard. It is a mask, of course, and we are allowed to
see it move; but this stratagem had not been evolved at the time of *Hansel and Gretel* –
which to adult tastes especially remains in mood and colour a sombre, wistful, but

164 *Look What I've Got*, 1980   165 (facing) *Hansel and Gretel*, 1981

challenging performance. The danger of a drift towards gloom and nostalgia may have prompted the subsequent revision of his colour palette in the child's favour.

In the year 1963–64 Anthony Browne attended the foundation course at Leeds College of Art. This was run by Harry Thubron, and all accounts place it in a pioneering and influential role by any standards at that time. Anthony found it an education in itself, but the following three years of Dip AD studies at Leeds were not to be such happy ones. A great divide existed between the fine art and graphic design courses, and he had opted for the latter; considering that – although his primary abilities were painting and drawing – graphics might fit him to earn a living. The course was advertising-orientated, and he hated it. The revival of interest in illustration in the colleges had not yet taken place, and would-be illustrators were regarded as second-class citizens. The life class was the only bright spot, and he found the influence of the painter Derek Hyatt very beneficial.

A period of unemployment followed college, until by chance he came to hear of a course in medical illustration offered periodically at St Bartholomew's Hospital in London. And so: 'I dissected some rats, I'd been to the butcher's and I'd painted rabbits' legs and I knew that what I'd done was good and felt really confident. I was shattered to learn that I hadn't been accepted.'[2] But a telephone call from a consultant at Manchester Royal Infirmary, who had been on the interviewing panel, led to two and a half years' work there: 'I like drawing the insides of peoples' bodies as well as the outsides.'

Photography is no substitute for analytic drawing in the operating theatre (and sometimes the mortuary as well) in recording and presenting new techniques for books, papers or slides. In his two extant anatomy lesson paintings,[3] Rembrandt virtually created a new genre; but the work of today's medical illustrators has no artistic significance beyond its scientific and humanitarian *raison d'être*. Anthony Browne was apparently happy in this work; but a fear of total anonymity, of producing endless drawings that no one for a moment would ever regard as drawings, drove him to seek a change. And yet this spell of exacting anatomical draughtsmanship brought a hidden bonus, for without it I doubt that we should have *Gorilla* or *Willy* as they are. But the change, when it came, was to be an unfortunate one: an entanglement with the advertising world which exceeded his worst apprehensions, and which he prefers to forget.

The next turn in events brought Anthony Browne into the 'smile-please!' world of greetings cards, in which he was to become highly successful. 'No-one wants to send someone a miserable-looking greeting.' Every quality children's book publisher flinches at the sight of a greetings-card artist's portfolio: normally the engrained sentimentality and superficiality is there for keeps. Anthony Browne is one exception, Jan Pieńkowski is another: what they have in common is that each is an innovator at the quality end of the greetings market; and both had thought out their respective motivations and the forms that their contribution to the children's book world would take. Both also found for themselves perceptive publishers.

Hamish Hamilton's was one of the addresses suggested by Gordon Fraser to Browne when the time came that he was in danger of over-producing cards and his thoughts were turning in the direction of picture books, and it was there that he met Julia MacRae. Her authors and illustrators all enjoy a sense of freedom and tremendous support for getting on with their own thing, and welcome the accord as a personal and creative one as well as a business relationship. Julia was Anthony's editor for several years at Hamilton; and when she left to found her own independent imprint he was fortunate enough to find himself with two excellent publishers in place of one.

So far Anthony Browne's artistic career may appear to have been a mass of astounding contradictions, but a unifying factor is present: surrealism. By the time he came to book illustration he was in command of what Koestler regarded as the essential prerequisite for making anything from a new joke to a scientific breakthrough: the ability to cause interaction between sets which are not normally brought into juxtaposition.[4] This could also serve as a definition of surrealism.

> It's a part of not losing that visual openness that kids have . . . surrealism
> corresponds to a childlike view of the world, in that everything can be made
> new by putting unrelated objects together.

Browne's artistic enthusiasms range from René Magritte to Francis Bacon, taking in a great deal on the way. If there is a single focus, as I believe there to be, it is in the persistence of an image, the physical or imagined time taken to view it, and the ineradicable place it can establish for itself in the memory cells. One passes through the magic mirror *alias* looking-glass, and emerges slightly altered. As an illustration of this, Magritte's depiction of a locomotive emerging from a fireplace will serve as well as Holman Hunt's 'The Light of the World' – which is visually quoted on p.3 of *Hansel and Gretel.* These are 'time-freeze' pictures which trap attention within the volume and limits of their own frames.

It is exciting to observe that the whole action of *Hansel and Gretel* takes place within such confined boxes; and that the effect of cutting away these backgrounds is to liberate the movement of characters in *Gorilla, Willy,* and subsequent titles. They can now take a walk across the pages, and the storyteller's technical and expressive resources have been augmented and enhanced.

Anthony Browne discovered *Alice,* one of the surrealists' favourite books, when he was nine years old; some thirty years later he was to re-illustrate it. He read *Through the Looking Glass* much later, in his college days, and with a greater detachment from Tenniel's contribution:

> When I'm doing children's books, I try to remember the child I was and to
> make the kinds of book that I would have *liked* to have seen as a child. At
> present I tell myself I'll see through my own children's eyes the things I can't

remember. I can't remember what it was like to have been two and three or four and what sorts of book I would have liked then. I'm still waiting for changes in my work as they grow older, but perhaps not too much importance should be attached to this . . .

The nostalgia many illustrators and others express for vintage children's books is not particularly shared by Browne, a firm believer in books for our own age: 'The only time it did happen was in *Hansel and Gretel* – which the critics thought had been brought up-to-date – but, if I'm honest, it's actually set in my own childhood in the 1950s, rather than in the 1970s or 1980s.'

166 *Gorilla*, 1983

167 (facing) *The Visitors Who Came to Stay*, 1984

Asked whether the illustration of any particular adult title or classic might appeal to him in the right circumstances, his response was that: 'I would be very wary of it. I can't imagine many adult novels that would be improved by illustration.' The Grimm and Carroll projects had attracted him for a very long time, but apart from that he had always produced his own texts, aspiring to reach Maurice Sendak's level: 'where the words are as good as the pictures'. And so there seemed little prospect that any other contemporary writer would even get a look into his idiosyncratic, frequently dark but always humane world, let alone be able to make a creative partnership. That is why the two titles that he has produced with Annalena McAfee came as a surprise and a delight, as opening up new possibilities for development. The story of *The Visitors Who Came to Stay*, which was awarded the Deutscher Jugend Literaturpreis in 1985, may have helped him to break new ground whilst retaining established elements of his style almost in the form of self-quotations; this becomes apparent if his development from one key book to the next is considered in sequence. [5]

The picture book pioneers concede that it was all much easier for them a quarter of a century or more ago, when it was still possible to stake out a vast territory and cultivate it relatively free from rivalry and competition. Each successive influx of illustrators must have found the search for land of their own more taxing, and the constant need to extend and cultivate it intensively more imperative. Inevitably, many names spring to mind of illustrators who burst on this scene with an interesting first book or new theme, and then failed to live up to their early promise. Anthony Browne is among the most interesting of the exceptions to this rule.

There are three things to date which he does supremely well: the characterisation of his inimitable gorilla; the atmosphere he conveys through colour mood in certain settings, whether of enveloping woods or interiors or distanced townscape; and the undercurrent of pop culture which elides from the everyday into the surreal world of the comic paper and seaside postcard. *Gorilla* (which received both the Kate Greenaway and Emil/Kurt Maschler Awards in 1983) has already achieved classic status – a paid-up member of the exclusive club of immortal anthropomorphics. Despite successful prefigurations in the earlier books (notably in *Look What I've Got*) and greetings cards, and later in junior guise (as *Willy the Wimp*), the need to create fresh characters must have become apparent to the artist, and in *Piggybook* he shows himself entirely capable of doing this.

Hansel and Gretel (a Kate Greenaway commended book for 1981), has already been mentioned as a sustained composition in an integrated style which is dominated by the motif of confinement, and which, although some claim to find the imagery sad and gloomy, is nevertheless an illustrative view fully consonant with the text. It is clear where Anthony Browne lets one aspect of his complex artistic personality take the initiative, as here in *Hansel and Gretel*, and where he is prepared to allow incongruous elements to co-exist, held in balance through the purest surrealism, as in the case of *The Visitors Who Came to Stay*.

168 *Trail of Stones*, in preparation, 'The Seventh Dwarf'

Anthony Browne's pictures contain such an inexhaustible blend of puzzlement and precision, jokes and hidden references, invention and reality, that descriptive analysis is ultimately unrewarding and the best thing to do is to return to them frequently and with enjoyment. Equally, the question of artistic progress from book to book in terms of either technique or content seems less important than in the case of some other illustrators, since he came into the field already well equipped, both technically and intellectually, to cope with any imbalances left over from his earlier experiences; indeed, much of the vitality in his artwork is generated through this interplay of experiences.

Is there a swing between blackness and happiness from book to book, and sometimes even within the same book? Decidedly so, but then the unaccountable darkness of the Grimms' material,[6] the gruesomeness of *Struwwelpeter* and the quirkiness of Carroll are facts of children's literature – and life. Doubtless nineteenth-century educationists erected these pre-Freudian lightning conductors with benevolent intent, and it may not be unfair to see the best aspects of this tradition more gently perpetuated in the work of Maurice Sendak and Anthony Browne.

169/170 *Alice's Adventures in Wonderland,* 1988

NOTES

1. Quoted by Tony Bradman, in 'Through the magic mirror: the work of Anthony Browne', *British Book News* (Children's Books, Autumn 1984), 2–5.
2. Unless otherwise attributed, quotations are transcribed from a discussion with the author recorded in London, 26 March 1987.
3. 'Anatomy Lesson of Dr Nicolaes Tulp', 1632, The Hague, Mauritshuis; and 'Anatomy Lesson of Dr Joan Deijman', 1656, Amsterdam, Rijksmuseum.
4. This is the central thesis of Arthur Koestler's *The Act of Creation* (Macmillan, 1964).
5. A useful book-by-book discussion appears in Jane Doonan, 'The object lesson: picture books of Anthony Browne', *Word & Image*, 2/2 (April-June 1986), 159–72. On *Hansel and Gretel* see also Aidan Chambers, 'Letter from England: making them new', *The Horn Book Magazine* (December 1981), 706–8.
6. cf. Andrew Lang's Introduction to *Grimm's Household Tales*, translated and edited by Margaret Hunt (2 vols., London, 1884) xi-lxxv.

BIBLIOGRAPHY

1976
THROUGH THE MAGIC MIRROR   Anthony Browne   Hamish Hamilton/Greenwillow

1977
A WALK IN THE PARK   Anthony Browne   Hamish Hamilton/Macmillan

1978 –

1979
BEAR HUNT   Anthony Browne   Hamish Hamilton/Atheneum

1980
LOOK WHAT I'VE GOT!   Anthony Browne   Julia MacRae/Knopf

1981
HANSEL AND GRETEL   The Brothers Grimm   Julia MacRae/Knopf

1982
BEAR GOES TO TOWN   Anthony Browne   Hamish Hamilton

1983
GORILLA   Anthony Browne   Julia MacRae/Knopf

1984
THE VISITORS WHO CAME TO STAY   Annalena McAfee and Anthony Browne   Hamish Hamilton/Viking Kestrel
WILLY THE WIMP   Anthony Browne   Julia MacRae/Knopf

1985
KNOCK, KNOCK! WHO'S THERE?   Sally Grindley and Anthony Browne   Hamish Hamilton/Knopf
WILLY THE CHAMP   Anthony Browne   Julia MacRae/Knopf

1986
PIGGYBOOK   Anthony Browne   Julia MacRae/Knopf

1987
KIRSTY KNOWS BEST   Annalena McAfee and Anthony Browne   Julia MacRae/Knopf

1988
ALICE'S ADVENTURES IN WONDERLAND   Lewis Carroll   Julia MacRae/Knopf

1989
I LIKE BOOKS   Anthony Browne   Julia MacRae/Knopf
THINGS I LIKE   Anthony Browne   Sainsbury Walker/Knopf
THE TUNNEL   Anthony Browne   Julia MacRae/Knopf

16 · MICHAEL FOREMAN

SOME OF MICHAEL FOREMAN'S earliest memories are of living by the sea at a time when all the beaches were mined and totally cut off by a Berlin Wall of barbed wire. His later pacifism and compulsive globe-trotting may both be rooted in these circumstances, but only as his fiftieth birthday approached was he ready to begin to shape this mental imagery which still haunted him into a book.[1]

He was born in 1938 in Pakefield, at the edge of the Suffolk fishing port of Lowestoft, where his mother kept the village shop. His father had died a month before he was born, but '. . . during the war the other boys' fathers were away, and that helped me; not having a father didn't seem unusual'.[2]

In other respects his childhood and schooldays were unremarkable. He grew up without books, but he did see all the magazines and comics in the interval between when they arrived at the village shop from the wholesalers and when they were sent out with the Sunday newspapers. In this way he discovered favourites among illustrators (notably an artist named Rose who peopled his cover scenes for *John Bull* with hundreds and hundreds of figures), and began to draw a lot in his spare time.

He had no particular ambitions, and admits that anything might have become of him but for a chance educational emancipation of a kind that must have been rare even at that time and would be virtually impossible today. On one of his morning newspaper rounds he was asked by a regular customer if he and his friends would be prepared to dig out some clay from the cliffs, and take it round to the local art school so that they could find out whether it was usable for modelling. This odd request came from Tom Hudson,[3] an art teacher whom he got to know and who quickly recognised his talent for drawing and arranged for him to join a Saturday morning art class for schoolchildren.

To encounter one inspiring teacher at an early stage is good fortune, to find two can be to discover a direction in life. Michael Foreman found this to be so, and events moved swiftly. Tom Hudson approached his headmaster, Michael Duane, and the latter readily agreed to excuse the young Foreman from school to attend the Lowestoft Art

172 From 'Lappland Sketchbook', 1985

School for two additional afternoons each week, as he was more talented in that area than in any other. And so at thirteen years of age, he found himself in the regular company of full-time art students some years his senior.

When he left school without any 'O' Levels at fifteen, he was accepted at Lowestoft but lumped together at first with the apprentices who were on day-release. After a few days, Tom Hudson spotted him: '. . . and took me into another room where there was a big pink nude woman. I thought, "I'm an artist!" But the principal was horrified. She thought I was too young, or too dumb, and put me back for a year.'

Lowestoft was a very small school, but Michael Foreman was able to follow the four-year course leading to the NDD in Painting, although it was necessary to visit the neighbouring schools at Ipswich and Great Yarmouth for access to printmaking facilities. The prospect of National Service awaited him at the end of this course, but both his older brothers, who had been called up, advised him to avoid it by the expedient of a further year's study in the course of which compulsory military training would be phased out. This coincided with his realisation that, in common with most provincial art students, he had been led by the nose to a certain extent and had applied himself to the fine art curriculum with little idea of what might happen later. It

171 *The General*, 1961

therefore seemed reasonable to argue that training for a 'proper' job would be a wiser use of public resources, and so the academic year 1958–59 was spent studying commercial art at St Martin's School of Art in London.

He still remained closely involved with painting, in an almost totally abstract idiom, both at St Martin's and at the Royal College, but increasingly painting and graphic design or illustration came to be seen as quite separate fields of activity.

> The thing that gives me most pleasure in being an illustrator now is that almost everything I do in the normal course of life has a bearing on the work in progress. It's all totally enmeshed, and anything that affects you in the newspapers or television or in your own personal experience can be a jumping-off point. Whereas had I remained an abstract painter – and I'm certain in any case that I wouldn't be abstract any longer by now – there would still be a division between pursuing a very narrow aesthetic path on the one hand and living a normal life on the other.

At St Martin's he was drawn to the teachers in the sculpture school at the time, Anthony Caro and Elizabeth Frink; he did as much life drawing as possible, and just enough commercial stuff to keep his place in the department.

He then sought entry to the Royal College of Art, but had to consider how to make the best use of the year that would elapse between applying and getting in. The freelance market had to be explored; outlets for commercial drawings for the press in his Camden Town locality were readily established, but he was conscious that the fine art bias of his portfolio was ill-calculated to achieve a breakthrough at a wider and more viable level.

To remedy this, he worked on a tentative story-line and began to produce sample drawings for a picture book. These were submitted to Routledge & Kegan Paul. They were not at the time active publishers of children's books, but Sir Herbert Read, then a director of the company, was actively committed to the Campaign for Nuclear Disarmament, and so the book came to be published as *The General* with a text by Janet Charters, Michael Foreman's first wife.

The book had quite an impact; it was recognisable as a pacifist tract for the times (that made it 'communist-inspired' in the United States), but it was also hailed by art students as a breakthrough by a contemporary. It remains remarkably fresh and immediate, despite a well-discharged debt to André François in the handling of certain passages. Routledge offered him a couple of other titles to illustrate in this same year, but apart from that he was destined to be absent from the book publishing scene for almost six working years.

The years 1960–63 were spent at the the RCA, where there was then no illustration course as such, and graphics was divided into typography and advertising graphics on the one hand – Foreman has always resisted the pressures of advertising deadlines – and decorative graphics on the other. Although ostensibly studying the latter, in the department headed by Edward Bawden, he gravitated once more towards painting. These were vintage years, with David Hockney, Allen Jones and Zandra Rhodes just a token few luminaries among so many documented in the exhibition and history which marked the College's 150 years of existence.[4] Foreman also found himself effortlessly accepted into the charmed circle of pop musicians and photographers, restaurateurs and fashion designers who were poised to take the dominant initiative in 1960s styling all the way from King's Road and Carnaby Street to international status.

An RCA travel scholarship to the United States in the summer of 1963 enabled Michael Foreman to make the first of very many visits:

> I can remember walking down streets in New York thinking, in the words of
> that terrible Frank Sinatra song, 'If I can make it here, I'll make it anywhere.'
> At the Royal College, when I was a student there, Madison Avenue was Mecca.
> It didn't occur to me that there could be people here doing better stuff than
> they were doing on Madison Avenue, because that was where the Gods lived.
> Those were terrifically exciting times, and in a way I preferred to be struggling
> there rather than anywhere else.

173 'Houses of the Stars', from an unpublished sequence, 1968

174　*The Pig Plantaganet,* 1980　　　　　　　　175 (facing)　*Fairy Tales,* 1981

176 *The Stone Book Quartet*, 1976–8

He recalls New York as it was before the Beatles had even been heard of there, and of course prior to the Kennedy assassination. 'After the assassination America was no longer so optimistic – but remained dynamic . . . It had the whole British ''thing''. On my next visit the following year, everything that was happening in London was happening in America also.'

Returning to England later in 1963, and assessing the climate for illustration, he formed the view, which was to remain unchanged for several years, that:

> . . . with books at that point – somehow you had to be able to afford to take them on. Because of the experience of having done *The General,* receiving good reviews yet not getting another book to do, I concluded that you couldn't do it with books, you just had to be a general illustrator and go where the business was . . .

> . . . For me there was more happening in the magazines in America than over here. Here the early supplements – *The Sunday Times* for instance – tended to be locked into certain kinds of style, I think they still are. But in America because there were so many more magazines the situation was more open and you didn't have to adopt the camouflage of the season to be adopted by the press.

Accordingly, his involvement with teaching[5] dates from this time and he also set up a design group with two friends in London, producing book covers for Penguin and general graphics, to which he could return in the intervals between his visits to America. 'Then it was on to Chicago as an art director on *Playboy* magazine. It was a great life for a time, but after two months it became incredibly boring, turning out the

177 *The Stone Book Quartet,* 1976–8

178 *Classics of the Macabre*, 1988

179 'Waiting for the guests', etching with lithographed colour, 1980

same basic package for each issue. *Playboy* was trying to do predictable things with endless amounts of money.' He began to feel that he was on the wrong end of the telephone and longed for a situation in which he would be the one being offered commissions. After four months he returned to England, and was engaged in art direction for the magazine *King* for a while. This was a low budget operation by comparison, and he found that he was required to take on all the illustrations and cartoons himself, but under a range of pseudonyms. Work followed for the short-lived magazine, *Nova,* as well as for the Sunday colour supplements. Two very different journals have continued to engage his loyalties up to the present: Mobil's *Pegasus,* for which so many of his travel illustrations have been commissioned; and the little magazine, *Ambit,* which is now past its hundredth issue, all but the opening few under the unpaid art editorship of Michael Foreman.

To bring the magazine aspect of his work right up to date, he contrasts transatlantic styles in art direction:

> I do very little for magazines now in any case; but there are two or three art
> directors I've worked with for a long time in America, and I know that when
> the phone rings and they ask me to do something, then they'll have ironed-out
> all the wrinkles and it's going to be fun to do, and what they want is what I do.
> Whereas the risk in working with new art directors here is that they don't
> really know what you do. They've seen one piece of work and they think that's
> what you do like sausages, they all come out the same. But the ones I enjoy
> working with are those that like you to put in your ideas as well as just
> producing that image they expect.

Michael Foreman's return to book illustration in 1967 was signalled by the publication of two new picture books to his own texts, *The Perfect Present* and *The Two Giants.* He did these largely because he recognised that he was no longer known in the field and therefore people simply weren't offering him books to illustrate. *The Two Giants* makes brilliant use of torn-paper technique, which suggested itself as an answer to some of the technical problems to be encountered in subsequent adaptation to film animation:

> I was approached by some young people in Denmark for permission to make
> an animated film of *The General.* They had no money, but they liked it, and so I
> said 'Sure', and went over to do extra drawings and we became very friendly,
> but I saw how difficult it was to animate pictures of that kind. So I thought of
> torn-up paper shapes for *The Two Giants* as these could be easily manipulated
> in order to overcome many of these problems.

Technical problems of this sort have apparently always held a fascination for Michael Foreman. He evinces similar concern for print quality, and visits colour printers whenever possible to discover how far the artist's presence or intervention can influence the final result. There is a preoccupation with transcribing the quality, tone and texture of the paper which the artist has used to that on which the book is to be printed. Reproduction houses are quite used to capturing the colour image from the sheet, whilst suppressing most of the effect from this substrate; but Foreman builds up his effects with a reliance on the integrity of the paper surface to the extent that he must start again if things go wrong. His celebrated 'grainy' watercolour effect depends not only on the printer's facsimile reproduction of the texture of rough handmade paper, but on his own skill in causing and controlling the precipitation of watercolour pigment particles from the wash. Foreman claims that he sometimes mixes-in sugar, gravel or even boot polish to build up these luminous washes and reticulated textures. He uses concentrated watercolour in preference to the traditional 'cakes' for the added brilliance they confer, combining the best properties of watercolour with those of coloured inks. But at the end of the day he recognises that it is the objective printed result which has to count, and admits that the grainy effect often becomes more pronounced along the way.

In taking 1967 as the year in which it becomes possible to identify book illustration as the clear path that Michael Foreman has chosen for the future, it is interesting to observe that the approximate total of books illustrated in the decade 1967−76 (27) is doubled by that for 1977−86 (54). The rate of output for his own picture books however remains steady (8 and 7 respectively), and this is perhaps to be explained by the fact that as entrepreneur he was taking his own book output to his publisher on a package proposal basis, whereas publishers were slower to commission him to illustrate other kinds of book and to identify those fields in which he would excel. His earlier remark that at first he could not afford to do more book illustration still has some force, but should not be taken simply at its economic face-value − for then all illustrators could say the same; rather it has to do with his whole working approach, above all with his need to travel to specific locations, which under-powered commissions could not hope to fund even in part.

At this point it may be more rewarding to discuss this obsession with travel, and to try to map out some other underlying features which characterise his individual approach, although this entails disregarding the chronology of the books he has illustrated.

It was for his work as a *travel* illustrator that he was honoured with the designation 'Royal Designer for Industry', and travel and its converse − staying at home − provide a key to his visual inspiration. In over-simplified terms, he believes that ersatz experience or the second-hand image can never suffice, for children least of all. And so Alan Garner leads inexorably to Alderley Edge, Madhur Jaffrey to a four-week journey through India. *Panda and the Bushfire* required a seven-week trip to Australia, and he revisited the southern hemisphere recently to gain background for some retellings of Maori legends. These are merely a few episodes taken at random from the log of a prodigious traveller, who heads for Heathrow rather than to the reference library in

search of authenticity. There are few countries he hasn't visited by now, at times following up a given assignment, at others pursuing a momentary impulse that may relate to some as yet undefined project.[6]

Sometimes a chance synthesis of some of this material seems within reach, as when a publisher found him uniquely placed to illustrate an anthology of universal prayer drawn from cultures all round the world.[7] However, the corpus of unpublished sketchbooks and finished works resulting from his travels constitute Foreman's visual autobiography, which will surely start to find its way into print in due course.

If travel brings back a cargo which adds something to the text for children unable to make the voyage for themselves, then this is rationale enough for his work as an illustrator; but staying at home can be equally special. In the way in which Stanley Spencer saw biblical events taking place in his native Cookham, if to a lesser degree, Michael Foreman draws family, friends and places, in Fulham or at St Ives, Cornwall. They appear unexpectly in his illustrations for a wide range of authors. This is a coinage not to be debased: it belongs to a personal vision and to literary affinities freshly discovered:

> As a child we had no books in the house at all. I didn't really have that habit.
> But now I tend to come to read books for the first time, that's to say classics,
> when I'm asked to illustrate them. To some extent I think that's a little bit
> fortunate, because I haven't had other artists' pictures in my brain before . . .

Foreman speaks quietly and economically, personally and through his work, although one never underestimates the power which is held in reserve. There are superficial characteristics which make his style instantly recognisable from book to book, and yet each is very different. Many of the gentler watercolours and line drawings rest on the page, sharing a common reading plane with the typography, and in this way the poetry of the illustrations unfolds in pace with the text. In practice it is rare for words and pictures to be brought together so naturally, and illustrators frequently lack this technical ability to *accompany* a text, depending on others to find the best compromise between their drawings and what is possible in terms of typography and book production. Foreman attributes many insights in this area to his long friendship and numerous collaborations with the distinguished book typographer, Derek Birdsall.

Technical mastery of the whole picture surface is fundamental to his skill in resolving three dimensions into two, whatever the depth of field; that is to say, there are no 'throw- away' areas, weak passages or ill-considered edges. Unless the intention is contrary, this induces an initial effect of calm which is qualified into a precise mood after a few moments of the observer's attention. Calm resolves into childhood recall or dreamland, isolation or engrossment. Sentimentality is absent, and the sharp factual recapture of a childhood activity precludes nostalgia. This can perhaps be seen at its best in *A Child's Garden of Verses* – a wonderfully illustrated book.

180 *A Child's Garden of Verses,* 1985

181 *Shakespeare Stories, 'Macbeth', 1985*

Foreman believes that every manuscript or text should set the artist off on a new line of enquiry, and yet it suits his working method to have two or more projects in concurrent progress, since he likes to be able to dodge from one to another should a temporary block develop. Each published title works on its own terms for the reader, but the range and variety of handling and style only really become apparent when a collection of his books are studied comparatively. The selection of favourites becomes a subjective matter where standards and output are are so uniformly high, as has been the case throughout the past decade; but my personal short-list would have to include his two early picture books, *The General* and *The Two Giants,* for their verve, directness and staying power. *Moose* and *Dinosaurs and all that Rubbish* are fine examples of his middle-period picture books for Hamish Hamilton. Alan Garner's *The Stone Book*

Quartet is a splendid achievement, and Foreman has written a brief but graphic account of how these illustrations came about. [8]

Michael Foreman's work for children's books has been widely honoured, [9] but the popularity ratings accorded by children themselves must count for even more. He is greatly sought after these days, and has to turn away more titles than some equally professional colleagues possessed of a more catholic range. He has always had the integrity to do that whenever confronted by a project for which he felt insufficient commitment, and which might have yielded a result below his consistent personal best.

Life has become simpler since relations with his respective publishers have tended to fall in recent years into a stable, compartmentalised pattern which he finds ideal: for instance, currently Andersen Press publish his own picture books; Pavilion Books come to him with titles by modern writers of distinction such as Edna O'Brien, Terry Jones and Madhur Jaffrey; Gollancz afford him an opportunity to illustrate the classics, so far ranging from Shakespeare (in Leon Garfield's retelling), by way of Grimm, Andersen and Stevenson, to Daphne du Maurier's *Classics of the Macabre;* Viking Kestrel offer projects which have ranged from Kipling to Causley. [10]

With typical modesty he states that for the future he would just like to do more of the same, and that perhaps he could even re-illustrate some of the books he has done in the past and improve on them:

182 *Shakespeare Stories,* 'The Merchant of Venice', 1985

This is best explained by a sense of privilege, luck, good fortune or whatever, that I experience whilst sitting at my table making pictures and when surrounded by my family. Coming from where I did – and with those chance encounters along the way – heightens these feelings of fortune and my determination to make the most of it. Also having an incendiary bomb drop through my bedroom ceiling when I was 3 years old has left me feeling that every day is precious and a blessing.[11]

NOTES

1. At the time of writing, this project was in an early stage of development under the working title *War Boy,* to be published by Pavilion Books.
2. Quotations, unless otherwise stated, are from an interview recorded in Fulham, West London, on 15 December 1986.
3. Tom Hudson was a charismatic teacher, deeply influenced by Victor Pasmore's post-war conversion to pure abstraction. The neo-Bauhaus approach to pre-diploma studies was largely a creation of the Pasmore/Thubron/Hudson trio, and formed one of the strands in the colleges that heralded the self-confidence and style-consciousness of the 1960s. Michael Foreman's early encounter with Hudson's theories must have been a formative one, but like most artists he rightly speaks of influences only in general rather than specific terms, and acknowledges that the didacticism which he found stimulating at the time may have proved of questionable benefit to many.
4. For the post-war history of the RCA see Christopher Frayling, *The Royal College of Art: 150 years of Art & Design* (Barrie & Jenkins, 1987), 128–97.
5. He lectured part-time at St Martins (1963–65), the London College of Printing (1967–68), the Royal College of Art (1968–70, and intermittently until 1981), and at the Central School of Art and Design (1972).

6. 'I did a lot of my own sponsored travelling right from the start. Now publishers know I have been to so many places and they seek me out. For a long time people haven't been saying we have got a job for you, they talk about the trip instead.' Michael Foreman, 'An honourable profession', *Graphics World,* 58 (January/February 1986), 28–32.
7. 'I declined to do this book eventually as I found what I wanted to do was not what the publisher visualized. Unfortunately I did quite a lot of work before discovering this.' Letter of 21 November 1987.
8. Michael Foreman, 'Illustrating Garner', *School Bookshop News* (Autumn 1979), and reprinted in *Labrys,* 7 (November 1981), 123–6, an issue devoted to Alan Garner's work.
9. He has been awarded first prize in the Francis Williams Book Illustrations Award (1972 and 1977), the Silver Eagle Prize at the Nice International Festival of the Book (1972), the Graphics Prize at Bologna (1982), the Emil/Kurt Maschler Award (1982) and the Kate Greenaway Medal (1982).
10. A fine and well-illustrated survey of Michael Foreman's recent works is to be found in *HQ, High Quality* Heft II (Heidelberg, 2/1988), 18–25.
11. From a letter dated 21 November 1987.

BIBLIOGRAPHY

1961

COMIC ALPHABETS   Eric Partridge
    Routledge
THE GENERAL   Janet Charters and Michael
    Foreman   Routledge/Dutton
THE KING WHO LIVED ON JELLY
    Cledwyn Hughes   Routledge

1962–65 –

1966

HUIT ENFANTS ET UN BÉBÉ   [text in French
    and English]   Leonore Klein
    Abelard-Schuman
MAKING MUSIC   Gwen Clemens   Longman

1967

THE BAD FOOD GUIDE   Derek Cooper
    Routledge
THE PERFECT PRESENT   Michael Foreman
    Hamish Hamilton/Coward
THE TWO GIANTS   Michael Foreman
    Brockhampton/Pantheon
I'M FOR YOU – AND YOU'RE FOR ME
    Mabel Watts   Abelard-Schuman

1968

THE GREAT SLEIGH ROBBERY   Michael
    Foreman   Hamish Hamilton/Pantheon
LET'S FIGHT!, AND OTHER RUSSIAN
    FABLES   Sergei Mikhalkov   Pantheon [USA]

1969

ESSEX POEMS, 1963–67   Donald Davie
    Routledge

1970

ADAM'S BALM   Bill Martin   Bowmar [USA]
THE BIRTHDAY UNICORN   Janice Elliott
    Gollancz
HORATIO   Michael Foreman   Hamish
    Hamilton/Pantheon [as THE TRAVELS
    OF HORATIO]

1971

JAMES AND THE GIANT PEACH   Roald Dahl
    [ed.]   BBC Publications
THE LIVING ARTS OF NIGERIA
    William Fagg   Studio Vista/Macmillan
MOOSE   Michael Foreman   Hamish Hamilton/
    Pantheon

1972

DINOSAURS AND ALL THAT RUBBISH
    Michael Foreman   Hamish Hamilton/Crowell
FISCHER V SPASSKY, REYKJAVIK 1972
    C. H. O'D. Alexander   Wildwood House with
    Penguin/Vintage

1973

ALEXANDER IN THE LAND OF MOG   Janice
    Elliott   [ill. with Freire Wright]
    Brockhampton
THE LIVING TREASURES OF JAPAN
    Barbara Adachi   Wildwood House
MR NOAH AND THE SECOND FLOOD
    Sheila Burnford   Gollancz/Praeger

1974

RAINBOW RIDER   Jane Yolen   Crowell [USA]/
    Collins
WAR AND PEAS   Michael Foreman
    Hamish Hamilton/Crowell

1975

PRIVATE ZOO   Georgess McHargue
    Collins/Viking
TEENY-TINY AND THE WITCH-WOMAN
    Barbara K. Walker   Pantheon [USA]/
    Andersen Press 1977

1976

ALL THE KING'S HORSES   Michael Foreman
    Hamish Hamilton/Bradbury
HANS ANDERSEN, HIS CLASSIC FAIRY
    TALES   Erik Haugaard [ed.]   Gollancz/
    Doubleday
MONKEY AND THE THREE WIZARDS
    Peter Harris [ed.]   Collins/Bradbury
THE PUSHCART WAR   Jean Merrill   Puffin
THE STONE BOOK   Alan Garner   [the other
    volumes of The Stone Book Quartet were
    published in 1977–78]   Collins

1977

GRANNY REARDUN   Alan Garner   Collins
KÜCHENGESCHICHTEN   Kurt Baumann
    Nord-Süd [Germany]/Andersen Press [as
    MICKY'S KITCHEN CONTEST]
PANDA'S PUZZLE, AND HIS VOYAGE OF
    DISCOVERY   Michael Foreman   Hamish
    Hamilton/Bradbury
TOM FOBBLE'S DAY   Alan Garner   Collins

1978

THE AIMER GATE Alan Garner Collins
BORROWED FEATHERS, AND OTHER FABLES
  Bryna Stevens [ed.] [ill. with Freire Wright]
  Hamish Hamilton/Random House
POPULAR FOLK TALES [by] THE BROTHERS
  GRIMM Brian Alderson [ed.]
  Gollancz/Doubleday
THE SELFISH GIANT Oscar Wilde [ill. with
  Freire Wright] Kaye & Ward/Methuen

1979

THE GIRL OF THE GOLDEN GATE
  Alan Garner Collins
THE GOLDEN BROTHERS Alan Garner
  Collins
HOW TO CATCH A GHOST Bill Martin
  Holt, Rinehart [USA]
THE PRINCESS AND THE GOLDEN MANE
  Alan Garner Collins
THE THREE GOLDEN HEADS OF THE WELL
  Alan Garner Collins

1980

AFTER MANY A SUMMER Aldous Huxley
  Folio
FAIRYTALES OF GOLD Alan Garner [the
  4 books from 1979 reprinted in one volume
  under this title] Collins/Philomel
THE FAITHFUL BULL Ernest Hemingway
  Emme Edizioni [Italy]/Hamish Hamilton
PANDA AND THE ODD LION Michael
  Foreman Hamish Hamilton
THE PIG PLANTAGANET Allen Andrews
  Hutchinson/Viking
CITY OF GOLD AND OTHER STORIES FROM
  THE OLD TESTAMENT Peter Dickinson
  Gollancz/Pantheon
THE TIGER WHO LOST HIS STRIPES
  Anthony Paul Andersen Press/Harcourt Brace

1981

FAIRY TALES Terry Jones Pavilion/Schocken
OVER THE BRIDGE John Loveday [ed.]
  Kestrel
SEVEN IN ONE BLOW [after Grimm]
  [ill. with Freire Wright] Random House
  [USA]
TRICK A TRACKER Michael Foreman
  Gollancz/Philomel

1982

THE CRAB THAT PLAYED WITH THE SEA
  Rudyard Kipling Macmillan/Bedrick
LAND OF DREAMS Michael Foreman
  Andersen Press/Holt, Rinehart
LONG NECK AND THUNDER FOOT
  Helen Piers Kestrel
THE MAGIC MOUSE AND THE MILLIONAIRE
  Robert McCrum Hamish Hamilton
THE SLEEPING BEAUTY, AND OTHER
  FAVOURITE FAIRY TALES Angela Carter
  Gollancz/Schocken

1983

THE BRONTOSAURUS BIRTHDAY CAKE
  Robert McCrum Hamish Hamilton/
  Simon & Schuster
A CHRISTMAS CAROL Charles Dickens
  Gollancz/Dial
POEMS FOR 7 YEAR OLDS AND UNDER
  Helen Nicoll [ed.] Kestrel
THE SAGA OF ERIK THE VIKING
  Terry Jones Pavilion/Schocken
TREASURE ISLAND Robert Louis Stevenson
  Penguin

1984

CAT AND CANARY Michael Foreman
  Andersen Press/Dial
A CAT AND MOUSE LOVE STORY Nanette
  Newman Heinemann/David & Charles
PANDA AND THE BUNYIPS Michael Foreman
  Hamish Hamilton/Schocken
POEMS FOR 9 YEAR OLDS AND UNDER
  Kit Wright [ed.] Kestrel
POEMS FOR OVER 10 YEAR OLDS
  Kit Wright [ed.] Kestrel

1985

BRONTOSAURUS SUPERSTAR! Robert McCrum
  Hamish Hamilton
CHARLIE AND THE CHOCOLATE FACTORY
  Roald Dahl Allen & Unwin with Puffin
A CHILD'S GARDEN OF VERSES
  Robert Louis Stevenson Gollancz/Delacorte
CHARLIE AND THE GREAT GLASS
  ELEVATOR Roald Dahl Allen & Unwin
  with Puffin
I'LL TAKE YOU TO MRS COLE Nigel Gray
  Andersen Press/Bergh
NICOBOBINUS Terry Jones Pavilion/Bedrick
PANDA AND THE BUSHFIRE Michael
  Foreman Hamish Hamilton/Prentice-Hall

POETIC GEMS   William McGonagall   Folio
SEASONS OF SPLENDOUR   Madhur Jaffrey
    Pavilion/Atheneum
SHAKESPEARE STORIES   Leon Garfield
    Gollancz/Schocken

1986
BEN'S BOX   [a pop-up fantasy]   Michael
    Foreman   Hodder & Stoughton
EARLY IN THE MORNING   Charles Causley
    Viking Kestrel
LETTERS FROM HOLLYWOOD
    Michael Moorcock   Harrap
THE MAGIC OINTMENT AND OTHER
    CORNISH LEGENDS   Eric Quayle
    Andersen Press/Simon & Schuster [as THE
    LITTLE PEOPLE'S PAGEANT OF
    CORNISH LEGENDS]
TALES FOR THE TELLING   Edna O'Brien
    Pavilion/Atheneum

1987
BEN'S BABY   Michael Foreman   Andersen
    Press/Harper & Row
FUN   Jan Mark   Gollancz
THE JUNGLE BOOK   Rudyard Kipling
    Viking Kestrel
JUST SO STORIES   Rudyard Kipling
    Viking Kestrel

1988
ANGEL AND THE WILD ANIMAL
    Michael Foreman   Andersen Press
THE CURSE OF THE VAMPIRE'S SOCKS
    AND OTHER DOGGEREL   Terry Jones
    Pavilion
DAPHNE DU MAURIER'S CLASSICS OF
    THE MACABRE   Daphne du Maurier
    Gollancz/Doubleday
PETER PAN AND WENDY   J. M. Barrie
    Pavilion

1989
EDMOND WENT FAR AWAY   Martin
    Bax   Walker/Harcourt Brace

183 *Letters from Hollywood, 1986*

GENERAL BIBLIOGRAPHY

This brief listing aims to provide some pointers to the literature available on a number of equally distinguished illustrators not dealt with elsewhere in this book, and to the basic surveys and reference sources that have been found most useful in its compilation. Bibliographical sources given in the notes to each chapter are not repeated here except where they have wider applications. In the case of monographs and catalogues, the main ascertainable contributor is given as author (although variously described as editor, compiler, introducer, etc., within the publication).

Brian Alderson, 'Edward Ardizzone:
  a preliminary hand-list of his illustrated books, 1929–1970', *The Private Library,* 2nd series, 5/1 (Spring 1972), 2–64
– *Sing a Song for Sixpence: The English Picture Book Tradition and Randolph Caldecott* (CUP, 1987)
Edward Ardizzone, 'The born illustrator', *Motif,* 1 (November 1958), 37–44; also reprinted in *Folio* (January–March 1962), 1–16 [cf. Lamb, 'The true illustrator']
– 'Brian Robb', *Signature,* new series, 11 (1950), 37–45
– *Diary of a War Artist* (Bodley Head, 1974)
– *Indian Diary* (Bodley Head, 1984)
– 'On the illustrating of books', *The PLA Quarterly,* 1st series, 1/3 (July 1957), 25–30
– *The Young Ardizzone: An Autobiographical Fragment* (Studio Vista/Macmillan, 1970)
Edward Bawden, *Travels of a War Artist: 1940–45* (Imperial War Museum, 1983)
Helen Binyon, *Eric Ravilious: Memoir of an Artist* (Lutterworth Press, 1983)

David Bland, *A History of Book Illustration* (2nd edn, Faber/Univ. California Press, 1969)
– *The Illustration of Books* (3rd edn, Faber, 1962)
Douglas Percy Bliss, *Edward Bawden* (Pendomer Press, 1979)
James Boswell, 'English book illustration today', *Graphis,* 7/34 (1951), 42–57
Simon Brett, *Engravers: A Handbook for the Nineties* (Silent Books, 1987) [invaluable survey of the work of 47 members compiled for the Society of Wood Engravers]
British Book Illustration 1935–45 (National Book League, 1949) [exhibition catalogue 48pp]
Edward Burrett, *Tribute to Diana Bloomfield: A Pot Pourri of Her Wood Engravings and Drawings* (Penmiel Press, 1985)
Mel Calman, 'The Gentleman touch', *Penrose Annual,* 69 (1976), 157–68
– *What Else Do You Do?* (Methuen, 1986)
Frances Carey, *Henry Moore: A Shelter Sketchbook* (British Museum Publications, 1988)
Humphrey Carpenter and Mari Prichard, *The Oxford Companion to Children's Literature* (OUP, 1984)
David Chambers, *Joan Hassall: Engravings and Drawings* (Private Libraries Association, 1985)
David Chambers and Christopher Sandford, *Cock-a-Hoop: A Bibliography of the Golden Cockerel Press* 1950–61 (Private Libraries Association for the Golden Cockerel Press, 1984) [The fourth volume: following upon *Cockalorum 1943-49,* n.d., and containing examples of work by Clifford Webb, Gwenda Morgan, Mark Severin, Derrick Harris and Geoffrey Wales]

INDEX